First World War
and Army of Occupation
War Diary
France, Belgium and Germany

1 DIVISION
3 Infantry Brigade
Welsh Regiment 1/6th Battalion,
South Wales Borderers
51st, 52nd and 53rd (Grad) Battalions,
Light Trench Mortar Battery
and Machine Gun Company
1 August 1915 - 28 February 1918

WO95/1282

The Naval & Military Press Ltd
www.nmarchive.com
Published in association with The National Archives

Published by

The Naval & Military Press Ltd

Unit 10 Ridgewood Industrial Park,

Uckfield, East Sussex,

TN22 5QE England

Tel: +44 (0) 1825 749494

www.naval-military-press.com

www.nmarchive.com

This diary has been reprinted in facsimile from the original. Any imperfections are inevitably reproduced and the quality may fall short of modern type and cartographic standards.

© Crown Copyright
Images reproduced by permission of The National Archives, London, England, 2015.

Contents

Document type	Place/Title	Date From	Date To
Heading	##		
Heading	##		
Heading	WO95/1282/1 6/Welsh Rgt Nov' 15-May' 16		
Heading	1st Division 3rd Brigade 6th Battalion Welsh Regiment 1915 Nov-1916 May From 28 Div 84 Bde To 1 Div Troops Pearson		
Heading	3rd Infantry 1st Division War Diary 6th Battn. Welsh Regiment November 1915		
War Diary		01/11/1915	29/11/1915
Heading	3rd Infantry 1st Division War Diary 6th Battn. Welsh Regiment. December 1915		
War Diary		01/12/1915	30/12/1915
Heading	1st Division 3rd Brigade 1-6th Battalion The Welsh Regiment Jan-May 1916		
Heading	3rd Brigade 1st Division 1/6th Battalion The Welsh Regiment January 1916		
Heading	6th Welsh War Diary January 1916		
War Diary		01/01/1918	31/01/1918
Heading	3rd Brigade 1st Division 1/6th Battalion The Welsh Regiment February War Diary For 1916 Missing		
Heading	1/6th 3rd Brigade 1st Division Battalion Welsh Regiment March 1916		
War Diary	Bracquemont	01/03/1916	03/03/1916
War Diary	South Maroc	04/03/1916	06/03/1916
War Diary	Left Sub Sector Maroc	01/03/1916	09/03/1916
War Diary	Les Brebis	10/03/1916	10/03/1916
War Diary	South Maroc	11/03/1916	12/03/1916
War Diary	Left Sub Sector Maroc	13/03/1916	13/03/1916
War Diary	Maroc	14/03/1916	15/03/1916
War Diary	Les Brebis	15/03/1916	21/03/1916
War Diary	North Maroc	23/03/1916	24/03/1916
War Diary	Loos Right Battn Hqs	27/03/1916	27/03/1916
War Diary	Old German Front Line O.G. 1	28/03/1916	30/03/1916
War Diary	Loos	31/03/1916	31/03/1916
Heading	3rd Brigade 1st Division 1/6th Battalion The Welsh Regiment April 1916		
War Diary	Loos	01/04/1916	02/04/1916
War Diary	Les Brebis	03/04/1916	08/04/1916
War Diary	Maroc	09/04/1916	10/04/1916
War Diary	Maroc (left Sectior)	11/04/1916	14/04/1916
War Diary	S. Maroc (Area B)	15/04/1916	16/04/1916
War Diary	Maroc (Sector) Hqs.	17/04/1916	17/04/1916
War Diary	Maroc Left Section	18/04/1916	20/04/1916
War Diary	Petit Sains (Billets)	21/04/1916	26/04/1916
War Diary	North Maroc	27/04/1916	29/04/1916
War Diary	Loos	30/04/1916	30/04/1916
Heading	3rd Brigade & 1st Divisional Pioneers Became 1st Divisional Pioneers 15.5.16 1/6th Battalion The Welsh Regiment May 1916		
War Diary	Loos	01/05/1916	03/05/1916

War Diary	O.G.I.	03/05/1916	06/05/1916
War Diary	Les Brebis	07/05/1916	13/05/1916
War Diary	Les Maroc	14/05/1916	16/05/1916
War Diary	Harchies	17/05/1916	31/05/1916
Heading	WO95/1282/2 51/S. Wales Bords May 19-July 19		
Heading	1 Division 3 Brigade 51 S.W.B. 1919 Mar To 1919 July		
Heading	War Diary of 51st Bn South Wales Borderers.		
War Diary	Stowlangtoft (Suffolk)	10/03/1919	10/03/1919
War Diary	Thurston	10/03/1919	10/03/1919
War Diary	Dover	10/03/1919	11/03/1919
War Diary	Dunkerke	11/03/1919	12/03/1919
War Diary	Merris	12/03/1919	12/03/1919
War Diary	Baisieux	12/03/1919	12/03/1919
War Diary	Charleroi	13/03/1919	13/03/1919
War Diary	Huy	13/03/1919	13/03/1919
War Diary	Duren	14/03/1919	14/03/1919
War Diary	Munstereifel	14/03/1919	31/03/1919
Miscellaneous	Appendix 1 Copy Of Telegram Received From War Office, London, 8th March 1919	02/04/1919	02/04/1919
Miscellaneous	Appendix 2 Roll Of Officers Who Embarked With 51st Bn. South Wales Borders 11th March 1919		
War Diary	Munstereifel	01/04/1919	30/04/1919
Miscellaneous	51st Bn. South Wales Borders.		
Heading	War Diary of the 51st Battn South Wales Borderers. From May 1st To May 31st 1919 Volume No 3		
War Diary	Munstereifel	01/05/1919	31/05/1919
Miscellaneous	51st Bn. South Wales Borderers		
Heading	War Diary of the 51st. Bn. South Wales. Borderers. From June 1st 1919 To June 30th 1919 Volume. No. 4		
War Diary	Munstereifel	01/06/1919	18/06/1919
War Diary	Rhinbach	19/06/1919	19/06/1919
War Diary	Duisdorf	20/06/1919	30/06/1919
Miscellaneous	51st Bn. South Wales Borders		
Operation(al) Order(s)	51st Bn. South Wales Borderers Operation Order No. 2	29/06/1919	29/06/1919
Miscellaneous	March Table To Accompany 51st Bn. South Wales Borderers Operation Order No. 2		
Miscellaneous	Confidential To Headquarters, 3rd Western Infantry Brigade.	01/08/1919	01/08/1919
Heading	War Diary of the 51st Bn South Wales Borderers From 1st July To 31st July 1919 Volume No 5		
War Diary	Rheinbach	01/07/1919	01/07/1919
War Diary	Munstereifel	02/07/1919	31/07/1919
Miscellaneous	51st Bn. South Wales Borderers	31/07/1919	31/07/1919
Heading	WO95/1282/3 52/S. Wales Bords May 19 Jul 19		
Heading	1 Division 3 Brigade 52 S.W.B. 1919 Mar To 1919 July		
Miscellaneous	3rd Infantry Brigade.		
War Diary	Colchester	06/03/1919	22/03/1919
War Diary	Dunkirk	23/03/1919	23/03/1919
War Diary	Amritsar No 39	24/03/1919	24/03/1919
War Diary	Witterschlick	25/03/1919	30/03/1919
War Diary	Arloff	30/03/1919	30/03/1919
War Diary	Kirspenich and Arloff	01/04/1919	18/06/1919
War Diary	Obr Drees & Ndr Drees	19/06/1919	19/06/1919
War Diary	Endenich	20/06/1919	01/07/1919
War Diary	Obr Drees & Ndr Drees	02/07/1919	02/07/1919
War Diary	Arloff & Kirspenich	03/07/1919	31/07/1919

Heading	WO95/1282/4 53/S. Wales Bords May 19-July 19		
Heading	1 Division 3 Brigade 53 S.W.B. 1919 Mar To 1919 July		
War Diary	Dunkirk	22/03/1919	22/03/1919
War Diary	Munstereifel	23/03/1919	03/05/1919
War Diary	Alfter	28/06/1919	30/06/1919
War Diary	Munstereifel	01/06/1919	20/06/1919
War Diary	Alfter	21/06/1919	31/07/1919
War Diary	WO95/1282/5 3 Inf Bde Light T.M.B Aug 16		
Heading	1st Division 3rd Infantry Brigade 3rd Brigade Light Trench Mortar Battery August 1916		
War Diary	Millencourt	01/10/1919	16/10/1919
War Diary	Becourt Wood	17/10/1919	20/10/1919
War Diary	In Action	21/08/1919	26/08/1919
War Diary	Albert	28/08/1919	31/08/1919
Heading	WO95/1282/6 3 Inf Bde Light T.M.B. July 17-Jan 19		
Heading	1st Division 3rd L.T.M. Battery 3rd Infantry Brigade From 1st July To 31st December 1917		
Heading	War Diary 3rd. L.T.M. Battery. 3rd. Infantry Brigade. 1st. Division. July. 1917		
War Diary	Coxyde Bains	01/07/1917	14/07/1917
War Diary	Ghyvelde	15/07/1917	15/07/1917
War Diary	Cappelle	16/07/1917	17/07/1917
War Diary	Chateau Du Pont Le Ptr Synthe	18/07/1917	18/07/1917
War Diary	Le Clipon Camp	19/07/1917	31/07/1917
Heading	War Diary 3rd. L.T.M. Battery. 3rd. Infantry Brigade. 1st. Division. August. 1917		
War Diary	Le Clipon Camp	01/08/1917	31/08/1917
Heading	War Diary 3rd. L.T.M. Battery. 3rd. Infantry Brigade. 1st. Division. September. 1917		
War Diary	Le Clipon Camp	01/09/1917	30/09/1917
Heading	War Diary 3rd. L.T.M. Battery. 3rd. Infantry Brigade. 1st. Division. October. 1917		
War Diary	Le Clipon Camp	01/10/1917	19/10/1917
War Diary	Zeggers-Cappel	20/10/1917	21/10/1917
War Diary	Houtkerque	22/10/1917	31/10/1917
War Diary	War Diary 3rd. L.T.M. Battery. 3rd. Infantry Brigade. 1st. Division. November. 1917		
War Diary	Near Houtkerque	01/11/1917	05/11/1917
War Diary	Dambre Camp	06/11/1917	07/11/1917
War Diary	Irish Farm	08/11/1917	11/11/1917
War Diary	Damloe Camp	12/11/1917	18/11/1917
War Diary	Dirty Bucket Camp	19/11/1917	22/11/1917
War Diary	School Camp	23/11/1917	27/11/1917
War Diary	Piccadilly Camp	28/11/1917	30/11/1917
Heading	War Diary 3rd. L.T.M. Battery. 3rd. Infantry Brigade. 1st. Division. December 1917		
War Diary	Piccadilly Camp Near Proven	01/12/1917	05/12/1917
War Diary	Woesten Near	06/12/1917	10/12/1917
War Diary	Canal Bank Het Sas	11/12/1917	31/12/1917
Heading	3rd Infantry Bde 3rd French Mortar Battery From 1st January To 31st January 1919		
War Diary	Het Pas	01/01/1918	05/01/1918
War Diary	Canal Bank	06/01/1918	08/01/1918
War Diary	Canal Bank (Het Sas)	09/01/1918	23/01/1918
War Diary	Irish Farm Camp	24/01/1918	31/01/1918
War Diary	Near Lion Belge	01/02/1918	08/02/1918

War Diary	Siege Camp	09/02/1918	19/02/1918
War Diary	Canal Bank	20/02/1918	03/03/1918
War Diary	Hill Top Farm	04/03/1918	15/03/1918
War Diary	Canal Bank	16/03/1918	28/03/1918
War Diary	Hill Top	29/03/1918	05/04/1918
War Diary	Hospital Farm	06/04/1918	07/04/1918
War Diary	Bethune	08/04/1918	14/04/1918
War Diary	Gorre	15/04/1918	20/04/1918
War Diary	La Bourse	21/04/1918	22/04/1918
War Diary	Sailly La Bourse	23/04/1918	30/04/1918
War Diary	Hollenzollern Sector	01/05/1918	06/05/1918
War Diary	Noeux-Les-Mines La Bourse	07/05/1918	16/05/1918
War Diary	Noeux-Les-Mines Labourse Cambrin Sector	17/05/1918	24/05/1918
War Diary	Cambrin Sector	25/05/1918	04/06/1918
War Diary	Noeux-Les-Mines	05/06/1918	12/06/1918
War Diary	Hohenzollern Sector	13/06/1918	30/06/1918
War Diary	Noeux-Les-Mines	01/07/1918	10/07/1918
War Diary	Cambrin Sector	11/07/1918	31/07/1918
War Diary	Noeux-Les-Mines	01/08/1918	09/08/1918
War Diary	Hohenzollern Sector	10/08/1918	21/08/1918
War Diary	Sachin	22/08/1918	31/08/1918
War Diary	Arras	01/09/1918	08/09/1918
War Diary	On The Move	09/09/1918	13/09/1918
War Diary	Vermand	14/09/1918	22/09/1918
War Diary	Line	23/09/1918	31/12/1918
War Diary	Schweinhein	01/12/1918	31/12/1918
Heading	WO95/1282/7 3 Inf Bee M.G.C. Feb 16-Feb 18		
Heading	1st Division 3rd Brigade 3rd Machine Gun Company 1916 Feb-Sept 1916		
Heading	3rd Brigade 1st Division 3rd Machine Gun Company February 1916		
Miscellaneous	D.A.G. 3rd Echelon	04/03/1916	04/03/1916
War Diary	Le Brebis	14/02/1916	24/02/1916
War Diary	In the field	25/02/1916	29/02/1916
Heading	3rd Brigade 1st Division 3rd Machine Gun Company March 1916		
Miscellaneous	3 Bde The Gun Coy		
Miscellaneous	A Form Messages And Signals.		
War Diary	In The Field	01/03/1916	04/04/1916
War Diary	Field	05/03/1916	25/03/1916
War Diary	In The Field	25/03/1916	01/04/1916
Heading	3rd Machine Gun Company 1st to 28th April 1916 Missing		
Heading	3rd Brigade 1st Division 3rd Machine Gun Company 29th April-30th May 1916		
War Diary	Les Brebis	29/04/1916	30/05/1916
Heading	3rd Machine Gun Company June 1916		
War Diary	Bully	31/05/1916	28/06/1916
Heading	3rd Bde. 1st Div. War Diary 3rd Machine Gun Company July 1916		
War Diary	Bruay	02/07/1916	06/07/1916
War Diary	Viqna Court	07/07/1916	07/07/1916
War Diary	Rainneville	08/07/1916	08/07/1916
War Diary	Franvillers	09/07/1916	10/07/1916
War Diary	Albert	11/07/1916	12/07/1916
War Diary	Vignacourt	07/07/1916	07/07/1916

War Diary	Rainneville	08/07/1916	08/07/1916
War Diary	Franvillers	09/07/1916	10/07/1916
War Diary	Albert	11/07/1916	14/07/1916
War Diary	Field	15/07/1916	15/07/1916
War Diary	Albert	13/07/1916	14/07/1916
War Diary	Field	15/07/1916	15/07/1916
War Diary	Contalmaison	16/07/1916	18/07/1916
War Diary	Obi	19/07/1916	19/07/1916
War Diary	Maxse Redourt Albert	20/07/1916	23/07/1916
War Diary	Contalmaison	18/07/1916	18/07/1916
War Diary	Obi	19/07/1916	19/07/1916
War Diary	Maxse Redourt Albert	20/07/1916	23/07/1916
War Diary	Contalmaison	24/07/1916	31/07/1916
Heading	3rd Brigade 1st Division 3rd Brigade Machine Gun Company August 1916		
War Diary	Millencourt	01/08/1915	14/08/1915
War Diary	Becourt	15/08/1915	19/08/1915
War Diary	High-Wood T-Bazentin-Le-Petit	20/08/1915	26/08/1915
War Diary	Becourt	27/08/1915	31/08/1915
Heading	3rd Brigade 1st Division 3rd Machine Gun Company September 1916		
War Diary	Albert (Maxse Redoust)	01/09/1916	01/09/1916
War Diary	Mametz Wood	02/09/1916	05/09/1916
War Diary	Bazentin-Le-Grand (High Wood)	06/09/1916	10/09/1916
War Diary	Henencourt	11/09/1916	11/09/1916
War Diary	Franvillers	12/09/1916	15/09/1916
War Diary	Henencourt	16/09/1916	17/09/1916
War Diary	Black Wood (Albert)	18/09/1916	18/09/1916
War Diary	Mametz Wood	19/09/1916	22/09/1916
War Diary	Bazentin-Le-Grand (High Wood)	23/09/1916	25/09/1916
War Diary	Albert	26/09/1916	27/09/1916
Heading	3rd Brigade 1st Division 3rd Machine Gun Company October 1916		
War Diary	Albert	28/09/1916	28/09/1916
War Diary	Millencourt	29/09/1916	29/09/1916
War Diary	Henencourt Wood	30/09/1916	03/10/1916
War Diary	Hocquelus	04/10/1916	31/10/1916
Heading	3rd Brigade 1st Division 3rd Machine Gun Company November 1916		
War Diary	Bazieux	01/11/1916	05/11/1916
War Diary	Millencourt	06/11/1916	28/11/1916
War Diary	Mametz Wood	29/11/1916	30/11/1916
Heading	3rd Brigade 1st Division 3rd Machine Gun Company December 1916		
War Diary	Flers	01/12/1916	01/12/1916
War Diary	Bazentin Le Petit	03/12/1916	17/12/1916
War Diary	Mametz	18/12/1916	29/12/1916
War Diary	Becourt	30/12/1916	31/12/1916
War Diary	Holquelus	24/09/1916	27/09/1916
Heading	1st Division 3rd M.G. Company 3rd Infantry Brigade From 1st January. To 30th June 1917		
Heading	War Diary 3rd. M.G. Company. 3rd. Infantry Brigade. 1st. Division. January. 1917		
War Diary	Becourt	01/01/1916	22/01/1916
War Diary	Vadencourt	23/01/1916	31/01/1916

Heading	War Diary 3rd. M.G. Company. 3rd. Infantry Brigade. 1st. Division. February. 19117		
War Diary	Vadencourt Morcourt	01/02/1917	04/02/1917
War Diary	Barleux	05/02/1916	22/02/1916
War Diary	Chuignes	23/02/1917	28/02/1917
Heading	War Diary 3rd. M.G. Company. 3rd. Infantry Brigade. 1st. Division. March 1917		
War Diary	Chuignes	01/03/1917	01/03/1917
War Diary	French	02/03/1917	18/03/1917
War Diary	Chuignes	19/03/1917	23/03/1917
War Diary	Chuignes	24/03/1917	31/03/1917
Miscellaneous	Operation Order by Lieut L.P. Da Costa. Commanding 3rd M.G Company		
Heading	War Diary 3rd. M.G. Company. 3rd. Infantry Brigade. 1st. Division. April 1917		
War Diary	Chuignes	01/04/1917	06/04/1917
War Diary	Brie	07/04/1917	15/04/1917
War Diary	Curchy	16/04/1917	30/04/1917
Operation(al) Order(s)	Operation Order No 3 By Lieut L.P. De Costa Commanding 3rd K.G. Company.	09/04/1917	09/04/1917
Operation(al) Order(s)	Operation Order No 3 Lieut R.P. Da by (extra, Commanding 3rd M.G. Coy.	01/04/1917	01/04/1917
Operation(al) Order(s)	Operation Order No. 4 Lieut. L.P. Da. Costa, by Commanding 3rd M.G. Coy	06/04/1917	06/04/1917
Heading	War Diary 3rd. M.G. Company 3rd. Infantry Brigade. 1st. Division. May 1917		
War Diary	Curchy	01/05/1917	02/05/1917
War Diary	Peronne	03/05/1917	07/05/1917
War Diary	Eclusiere	08/05/1917	18/05/1917
War Diary	(Warfusee-Ablan Court)	19/05/1917	19/05/1917
War Diary	Lanotte-En Santerre	20/05/1917	24/05/1917
War Diary	La Motte	25/05/1917	26/05/1917
War Diary	R32 01.6.2 (Sheet 27)	27/05/1917	31/05/1917
Miscellaneous	1st Division No. G 441/12	10/05/1917	10/05/1917
Miscellaneous	General Idea.		
Miscellaneous	Special Idea (White).		
Map	Reference Sheets 62.c. 2 62.d. Scale: 1: 20.000.		
Heading	War Diary 3rd. M.G. Company. 3rd. Infantry Brigade. 1st. Division. June. 1917		
War Diary	R.32d 6-2 (Sheet 27.)	01/06/1917	10/06/1917
War Diary	Wallon-Cappel	11/06/1917	14/06/1917
War Diary	Wormhoudt	15/06/1917	15/06/1917
War Diary	St Pol-Sur-Mer	16/06/1917	18/06/1917
War Diary	Camp Kerkepanne	19/06/1917	19/06/1917
War Diary	Camp Gadel (Coxyde Bains)	20/06/1917	26/06/1917
War Diary	Coxyde Bains	27/06/1917	30/06/1917
Heading	1st Division 3rd M.G. Company 3rd Infantry Brigade From 1st July To 31st December 1917		
Heading	War Diary 3rd. M.G. Company. 3rd. Infantry Brigade. 1st. Division. July 1917		
War Diary	Coxyde Bains	01/07/1917	14/07/1917
War Diary	Ghyvelde	15/07/1917	15/07/1917
War Diary	Capelle	16/07/1917	18/07/1917
War Diary	Le Clipon Camp	19/07/1917	31/07/1917
Heading	War Diary 3rd. M.G. Company. 3rd. Infantry Brigade. 1st. Division. August. 1917		

War Diary	Le Clipon Camp	01/08/1917	31/08/1917
Heading	War Diary 3rd. M.G. Company. 3rd. Infantry Brigade. 1st. Division. September 1917		
War Diary	Le Clipon Camp	01/09/1917	30/09/1917
Heading	War Diary 3rd. M.G. Company. 3rd. Infantry Brigade. 1st. Division. October. 1917		
War Diary	Le Clipon Camp	01/10/1917	19/10/1917
War Diary	Eringhem	20/10/1917	20/10/1917
War Diary	Rubrouck	21/10/1917	24/10/1917
War Diary	Houtkerque	25/10/1917	31/10/1917
Heading	War Diary 3rd. M.G. Company. 3rd. Infantry Brigade. 1st. Division. November. 1917		
War Diary	Houtkerque	01/11/1917	05/11/1917
War Diary	Danbre Camp	06/11/1917	10/11/1917
War Diary	Irish Farm Dambre Camp	11/11/1917	18/11/1917
War Diary	Dirty Bucket Camp	19/11/1917	22/11/1917
War Diary	Schools Camp	23/11/1917	26/11/1917
War Diary	Putney Camp	27/11/1917	30/11/1917
Miscellaneous	Armoured Shorts Nile House D 14a 3095		
Map	Spriet 1:10,000		
Miscellaneous	Armoured Shorts Nile House D 14a 3095		
Heading	War Diary 3rd. M.G. Company. 3rd. Infantry Brigade. 1st. Division. December 1917		
War Diary	Putney Camp (Proven)	01/12/1917	10/12/1917
War Diary	Houthoulst Forest Sector.	11/12/1917	19/12/1917
War Diary	Bixschoote Sheet 28.B.3.a. 6.4 Eikhoek Camp	20/12/1917	28/12/1917
War Diary	A S On 20/12/17	29/12/1917	31/12/1917
Heading	1st Division War Diary 3rd Infantry Bde. 3rd. M.G.C. Absorbed by 1st Bn. M.G.C. From 1st January To 22nd February 1918		
War Diary	Sheet 28 N.W. B. 3.a. 6.4.	01/01/1918	12/01/1918
War Diary	B.I.d. 85.90 Sh. 28.NW.	13/01/1918	13/01/1918
War Diary	S.22.a. Sh. 20 1/40000	14/01/1918	21/01/1918
War Diary	B.I.d. 85.90 Sh. 28.NW.	22/01/1918	24/01/1918
War Diary	Canal Bank	25/01/1918	08/02/1918
War Diary	Siege Camp	09/02/1918	21/02/1918
War Diary	Canal Bank	22/02/1918	28/02/1918

B.E.F. FRANCE & FLANDERS.
1 DIV. 3 INF BRIGADE.
6 WELSH REGIMENT.
1915 NOV TO 1916 MAY.
51 SOUTH WELSH BORDERERS
52. S.W.B.
53. S.W.B.
1919 MAR TO 1919 JULY.
3 LIGHT TRENCH MORTER BATTERY.
1916 AUG.
1917 JULY TO 1919 JAN.
3 MACHINE GUN COMPANY
1916 FEB TO 1918 FEB

B.E.F. FRANCE & FLANDERS
1 DIV. 3 INF BRIGADE.
6 WELSH REGIMENT.
1915 NOV TO 1916 MAY.
51 SOUTH WELSH BORDERER
52. S.W.B.
53. S.W.B.
1919 MAR TO 1919 JULY.
3 LIGHT TRENCH MORTER
BATTERY.
1916 AUG.
1917 JULY TO 1919 JAN
3 MACHINE GUN COMPANY
1916 FEB TO 1918 FEB

1282

WO95/1282

6/ Welsh Regt

Nov '15 – May '16

1ST DIVISION
3RD BRIGADE

6TH BATTALION
WELCH REGIMENT
1915 NOV-DEC 1915 1916 MAY

From 28 DIV 84 BDE

(TO 1 DIV TROOPS Pioneers)

3rd Infantry Brigade.
1st Division.

Battn transferred
from 84th Bde,
28th Div. 28.10.15

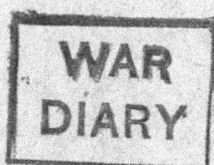

6th BATTN. WELCH REGIMENT.

NOVEMBER

1915

6th Battn. Welch Regiment.

November 1915

NOVEMBER 1st 1915.

The Battalion went a Route March through AUCHEL - LOZINGHEM - BURBERE, it was beastly wet.

Nov 2nd
The wet weather continues & this mornings original routine was cancelled, in place of which the Doctor gave a very useful & interesting lectures on Trench Foot to the men

Nov 3rd
Despite the still inclement weather some practice on the range was carried out & Companies practiced open order drill.
All men bathed today & were now supplied with clean clothes

Nov 4th
Companies practised close order drill & Bayonet fighting. In the afternoon a Bombing Competition was held for the longest & straightest throw.

November 5th

The men fired on the range with smoke helmets on, they are getting more confidence in them now, and will lose that suffocating feeling.

Companies also practised extended order attack whilst a class for our Lewis-s for junior N.C.O.s was held during the morning.

November 6th

Bayonet fighting was practised for the first hour. All men & billets were thoroughly cleaned & inspected by the C.O. during the morning.

In the afternoon we beat the 2nd Welsh at Rugby by 8 points to 3.

November 7th

A very enthusiastic service was held in the village school for the C of E's. Services were arranged for other denominations.

A travelling Concert entertainment was well patronised in the evening.

Nov 12th

We were to have practiced a Bombing Scheme today but owing to the Rain, the programme was cancelled. The men scrubbed their equipment & were inspection by the C.O.

A draft of 10 Officers joined us tonight as follows:—

2nd Lieut. A.G. AKENHEAD	11th Welsh
" " E.S. SEABOURNE	11th "
" " R.M. PROSSER	11th Welsh
" " H.J. EDMUNDS	11th "
" " D.M. MORGAN	11th "
" " F.W. JACOB	11th "
" " J.W.G. MORRIS	9th "
" " C.J.S. NICHOLL	9th "
" " T.T. ELLISON	9th "
" " C.D. ETCHELLS	9th "

Nov 13th

Another soaking wet day, the usual programme was cancelled. The Commanding Officer went carefully through the movement orders with all concerned. An inspection of Billets with the M.O. followed.

November 8th
Weather continued to be wet.
The Battalion went a
Route March via BORDUEL
MARLES-LES-MINES & RAIMBERT

November 9th
Companies received instruction
on extended order drill.
The Battalion practised
the attack. The Machine
Gunners fired on the Range
while Lewis gun squads
were given instruction in
the use of the snipescope
on the Range.

Nov 10th
The new Brigade was
inspected by GENERAL RAWLINSON
the IV Corps Commander
today, who spoke words
of praise & encouragement
to the men.

Nov 11th
Weather still changeable.
The Battalion practised
Bayonet fighting, and
Fire discipline & Control.
Scouts had instruction in
Map reading

Nov 14th — This was the last day of the divisional training, and was spent, after the usual (Sunday) divine services, in making preparation for the move on the following day. Lieut E.H. Blany, who had been acting adjutant since Major Carleton assumed command of the Battalion, left for leave to-day, and his duties were taken up by Lieut P. Bell.

Nov 15th — The Battalion moved off in lovely autumnal weather to their new destination, MAZINGARBE at 8.30 a.m. The whole population turned out to see them off, and ~~the soldier~~ it was very evident that the regiment was extremely popular with the inhabitants. The Battalion arrived at MAZINGARBE at about 6 p.m., having marched a distance of 18 kilometres.

Nov 16th — The morning was spent in cleaning up the roads in front of the billets which were in a very bad condition. The billets were very poor and very dirty.

Nov 17th — The morning was spent in battalion and coy. drill. Instruction was also given to the new officers in bombing.

Nov 18th — Captain J.M. Goldberg took the Battalion for an hour in the morning in drill, after which the companies practised moving over rough ground and giving orders with their smoke helmets on.

Nov 19th. – Cleaning up billets and getting ready for moving into the trenches. The Coy. officers went up in the morning to reconnoitre and take over stores. Lieut R.C. Lindsey-Brabazon took charge of the machine gun section in the place of Lieut J.H. Mills, who left for leave to don. The Battalion moved off at 4.30 pm. for the trenches, and relieved the London Scottish, 1st Brigade. The relief was completed by 7p.m. The Battalion took up the following positions. – "B" Coy. on the right from Puits 14 Bis. and A Coy from the left of B Coy, a frontage of about 1000 yards in the firing line with C and D Coys in support. The South Wales Borderers were on our right, and the "2nd Bn Royal Sussex" were on our left in the firing line.

Nov 20th. – Trenches in very bad condition; over two feet of water in POSSEN ALLEY, leading up to firing line; artillery very active on both sides, and our trenches on the south were enfiladed by enemy battery from HULLOCH. Distance of enemy trenches varies from 300 yds on the south to 60 yards on the North. Our wire is very poor. The enemy opposite us are apparently Saxons, and are very friendly; very little rifle fire.

Nov 21st In the afternoon party of miners' leaders, including Mr Tom Richards, M.P.,

Alfred Onions and others, came round the trenches, and were very much impressed with the cheerfulness of our Officer and men. The enemy bombarded our supports during their visit. One man accidentally killed through sniperscope going on (Pte Simmons)

Nov. 22nd — This day we were relieved by the 2nd Welsh and took over their billets in old German fire trench. There were some very fine dug outs in these trenches. Casualties, two killed by rifle bullets, one whilst working on the top in support line, and the other at FORT GLATZ.

Nov. 23rd and 24th & 25th Very uneventful. The whole battalion was employed in working parties draining and pumping communication trenches.

Nov 26th — First fall of snow. The Battalion were relieved in the same line by 2nd R.W. Welsh Regt. and went back to billets in PHILOSOPHE where they took over from the 1st/9th Kings Regt. The billets were very good, although it was shelled on most days by the enemy.

Nov 27th — Lieut E.H. Clarry commenced a staff course. The day was spent in cleaning up and a working party of 50 men worked four hours at night in POSSEN ALLEY.

Nov 28th — C. of E. service, by companies, was held in a broken down house. Party of 150 men worked for four hours on a new support trench.

Nov 29th. — Every available man in the Battalion was employed on a digging fatigue repairing the trenches which had fallen in near Pint 14.

Nov 30th. — Pte Plane was killed by a shell and two others wounded — L/Cpl Pritchard & Pte Hopkins — when working on signal wires. Battalion was employed on fatigues during the night.

3rd Infantry Brigade.

1st Division.

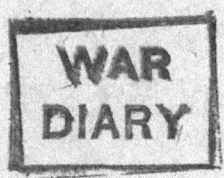

6th BATTN. WELCH REGIMENT.

DECEMBER

1915

6th Battn. Welch Regiment.

December 1915.

December 1st. — The day was spent in cleaning up billets, preparatory to handing over on the morrow.

December 2nd. — The Battalion handed over their billets at PHILOSOPHE to 4th K.R.R's, 2nd Brigade and proceeded to NOEUX-LES-MINES, where they took over billets from 2nd Royal Sussex, 1st Brigade. Lieut R.C. Lindsay-Brabazon took over the adjutancy from Lieut Pearson Bell, who took over the command of "C" Coy.

December 3rd. — Lieut L.C. Frisby took over command of "A" Coy in place of Capt. J.M. Goldberg, who became second in command. The day was spent in cleaning clothes and equipment and billets.

December 4th. — Fatigues were employed every day in cleaning roads and laying down slag on paths and around billets. Parades, 7-7.30 doubling; 9 a.m. to 12 a.m.

inspection of kit and scrubbing of equipment.
Dec 5th. — C. of E. parade 10 a.m.; R.C. parade
11 a.m. The remainder of the day was
spent in bathing.
December 6th. — Two hundred & 30 men on biv.
fatigue, remainder, bombing instruction
and practice in smoke helmets from 9 to 12:30 p.m.
All officers and one NCO per platoon attended
a course of instruction in rivetting at 2 p.m.
Coy. commanders attended a lecture at 5.30
p.m. at MAZINGARBE on "Trench maintenance."
All billets were inspected by the Brig.- Gen. and
by the A.D.M.S., who were very satisfied with them.
Dec 7th. — 7.15-7.45 physical drill; 9-10, coy. drill;
10-11, fire control, musketry;
11-12:30, bombing instruction and practical
with smoke helmets.
Dec 8th. — The battalion handed over billets to
Cameron Highlanders and took over trenches
in front of HULLOCH from VENDIN Alley to
Kingsway Alley, a distance of 1200 yards
from 1st Black Watch and 10th Gloucesters. "A",
"C" and "D" were in the firing line, and "B" Coy
in supports. The 1st Batt. the South Wales Borderers
were on our left, and the 2nd Brigade on our right.
The trenches were in bad condition and continually
falling in. There were three saps in our line,
being old German communication trenches,

which had been barricaded by the Germans and ourselves at a distance of about 30 yards apart.

Dec 9th. — Rifle grenade fired by enemy killed one man — Pte Levi Davies — and wounded four, Pte Sergt Wyatt, Pte Turton, Pte Crabbe, and Cpl. Lowery, in the Northern sap. Two men were also wounded this day, one by a grenade, and the other by shell. The enemy blew the trenches in in several places.

Dec 10th. — Trenches were visited by 1st Divisional General, Major-Gen. Holland, who was very pleased with the work that had been done. A very wet day and the water affecting the chalk caused many falls, which had to be continually repaired.

Dec 11th. — Still raining. Communication trenches knee deep in water. Work repairing falls and cleaning trench. Relieved by 1st/9th Kings and took over trenches in old British line and 1st German firing line.

Dec 12th. — A very quiet day except for normal artillery bombardments on both sides, in which, we, as usual predominated. The morning was spent in cleaning up trenches and in the night every available man was

employed in digging a new support
trench between Sixth and Seventh avenues,
a distance of about 250 yards
long, and about 100 yards from the
firing line. A depth of 3ft 6in was
dug without sustaining any casualties.

Dec 13th. — Work was continued on
new support trench, which was
considerably deepened and widened, and
a new support trench was mapped out
and on the left of the first trench for a
distance of about 100 yards, and
dug to a depth of about three feet.

Dec 14th. — We relieved the 1/9th Kings
in the firing line, but took over
a shorter line, the part previously held by
D Coy being taken over by the 2nd Welsh with
the 2nd Brigade on our right. We were
shelled whilst relieving, but there were
no casualties. Position; C, B, and D Coys
in the front line; A Coy in support.

Dec 15th. — A tremendous amount of
work was done in revetting the
trenches with sandbags and taking up
old trench boards, which in some cases
were found in layers under the mud
from two to three deep. Digging deep
sump holes under trench boards

and relaying same.

__Dec 16th__ — Trenches were inspected by Major-Gen. Holland, who praised the regiment very highly for the cleanliness of the trench & the large amount of work that had been done. A very wet night.

__Dec 17th__ — Relieved by 1/9th Kings and again took over our old position in reserve trenches.

__Dec 18th__ — The morning was spent in cleaning up the trenches. The Commanding Officer (Major Cas. Carleton, D.S.O.) went on leave to-day, and his place was taken by Capt. J.A-S. Hinton. Work continued in the night on new support trench.

__Dec 19th__ — The day was spent in erecting shelters in old German line and throughout the stay in reserve trenches the battalion practised fixing their smoke helmets in 20 seconds. At night work was continued on the support trench which now was dug to the required depth and width ready for revetting. Specimen fire steps were erected & and have since been adopted throughout the university.

__Dec 20th__ — The 15th Bn Loyal North Lancs., 2nd Bde, relieved us and the Bn proceeded to the same billets in NOEUX-LES-

MINES

Dec 21st. – 10 a.m. parade for inspection of rifles, smoke helmets, etc. The remainder of the day was spent in cleaning up kit and refitting under coy. arrangements.

Dec 22nd. – 9–10, inspection and coy. drill. 10.30–11.30, practice with smoke helmets. 11.30–12.30, bombing practice. A small fatigue was also employed in cleaning up the streets.

Dec 23rd. – This day was allotted for baths. Coys. also held kit inspection during the morning and billets were inspected by the C.O. at 12 a.m. A battalion dinner for the officers was held at a café in NOEUF-LES-MINES and was a great success. After dinner the evening was devoted to a musical programme supplied by the members which was greatly appreciated by all.

Dec 24th. – The Commanding Officer & the Adjutant went up the

line" to reconnoitre the trenches.
A party of 5 officers, 16 N.C.O.'s and 200 men were employed on fatigue in communication trenches leading up to the firing line.

Dec 25th. — Divine Service at 11 o'clock.
In the evening a concert was held in which the 6th Welsh Flee Part took part.

Dec 26th. — The morning was spent in cleaning up billets preparatory to moving up to "the line". The Bn. fell in at ~~3.30~~ 2 p.m. and marched to the trenches where they took over from the 10th Gloucesters in the old German line.

Dec 27th. — The day was spent in cleaning up and draining trenches, and in digging sump pits and laying new trench boards. In the night two platoons were employed ~~on the Northern~~ making a redoubt to be known as

"Northern Sap Redoubt", and the remainder of the Bn. worked on a communication trench, south of VENDIN alley, which was to be converted into a new support trench, a depth of about 250 yards.

Dec 28th :— Work was continued on "Northern Sap Redoubt" and also on new support trench. A shell burst on the doorway of the Headquarters, but beyond breaking the door did no damage. The enemy from about this date showed increased activity in artillery bombardments which up to now compared very unfavourably with our own artillery.

Dec 29th :— We relieved the 1/9th Kings in the firing line. Our right being on POSSEN alley (a distance of about 100 yards from PUITS 14) and our left on VENDIN alley, a little south of Hulloch. Position as follows:— "A" "B" and "C" in firing line, and "D" in support. Our anti-air craft brought down a large French battle plane.

Two platoons of the 9th Dublins (16th Div.), were attached to us in the firing line, and two platoons in support for purpose of instruction.

Dec 30th. – Considerable work was done in the trenches in revetting with sand bags, draining, digging sump holes, and laying new trench boards; also, in putting up new wire. Several patrols were sent out to examine enemy wire, which on the whole was in a good condition. No enemy patrols were met. Several working parties were seen, fired on, and dispersed.

Dec 31st. – Major Carleton returned from leave and took over command from Capt. Hinton. Enemy artillery shelled our new reserve trench and POSSEN alley with 6 in. shells, but very little damage was done. Patrols were sent out and one of them was observed and fired on, but suffered no casualties.

1ST DIVISION
3RD BRIGADE

1-6TH BATTALION
THE WELCH REGIMENT
JAN - MAY 1916

3rd Brigade.

1st Division.

1/6th BATTALION THE WELCH REGIMENT ::: JANUARY 1916

6th Welsh Regt.
January 1916

vol 7.

6th Welch.
War Diary.
January 1916

Jan 1st. — We were relieved by 1st/9th Kings
and took up our old position in
reserve trench. Two companies remained
behind & worked for four hours in
new support trench, North of VENDIN Alley.
Mr Millar, of 'B' Co, was wounded by
enemy shrapnel. A draft of 76 other
ranks joined the battalion.

The ration party were shelled when
bringing up rations on the railway
running up to reserve line, but although
the railway was destroyed,
suffered no casualties.

January 2nd. — The enemy shelled new
reserve trench and POSSEN station.
Three platoons employed all day working
on "Northern Sap Redoubt", which was
inspected by C.R.E., 1st Division, who
was highly pleased with the work which
had been done. Two companies worked
four hours on new support trench.

January 3rd. — Cleaning, draining,
digging sump pits and laying new
trench boards in reserve trench. Work
was continued on "Northern Sap Redoubt",
and two companies continued work on
new support trench.

Jan. 4th. — Practice in putting on and
fixing smoke helmets in 20 seconds
was carried out daily during the stay
in reserve trenches. Work was continued
on Northern Sap Redoubt, and this

was inspected by Officers of the General Staff, who expressed themselves as very pleased with the work done.

We relieved 1/9th Kings in firing line and took over the same position vis-à-vis trenches.

Jan 5th. — We were asked to make a special effort to dig a new support trench on the North of POSEN alley, 200 yds long, and 50 yds from our firing line. We were assisted by 200 of 1/9th Kings and two platoons of the 9th Dublins were attached to us. The trench was dug along the entire length, 4ft 6in deep, and 3 ft broad. The Brig.-Gen. was very pleased with the work done. The 1/9th Kings left the Brigade together with the 5th King's Own Lancasters & proceeded to join the 3rd Army.

Jan 6th Work continued on the support trench. VENDIN alley drained, sump pits dug, and new trench boards laid for a distance of 75 yds. Officer's patrol sent out to confirm position, located same and were heavily fired on but suffered no casualties. An order was issued from G.H.Q. asking Bde to cut

30 yards of German wire at a position in front of our line. Volunteers were asked for and No 2370 Pte Thomas, J.R. of our battalion was one of the volunteers. The party was made up as follows. Pte Thomas and a man from the 2nd Welsh together with the Bde Scout Officer & the Bde Bombing Officer. Each man cut 12 yards of German wire, which was about six yards deep and five yards from the enemy trench. There was a German sentry opposite the place where the wire was cut by Pte Thomas, but they were unobserved until they completed their task when they were fired upon but all returned safely to their own lines. Pte Thomas received a note of appreciation from the Div. General & he stated that he was forwarding a report on his action to higher quarters.

Jan 7th. — The battalion was relieved by the Northamptons & the Coy of the Loyal North Lancs of the 2nd Bde. A coy of the Loyal North Lancs relieved our coy on the left. After relief the Bn moved into billets

Jan 8th
at MAZINGARBE taking over from
~~Loyal~~ Bn. Loyal North Lancs.

Jan 8th The day was spent in bathing
and general cleaning up.

Jan 9th In the morning the Battalion
attended Divine Service. In the
afternoon a party of 5 Officers & 200
men went up the trenches on fatigue.
  Also a party of 30 men and an
Officer were employed during the day
maintaining La Rutoire Alley.

Jany 10
  The day was occupied by bathing
at the Divisional Baths. ~~unfatigue~~
Small fatigues were also found for
cleaning up the roads &c. Four or five
shells dropped fairly close the Orderly
Room but no damage was done.

Jany 11th Two fatigue parties of 1 Officer
and 50 men each were detailed to work
at Tower No 1 and Tower No 3 near
Noeux les Mines. The party for Tower No
3 was cancelled after the party had
left. Two further fatigues at of same size

party at same place were also detailed for 12 noon but the party for Tour No 2 was cancelled. The party at Tour No 1 at 12 noon were unable to find R.E. Officer who should have met them and consequently no work was done by them. A party of 1 Officer & 20 men were also employed working on maintenance of Rotten Alley.

The Commanding Officer inspected Billets at 11-30 am

Jany 12 A fatigue party of 5 Officers & 300 men was employed for 6 hours working in the trenches. A party of 1 Officer & 30 men were detailed to unload lorries in magazine of the Battalion has moved up to work under R.E.

Jany 13 The 3rd Bde. were relieved by the 4th Brigade. The Battalion (with the remainder of the Brigade) marched to Heure by train where they entrained at about 10 am arriving at Hillers at about 11 when they detrained and marched to Rainbert where we were billeted for the Divisional Rest.

January 14th

The whole of the day was spent in clearing up the mess left by the last Battalion. The mens appearance was also improved, & some drill was carried out.

Lieut E.O.C. OWENS joined the Battalion from the 2/6th Welsh & was temporaly posted to B. Coy

January 15th

Physical drill & arm drill on the Bn parade ground in the morning.

A scratch football match took place in the afternoon.

2nd Lt. H.H. BUCKNELL & 2nd Lt. A.T. DAVIES joined Battalion from the 2nd/6th Welsh the former was posted to A. Coy & the latter to D. Coy.

January 16th

Church Parade at the school in RAIMBERT after which the men were free for the rest of the day.

2nd Lt. H. Pw. M EVANS joined Battn from 2nd/6 Welsh & was posted to B. Coy

Jan 17th
The Battalion continued its training which included Physical drill, Section & Platoon drill & Musketry. Details such as M.G's, Scouts etc specialised in their own particular branch.

Jan 18th
Preliminary training proceeds & men already show marked improvement both in spirits & smartness.

Jan 19th
Lectures were given to Platoon Commanders & senior N.C.O's. Practice exercises in Fire Control & Orders etc. together with a little Coy. drill occupied the day.

Jan 20th
The whole morning was taken up with Ceremonial & general cleaning up. 2nd LT H.H. BUCKNELL took over duties as Adjutant 2ND LT E.H. CLARRY proceeding to England on leave. We lined the streets for General JOFFRE who passed through RAIMBERT

Jan 21st
Physical drill & bayonet fighting and extended order drill was the order of the day. A good attendance at a Cinema Concert given by MAJOR BLACKBURN in the evening.

Jan 22nd
The men practised Platoon extended order drill, & Musketry & fire control.
A draft of 1 S.N.C.O & 9 men joined us from England & the Base.
The Brigade Machine Gun Company was formed today.

Jan 23rd
Divine Service & C.O's inspection of Billets & Area was all that we did today.

Jan 24th
One Company spent the day on the range. The remaining Companies as well as details carried out their own scheme of training.

Jan 25th
Company training continues.

Jan 26th
Independent Company training including the attack & outposts.

Jan 27th
The men indulged in a good hot bath today. One company was on the range, the other companies continued their special training.

Jan 28th
Instruction for Lewis gun team on the range. Musketry & Company training details carried out their own programme.

Jan 29th
Companies practiced attack in Artillery formation. Some word fighting was also done.

Jan 30th Divine Service & Company programme carried out. First D.C.M. in Battalion 2370. Pte. J H Thomas D Coy. for successfully cutting German wire

Jan 31st

This day was allotted for practicing backward work etc. this was duly carried out. 3rd Brigade boxing tournament in the afternoon & evening in which we won one 1st prize, two 2nd prizes & one best loser prize.

3rd Brigade.

1st Division.

MISSING

1/6th BATTALION THE WELCH REGIMENT

WAR DIARY FOR FEBRUARY 1916 MISSING

3rd Brigade.

1st Division.

1/6th BATTALION WELCH REGIMENT ::: MARCH 1916.

WAR DIARY or INTELLIGENCE SUMMARY

Army Form C. 2118

Place	Date	Hour	Summary of Events and Information	Remarks and references to Appendices
BRANDHOEK	1/3/		As usual - The morning was devoted to Company drill and specially details classes for Lewis gun and Lewis Gun. The Regimental Band played in the afternoon in the Band Stand. St Davids Day tickets were very popular. A very good Regimental concert in honour of the day was given later in the evening and which the Band rendered much assistance.	

Army Form C. 2118

Instructions regarding War Diaries and Intelligence Summaries are contained in F. S. Regs., Part II. and the Staff Manual respectively. Title Pages will be prepared in manuscript.

WAR DIARY
or
INTELLIGENCE SUMMARY

(Erase heading not required.)

Place	Date	Hour	Summary of Events and Information	Remarks and references to Appendices
BRACQUEMONT	2/3/16		The Commanding Officer and Company Commanders went to SOUTH MAROC to reconnoitre line. All the Battalion were in billets in better down houses. The morning was spent as usual in Company drill, lecture, drill and Lewis Gun instruction, 2" trench R.C. howitzer, Stokes gun and the Adjutancy.	

WAR DIARY or INTELLIGENCE SUMMARY

Army Form C. 2118

Place	Date	Hour	Summary of Events and Information	Remarks and references to Appendices
BEAUCAMP	3/3/16		The morning was spent in clearing up billets preparatory to handing them over to 3 Berkshire Regt (2nd Brigade) whom we were relieving in the line. At about 5 pm the Battalion moved off and relieved the 1st Berkshires at about 7.30 pm in support in MARCE Scar, left Subsec. One Company was detailed to support and work with 2 Royal Munster Fusiliers at 1st C.T's. The remainder of the Battalion worked for 4 hours in the trenches.	

Army Form C. 2148

WAR DIARY
or
INTELLIGENCE SUMMARY

(Erase heading not required.)

Instructions regarding War Diaries and Intelligence Summaries are contained in F. S. Regs., Part II. and the Staff Manual respectively. Title Pages will be prepared in manuscript.

Place	Date	Hour	Summary of Events and Information	Remarks and references to Appendices
South MAROC	11/3/16		Very little movement could be seen & it was concluded by observation that our look on the support line (SEVENTH AVENUE) was rendered continuous as the afternoon. A certain amount of desultory shelling of our billets & reserve trenches but no damage was done.	

WAR DIARY
or
INTELLIGENCE SUMMARY

Army Form C. 2118

Place	Date	Hour	Summary of Events and Information	Remarks and references to Appendices
South. pare	5/3/16		A B bright clear day. Enemy shelled road about 200 yards from our billets with 8 inch (How.) but did little damage. Enemy aeroplane very active - several aerial engagements - one of the enemy attacked 2 of our aeroplanes managed to get back to its own lines. (Lt Brinzin) A Company of 8 Royal Irish Fusiliers were attached to us for instruction. Battalion worked all day on Support line.	

WAR DIARY
or
INTELLIGENCE SUMMARY

(Erase heading not required.)

Army Form C. 2118

Instructions regarding War Diaries and Intelligence Summaries are contained in F.S. Regs., Part II. and the Staff Manual respectively. Title Pages will be prepared in manuscript.

Place	Date	Hour	Summary of Events and Information	Remarks and references to Appendices
South Maroc	4/3/16		Battalion continued work on Support line in morning. The afternoon was devoted to cleaning up billets preparatory to handing over to 2nd Royal Munsters. At about 6pm we relieved 1st Glo'ster on left sub sector MAROC from huisine sheet 36 Cojeul Rouse (Aix La Chapelle) (M.11.b.4.5 to M.5.a.3.1.) Scale 1:10,000) Three Companies in front line one in Support and one in Reserve. At about 4pm a working party blown in at foot of Fosse 5 South Crassier and 11 men (Glo'ster + R.E.) were buried. They were dug out about 4 am 7/3/16 and no man lived. 2-Lt Ellison rejoined from Hospital.	

1875 Wt. W593/826 1,000,000 4/15 J.B.C. & A. A.D.S.S./Forms/C. 2118.

Army Form C. 2118

WAR DIARY
or
INTELLIGENCE SUMMARY
(Erase heading not required.)

Instructions regarding War Diaries and Intelligence Summaries are contained in F. S. Regs., Part II. and the Staff Manual respectively. Title Pages will be prepared in manuscript.

Place	Date	Hour	Summary of Events and Information	Remarks and references to Appendices
Hill 60 MARIC	1/3/16		The front line was blown in many places by enemy trenchfire. A number of the enemy were seen at dawn near this line and were fired on and dispersed. No 11175 Pte Jevons B Coy killed by a sniper. In the afternoon a large number of trench mortars were thrown by the enemy in the neighbourhood of our front line.	

WAR DIARY
or
INTELLIGENCE SUMMARY

(Erase heading not required.)

Army Form C. 2148

Instructions regarding War Diaries and Intelligence Summaries are contained in F. S. Regs., Part II. and the Staff Manual respectively. Title Pages will be prepared in manuscript.

Place	Date	Hour	Summary of Events and Information	Remarks and references to Appendices
LEFT SUB SECTS MARICO	8/7/16		The enemy again trenched our lines with trench mortars and field artillery rifles and trench mortars – our field mortars and field artillery replied with good effect. They also put heavy trench shells with delay time fuses. They were apparently reaching for our mine heads. Several trench attacks were made by us in front of the Southern Crassier. Our Stokes guns eventually drove them down – he suffered the casualties. The Company of R 131's attacked him – he went back to his billets in Petit Saens. We had 2 casualties from artillery in Hortzoff-Rasoiny father indep.	

WAR DIARY
or
INTELLIGENCE SUMMARY

Army Form C. 2118

Place	Date	Hour	Summary of Events and Information	Remarks and references to Appendices
Left sub sect 5 MARIC...	9/3/ 16		A comparatively quiet day. A party of 2 Officers and 30 men went to for a flammenwerfer exhibition. Were relieved at dusk by 9.30 by 1st Glosters and took over billets in REF BRE 815.16275 Company Sergeant Major Cuddigan No 2882 Lance Corporal Woollahr now being promoted 2nd Lieut serving on connected with recent enter Dublin	

Army Form C. 2148

WAR DIARY
or
INTELLIGENCE SUMMARY
(Erase heading not required.)

Instructions regarding War Diaries and Intelligence Summaries are contained in F. S. Regs., Part II. and the Staff Manual respectively. Title Pages will be prepared in manuscript.

Place	Date	Hour	Summary of Events and Information	Remarks and references to Appendices
LES BREBIS	1/3/16		A party of 30 men were employed cleaning roads. A large number of men were used in endeavour to clean up new Billets in South avenue. On the arrival of GB Battalion to trench of hours found enemy line. On the arrival of GB Battalion moved at to these new Billets which were on the whole quite comfortable	

Place	Date	Hour	Summary of Events and Information	Remarks and references to Appendices
South Maroc	18/3/16		The whole Battalion worked all day on what is known as Reserve line from 7' Avenue to beyond junction with South [?] - Party of 3 Officers and 100 Other ranks working for R.E. in evening. "A" Company & 8' Royal Irish Fusiliers were attached to us for instruction.	

Army Form C. 2118

WAR DIARY
or
INTELLIGENCE SUMMARY
(Erase heading not required.)

Place	Date	Hour	Summary of Events and Information	Remarks and references to Appendices
Souchez Mare	12/3/16		The Battalion worked in relief in same line – 2" L.P.C. Routing relieved from Lewis Gun Crews at Jetroy. He relieved 1st Gloster in left sub sector Mare at about 9-30 p.m. – At about 4 p.m. enemy defence depot at fort Maillon barracks was blown in and about 35 men were buried. Relief parties worked all night trying to dig them out but enemy shell fire was very accurate and caused many casualties. About 9 a.m. party were to dig themselves out as well as men still alive. A/CSM Turner was recommended by Lt 73 R.E. Coy for staying under fire in trying to rescue those men and for doing the best man's work to dig out what was in a very dangerous workings.	

WAR DIARY
or
INTELLIGENCE SUMMARY

(Erase heading not required.)

Army Form C. 2118

Instructions regarding War Diaries and Intelligence Summaries are contained in F.S. Regs., Part II. and the Staff Manual respectively. Title Pages will be prepared in manuscript.

Place	Date	Hour	Summary of Events and Information	Remarks and references to Appendices
Left Sub sector Hinges	13/5/16		Our 9.2 (Howr) bombarded enemy lines opposite trenches 15 (in particular) & Hulluch. Trenches have preneds of Cl. shells were fired. Enemy trench engaged returns stare was in our left and was dispersed by our machine gun fire. Enemy bombed our map on S. Chasses, a recent occurrence and was retaliated well very good effect. Two small enemy bombing parties attacked our map in Hulluch Crasses but were dispersed by our machine gun fire. Two huts although recently thrown were very inefficient. All available men worked on New Communication Trench connectly 69.1 and Laurette avenue (made site to map/71 feet 1/10,000) Capt J.S. Packard was wounded by bomb. No bato. were wounded by Bomb.	

1875 Wt. W593/826 1,000,000 4/15 J.B.C. & A. A.D.S.S./Forms/C. 2118.

WAR DIARY
or
INTELLIGENCE SUMMARY
(Erase heading not required.)

Army Form C. 2118

Place	Date	Hour	Summary of Events and Information	Remarks and references to Appendices
MAROC.	14/3/16		A nice day. The enemy totally damaged our front line & saps by shell fire & trench mortar bombs today. Our 9.2 hows (13 Siege Battery. LES BREBIS) bombarded the enemy lines opposite MINE 15. A large percentage of these shells were blind – a large amount of damage was done to the enemy trenches by the shells which exploded. The enemy bombed our sap on the SOUTHERN CRASSIER on several occasions. We retaliated with good effect, but Mills Bombs seem to be very effective when they burst in the enemy sap, as groans could be heard several times after we had thrown them. The enemy usually eased fire pretty abruptly when we got any of our Mills in his sap. A draft of 32. other ranks arrived from England at the BASE. About 4.30 pm, a rifle grenade fired by the Germans fell short in the sap on the SOUTHERN CRASSIER killing 2nd Lieut Ellison & Sergt Holmes. They died instantaneously. 2nd Lieut Ellison had only returned about four days from a Base Hospital. [struck out line] Sergt Holmes the was the Battalion bombing sergt. & had done some very good work. These two will be felt by all. It was a great shock to us all. Two other men were killed & 9 were wounded in the same sap during the day. At the Coy of Offr R.D.F. & orders received by another Coy of the same regiment	

1875 W. W593/326 1,000,000 4/15 J.B.C. & A. A.D.S.S./Forms/C. 2118.

Army Form C. 2118

WAR DIARY
or
INTELLIGENCE SUMMARY

(Erase heading not required.)

Instructions regarding War Diaries and Intelligence Summaries are contained in F. S. Regs., Part II. and the Staff Manual respectively. Title Pages will be prepared in manuscript.

Place	Date	Hour	Summary of Events and Information	Remarks and references to Appendices
MAROC	15/3/16		The enemy was very active during the day & threw bombs & fired rifle grenades on our SAPS on the NORTHERN & SOUTHERN CRASSIER. All available men worked on new trench between M & C 8.10 & M 4 d.1.7. Lieut. J. Evans joined the battalion today. The Battalion was relieved in the evening by the 1st Loyal North Lancs & marched to LES BREBIS. Here we took over billets. 2nd Lieut. Ellison was buried in the cemetery at MAROC. Several officers attended the funeral.	

Army Form C. 2118

WAR DIARY
or
INTELLIGENCE SUMMARY

(Erase heading not required.)

Instructions regarding War Diaries and Intelligence Summaries are contained in F. S. Regs., Part II. and the Staff Manual respectively. Title Pages will be prepared in manuscript.

Place	Date	Hour	Summary of Events and Information	Remarks and references to Appendices
LES BREBIS	15/3/16		The day was spent in general cleaning up & rest. The enemy shelled the village slightly during the morning with H.E. shrapnel. One man of this battalion was killed; five others being wounded at the same time. Rather a poor start! The rest of the day was uneventful.	

Army Form C. 2118

WAR DIARY
or
INTELLIGENCE SUMMARY
(*Erase heading not required.*)

Instructions regarding War Diaries and Intelligence Summaries are contained in F. S. Regs., Part II. and the Staff Manual respectively. Title Pages will be prepared in manuscript.

Place	Date	Hour	Summary of Events and Information	Remarks and references to Appendices
YPES BREGIS	1/3/16	—	The day was quite uneventful. Lieut Ranger re-joined the battalion from hospital.	

Army Form C. 2118.

WAR DIARY
or
INTELLIGENCE SUMMARY

(Erase heading not required.)

Instructions regarding War Diaries and Intelligence Summaries are contained in F.S. Regs., Part II. and the Staff Manual respectively. Title Pages will be prepared in manuscript.

Place	Date	Hour	Summary of Events and Information	Remarks and references to Appendices
LES BREBIS	18/3/16		The new draft was instructed in bombing by 2nd Lieut MORRIS. Lieut. J. R. Samuel arrived today from England and was taken on the strength of the battalion. The day was uneventful.	

Army Form C. 2118

WAR DIARY
or
INTELLIGENCE SUMMARY
(Erase heading not required.)

Instructions regarding War Diaries and Intelligence Summaries are contained in F. S. Regs., Part II. and the Staff Manual respectively. Title Pages will be prepared in manuscript.

Place	Date	Hour	Summary of Events and Information	Remarks and references to Appendices
LES BREBIS	19/8/16		The day was bright & sunny. Nothing of interest happened today, with the exception that leave recommenced (this is very interesting).	

Army Form C. 2118

WAR DIARY
or
INTELLIGENCE SUMMARY

(Erase heading not required.)

Instructions regarding War Diaries and Intelligence Summaries are contained in F. S. Regs., Part II and the Staff Manual respectively. Title Pages will be prepared in manuscript.

Place	Date	Hour	Summary of Events and Information	Remarks and references to Appendices
LES BREBIS	20/3/16		Nothing of interest happened today. Lieut R. K. Green arrived from England and was taken on the strength of the battalion. In the evening there were the usual fatigue parties.	

Army Form C. 2118.

WAR DIARY
or
INTELLIGENCE SUMMARY
(Erase heading not required.)

Instructions regarding War Diaries and Intelligence Summaries are contained in F. S. Regs., Part II. and the Staff Manual respectively. Title Pages will be prepared in manuscript.

Place	Date	Hour	Summary of Events and Information	Remarks and references to Appendices
LES BREBIS	2/1/16		A quiet day. Battalion went to the Baths (by companies) during the morning & afternoon. 2nd Lieut Cherry & 2nd Lieut Hugh Evans went to Hospital.	

Army Form C. 2118

WAR DIARY
or
INTELLIGENCE SUMMARY
(Erase heading not required.)

Instructions regarding War Diaries and Intelligence Summaries are contained in F. S. Regs., Part II. and the Staff Manual respectively. Title Pages will be prepared in manuscript.

Place	Date	Hour	Summary of Events and Information	Remarks and references to Appendices
North Maroc	22/3/16		A very quiet day practically no shelling on either side — found our new billets very comfortable. The men were employed in cleaning up Billets and making them more comfortable. As now all the Battalion were employed in this way.	

Place	Date	Hour	Summary of Events and Information	Remarks and references to Appendices
North Maroc	23/3/16		Another very quiet day. The whole Battalion were employed on fatigue at night	

Army Form C. 2118

WAR DIARY
or
INTELLIGENCE SUMMARY

(Erase heading not required.)

Instructions regarding War Diaries and Intelligence Summaries are contained in F. S. Regs., Part II. and the Staff Manual respectively. Title Pages will be prepared in manuscript.

Place	Date	Hour	Summary of Events and Information	Remarks and references to Appendices
North Maroc	24/3/16		Snow fell heavily during the night and was at least 3 inches deep in the morning. Headquarters were moved during the day as they were too far away from the Companies. A small mine was thrown by us in the Carency sector. There a small volume of earth but well into the air and went fair and immediate danger to enemy trolley lays. At about 9pm we relieved 1st Cheshires in trenches left Bangad. and trench and a week from Harness Cols to Corner and enclosive (M b 63b to M 5a 31 Scale 1:10,000) Two of our Companies hold the front line with a Company of 2 Royal Munster Fusiliers in support	

Army Form C. 2118

WAR DIARY
or
INTELLIGENCE SUMMARY
(Erase heading not required.)

Instructions regarding War Diaries and Intelligence Summaries are contained in F. S. Regs., Part II. and the Staff Manual respectively. Title Pages will be prepared in manuscript.

Place	Date	Hour	Summary of Events and Information	Remarks and references to Appendices
LOOS Right Battⁿ HQrs	29/3/16		A fairly quiet day. The enemy 'paywashed' our front line & supports in the vicinity of HARRISONS CRATER. Weather fairly warm, with occasional showers. During the afternoon some showers of rain. In the evening it we were relieved by the 1st Glosters who moved in about 7.30 pm. Relief was completed about 9 pm. Battalion then moved out, C company going to O.G.1. near HQs, A Coy being just N. of the LOOS CRASSIER (M36d5.5), B Coy in the ENCLOSURE & D Coy being in cellars in LOOS near the RIGHT BATTN HQrs. Headquarters left LOOS & proceeded to O.G.1, by via a road which runs to MAROC. A very dark night with wind & rain rendered walking somewhat difficult. The road running from LOOS to MAROC very wet & muddy. Very comfortable dugout + very safe - dugout being about 25 feet underground. Sleeping accommodation not so good - A great fault of all these German Dugouts is the need for artificial light all day. However acetylene is a good substitute. All ranks did not go on fatigue which was a good thing as they had had a very hard day working on their trenches in the line all day.	

Army Form C. 2118

WAR DIARY
or
INTELLIGENCE SUMMARY
(Erase heading not required.)

Instructions regarding War Diaries and Intelligence Summaries are contained in F. S. Regs., Part II. and the Staff Manual respectively. Title Pages will be prepared in manuscript.

Place	Date	Hour	Summary of Events and Information	Remarks and references to Appendices
Old German front line O.G.1.	28/3/16	—	A very nice sunny day on the whole, although rather a cold wind. Enemy exceptionally quiet — our artillery also very inactive. From about 11 am & onwards the Germans lines could be very plainly seen owing to the sunlight — therefore a splendid day for observation — the enemy evidently thought so too & kept very quiet with the result that very little movement was seen. Some 'pip squeaking' of our support & front line in places & of the MAROC end of PICCADILLY, one 'pipsqueak' broke a portion of the barricade erected on the side of the road to prevent movement being seen there — several men passing here had narrow escapes as it an enemy machine gun was very attentive. No definite news of the 'show' at VERDUN. In the evening sky clouded over — looks appears to be another snow storm coming or at least heavy rain. Wind very cold. 60 men of C Coy working in LOOS for the 26 Field Coy R.E.s.	

WAR DIARY
or
INTELLIGENCE SUMMARY
(Erase heading not required.)

Army Form C. 2118

Place	Date	Hour	Summary of Events and Information	Remarks and references to Appendices
Old German front line.	29/7/16		A very quiet day. There were some very artistic drawings on the walls of our Mess. Went up to MAROC as usual & had a good Observation report. There are a large number of rats in these trenches — the huns always seem to attract vermin. The dugouts here are very deep — almost like little coal mines. Went out in the evening & inspected the 'souvenir' left outside the wire entanglements by our four fellows on the 25th September. There is a 9" or 10" shell (German) lying out there — a most dangerous looking object. A few scraps between our aeroplanes & the Boches — but none of our aeroplanes were brought down. One could have a splendid view of the German lines from O.G. 1. It was very interesting watching the German shells bursting round HARRISON'S CRATER.	

Army Form C. 2118

WAR DIARY
or
INTELLIGENCE SUMMARY
(Erase heading not required.)

Instructions regarding War Diaries and Intelligence Summaries are contained in F.S. Regs., Part II. and the Staff Manual respectively. Title Pages will be prepared in manuscript.

Place	Date	Hour	Summary of Events and Information	Remarks and references to Appendices
Old German front line.	3/17/16		Our third day here. A beautiful sunny day. Very uneventful. Visited the Lieuts Glanachan Pvt in MAROC & obtained a very fine view of the enemy's lines. Strafed two enemy working parties with the aid of the artillery. The Huns appeared to be very annoyed about it & replied with shrapnel on ARTILLERY ROW. In the evening we walked down to LOOS, as we had to relieve the 1st Gloster regiment. A very nice evening — very little rifle fire. On the way down the Doctor & myself bandaged up 1 of one of the Munsters who was wounded in the thigh. Our relief was carried out alright as usual. Except for the enemy's rifle grenade fire the night was comparatively quiet. (We little knew what the Huns were preparing for us the next morning).	

Army Form C. 2118.

WAR DIARY
or
INTELLIGENCE SUMMARY
(Erase heading not required.)

Instructions regarding War Diaries and Intelligence Summaries are contained in F. S. Regs., Part II. and the Staff Manual respectively. Title Pages will be prepared in manuscript.

Place	Date	Hour	Summary of Events and Information	Remarks and references to Appendices
LOOS.	31/8/16		Huns started shrapnel'ing our front line between HART'S & HARRISONS CRATER. They suddenly appeared to have a grudge against this part of the line as they poured in shells two at a time, until after midday. At last our artillery replied but it did not seem to intimidate the Huns then. The front line resembled a badly metalled road in a very short time. Tried to get up to the front line but got caught by two shells, but um-hats' saved us again, so about three pieces of shells hit my hat! The Doctor considered that this was not a getting a bit too much of it; the stretcher bearers did very good work in getting the wounded men down from the front line. The weather was really glorious — just the sort of day to be in England. Sergt Powell was killed by a sniper-bullet on HARRISONS CRATER. Must interview that sniper tomorrow. Major Carrington, commdg. the 115 Battery, visited the HQs during the afternoon, & prepared his mins or everything in general. In the evening, the Doctor took our Liaison officer up to the front line to shew him what the Hun's had done. A fairly quiet night except for some rifle grenades on our front line. However, we fired them more back than they wanted.	

3rd Brigade.

1st Division.

1/6th BATTALION THE WELCH REGIMENT))) APRIL 1916.

Army Form C. 2118

1/6 Welsh Regt

Vol 10

WAR DIARY
or
INTELLIGENCE SUMMARY

(Erase heading not required.)

Instructions regarding War Diaries and Intelligence Summaries are contained in F.S. Regs., Part II. and the Staff Manual respectively. Title Pages will be prepared in manuscript.

8th BATTALION, THE WELSH REGIMENT

Place	Date	Hour	Summary of Events and Information	Remarks and references to Appendices
LOOS	1/4/16		A beautiful sunny day. This morning the 'Huns' strafed our trenches on the right of HARRISONS CRATER for about 1½ hours starting at 9 a.m. Our trenches there were very badly damaged, our front line being almost levelled. We lost four killed & five wounded — amongst the killed being Capt. Morris. He was with several men in the front-line when a shell hit the front line, killing all of them except two men, one of whom was wounded. (He was bombing officer of the Battalion & was a very plucky & efficient officer. He had been about 5 months with us & his loss will be felt by all.) Our artillery replied but a large number of their shells were blind. During the afternoon things became very quiet except for the usual desultory shelling of our lines by the enemy artillery. Visited the bombing sap on MORRISON'S CRATER to inspect an enemy sniper's post. Was not disappointed as we could distinctly see the openings in the reflection from his periscope which he pushed up. Enemy also strafed the house where the hospital is — they obtained several direct hits. Owing to the hot weather, the trenches have already started to smell a lot. The C.O was bad in the night — probably owing to the escape of acetylene gas ~~started~~ from our lamp. We have now adopted the lamp & use candles instead.	M.M.

Army Form C. 2118

WAR DIARY
or
INTELLIGENCE SUMMARY
(Erase heading not required.)

Instructions regarding War Diaries and Intelligence Summaries are contained in F.S. Regs., Part II. and the Staff Manual respectively. Title Pages will be prepared in manuscript.

8th BATTALION,
THE
WELSH REGIMENT.

Place	Date	Hour	Summary of Events and Information	Remarks and references to Appendices
LOOS.	2/8/16		A nice sunny day. The Huns 'shaped' our trenches in the same places as yesterday. About 60 yards of SOUTH STREET was knocked in & five bays of our front line trenches to the West of the D was also blocked. The enemy was evidently searching for minenshafts. In the evening we were relieved by the 1st Loyal North Lancs about 10.p.m. Battalion then marched to LES BREBIS & took over billets from 2nd K.R.R.O. Everyone glad to get back for 6 days as we had a pretty strenuous time for three days. The Commanding Officer proceeded to England on leave for 10 days.	

Army Form C. 2118

WAR DIARY
or
INTELLIGENCE SUMMARY
(Erase heading not required.)

Place	Date	Hour	Summary of Events and Information	Remarks and references to Appendices
Les Brebis	3/4/16		A nice fine day again. The enemy sent over one shell which did no damage. Roads very dusty already from this spell of fine weather. All the same we all hope it keeps fine as nothing is worse than wet weather out here. Lt. Owens proceeded on leave to England.	

Army Form C. 2118

WAR DIARY or INTELLIGENCE SUMMARY

(Erase heading not required.)

Place	Date	Hour	Summary of Events and Information	Remarks and references to Appendices
LES BREBIS	4/9/16		Weather still fine but atmosphere very heavy to today. The Huns sent over a shell into the town at varying intervals – none of them did any damage as far as can be gathered. Spent some of the morning looking for the Rifle Range here. In the afternoon Company Commanders, Major Shaw the Lewis Gun Officer went to reconnoitre a new sector of the line on the right below BULLY. Some of the Battalion on fatigue – parties to report at the HOLE in the WALL.	

Army Form C. 2118

WAR DIARY
or
INTELLIGENCE SUMMARY
(Erase heading not required.)

Instructions regarding War Diaries and Intelligence Summaries are contained in F. S. Regs., Part II. and the Staff Manual respectively. Title Pages will be prepared in manuscript.

Place	Date	Hour	Summary of Events and Information	Remarks and references to Appendices
LES BREBIS	5/4/16		A nice sunny day. The whole battalion was out on fatigue for the greater part of the day. I attended a Field Court-Martial in the morning. During the day the enemy sent over a fair number of shells on the town. One man of the M.Berlis was rather badly injured & two civilians, a woman & a child, were killed. The only casualties in this battalion were four of our band instruments, three being slightly damaged & one was damaged beyond repair. The band, at the time were having dinner somewhere else, so they had a very narrow escape.	

Army Form C. 2118

WAR DIARY
or
INTELLIGENCE SUMMARY
(Erase heading not required.)

Place	Date	Hour	Summary of Events and Information	Remarks and references to Appendices
LES BRÉBIS	6/4/16		A quiet day. The enemy did not send over any shells here yesterday. In the evening two fatigue parties under two officers each worked for the 173 Coy. R.Es. The first party left here at 6.45 p.m. & proceeded to MAROC; from here they carried timber down to bn H.Q. 13 a 7.2. Mines where they emptied sand bags from these mines for about three hours. About 10.30 p.m. it came on to rain rather heavily which made the roads & trenches very muddy & slippery.	

Army Form C. 2118

WAR DIARY
or
INTELLIGENCE SUMMARY
(Erase heading not required.)

Place	Date	Hour	Summary of Events and Information	Remarks and references to Appendices
LES BREBIS.	7/4/16		A quiet day. Weather rather dull. 100 men & two officers on fatigue tonight for the Trench Maintenance Company at ST PANCRAS KEEP. The enemy sent over a few shells on the town during the afternoon which did no damage to any of this battalion. 2nd Lieut Hugh Evans rejoined from Hospital. 2nd Lieut Edmunds went to Hospital.	

Army Form C. 2118

WAR DIARY
or
INTELLIGENCE SUMMARY
(Erase heading not required.)

Instructions regarding War Diaries and Intelligence Summaries are contained in F.S. Regs., Part II. and the Staff Manual respectively. Title Pages will be prepared in manuscript.

6th BATTALION, THE WELSH REGIMENT.
No.........
Date.........

Place	Date	Hour	Summary of Events and Information	Remarks and references to Appendices
LES BREBIS	8/4/16		A quiet day - nice sunny weather. The enemy sent over several shells on the town during the day. In the evening we marched to MAROC & took over billets from the 8th Berkshires. About 8.30 the Engineers (ours) blew up a small mine near the new craters to the E. of LOOS CRASSIER. Our artillery fired - the enemy sent up a large number of red rockets - also several green ones - as if to call on their artillery for support - their artillery replied in bursts. Our machine guns could be heard "going strong" - the enemy machine guns could also be heard. These are not bad Head quarters - it is really much nicer to be in houses when in support or reserve instead of in trenches - it feels a bit more "comfy". Also these houses are certainly cleaner than the old German lines which absolutely "swarm" in rats & beastly things.	

WAR DIARY
or
INTELLIGENCE SUMMARY

Army Form C. 2118

Place	Date	Hour	Summary of Events and Information	Remarks and references to Appendices
MAROC	9/4/16		A very nice day. The bombardment of the enemy trenches SW of PUITS 16 was postponed as I expect it will happen tomorrow. The 12" Howitzer at LES BREBIS fired on a block of houses in CITÉ ST AUGUSTE & made some good practice – however observation was almost impossible owing to the heat haze. During the night our field guns, which are very near these Headquarters, fired intermittently on the enemy lines – these guns <u>do</u> make a beastly row!	

Army Form C. 2118

WAR DIARY
or
INTELLIGENCE SUMMARY
(Erase heading not required.)

Instructions regarding War Diaries and Intelligence Summaries are contained in F.S. Regs., Part II. and the Staff Manual respectively. Title Pages will be prepared in manuscript.

Place	Date	Hour	Summary of Events and Information	Remarks and references to Appendices
MAROC	10/4/16		A nice sunny day. During the morning the battalion worked on Sickly Alley — cleaning & deepening same towards the old German line. During the afternoon there was some desultory shelling of our trenches. At 4.30 pm our artillery carried off a very successful bombardment on the enemy's front line to the S.W. of PUITS 16. The 'shrap' lasted for about 20 minutes — a large number of guns fired & the shooting was very accurate. The enemy wire was badly damaged in the guns then lifted on to the enemy's support. No infantry attack was made but the enemy evidently thought we were going to! He shelled our front line & support line at the same time as our bombardment was carried out. The bombardment was a fine spectacle to witness — I saw it from the infantry O.P. in NEUF ALLEY. We had another trial SOS in the evening about 5.45 pm.	

1875 Wt. W593/826 1,000,000 4/15 J.B.C. & A. A.D.S.S./Forms/C. 2118.

WAR DIARY or INTELLIGENCE SUMMARY

Army Form C. 2118

(Erase heading not required.)

Instructions regarding War Diaries and Intelligence Summaries are contained in F. S. Regs., Part II. and the Staff Manual respectively. Title Pages will be prepared in manuscript.

Place	Date	Hour	Summary of Events and Information	Remarks and references to Appendices
MAROC (Left Section)	11/4/16		A quiet day - & sunny. In the evening we moved down to the left section & took over the line from the 1st Gloster's. In the night, at 11.30.pm I went out to find two Lymans dead & if possible to bring them into our lines. However we only got 150 yards when, owing to the bright moonlight, a German sniper on the NORTHERN CRASSIER spotted us & sent several shots over 'rather' near. Patrol returned to our lines at 12.30pm. Two Lewis guns fired on the crater formed by the camouflet flown up by us today during the night. These bursts of fire kept the enemy from repairing his damaged sap. The enemy were working on their trenches in the triangle during the night - also some wiring on the apex of the △.	

Army Form C. 2118

WAR DIARY
or
INTELLIGENCE SUMMARY

(Erase heading not required.)

Instructions regarding War Diaries and Intelligence Summaries are contained in F. S. Regs., Part II. and the Staff Manual respectively. Title Pages will be prepared in manuscript.

Place	Date	Hour	Summary of Events and Information	Remarks and references to Appendices
MAROC (left section)	12/4/16		A Quiet day. It rained for the greater part of the day which made the trenches very muddy. Enemy very quiet today. Visited front line twice also NORTHERN CRASSIER, by means of a periscope a miniature found that those two dead lying out between the lines are French not German. Message came through that all leave to be stopped on the 18th & that everyone on leave must return by that date	

Army Form C. 2118

WAR DIARY
or
INTELLIGENCE SUMMARY
(Erase heading not required.)

Instructions regarding War Diaries and Intelligence Summaries are contained in F. S. Regs., Part II. and the Staff Manual respectively. Title Pages will be prepared in manuscript.

Place	Date	Hour	Summary of Events and Information	Remarks and references to Appendices
MAROC (left sector)	13/4/16		A quiet day – weather fairly fair. In the morning it rained very heavily but it cleared up nicely later & was nice & sunny in the afternoon. The enemy was very quiet to-day – except for some desultory shelling of our lines & SOUTH MAROC. 2nd Lieut Rowlands joined from the battalion from England & was taken on the strength.	

Army Form C. 2118

WAR DIARY
or
INTELLIGENCE SUMMARY
(Erase heading not required.)

Instructions regarding War Diaries and Intelligence Summaries are contained in F. S. Regs., Part II. and the Staff Manual respectively. Title Pages will be prepared in manuscript.

Place	Date	Hour	Summary of Events and Information	Remarks and references to Appendices
MAROC (left section)	14/4/16		A quiet day. Nothing important occurred - except the usual shelling of our lines by light shells. During the afternoon the enemy sent several heavy shells on the PYLONS (LOOS TOWERS) the NORTHERN TOWER fell down carrying away with it a lot of the connecting structure of the two towers. The remaining tower looks very gaunt & lonely - probably it is very shaky now & many come down of the shelling on this point continues. In the evening we were relieved by the 10th Gloucesters & took over billets in SOUTH MAROC - area B. Battalion worked on front line during the day, cleaning & improving. CRASSIER SAP, NORTHERN SAP, SOUTHERN SAP were cleaned & deepened. MIDDLE ALLEY & the SUPPORT LINE were also repaired where damaged by shell fire. The enemy exploded a mine at 9 pm in front of our SAP on the SOUTHERN CRASSIER - this happened during the relief. No damage was done to the sap but some of our men were buried. The enemy opened a barrage on our front & support line directly after the explosion but very little damage was done. Commanding officer returned from leave & Capt Downe returned from England.	6th BATTALION, THE WELSH REGIMENT. No............ Date............

1875 Wt. W593/826 1,000,000 4/15 J.B.C. & A. A.D.S.S./Forms/C. 2118.

Army Form C. 2118

WAR DIARY
or
INTELLIGENCE SUMMARY

(Erase heading not required.)

Instructions regarding War Diaries and Intelligence Summaries are contained in F.S. Regs., Part II. and the Staff Manual respectively. Title Pages will be prepared in manuscript.

Place	Date	Hour	Summary of Events and Information	Remarks and references to Appendices
S. MAROC (Area B.	15/4/16		Rather a windy day. During the morning, & for some time in the afternoon the enemy shelled NORTH and SOUTH MAROC with HE and shrapnel — several billets were damaged but we had no casualties fortunately. Nothing of importance occurred. A working party worked on the ADVANCE BATTLE HEADQUARTERS for the Brigade near MAROC CEMETERY. A working party, consisting of all the available men of the battalion worked on the RESERVE LINE. Lieut. C. Wells returned from England.	

8th BATTALION THE WELSH REGIMENT

Army Form C. 2118

WAR DIARY
or
INTELLIGENCE SUMMARY

(Erase heading not required.)

Instructions regarding War Diaries and Intelligence Summaries are contained in F.S. Regs., Part II. and the Staff Manual respectively. Title Pages will be prepared in manuscript.

Place	Date	Hour	Summary of Events and Information	Remarks and references to Appendices
S MAROC (AREA B)	16/4/16		Nothing of importance occurred - weather good. The enemy sent over H.E. and shrapnel on SOUTH MAROC during the afternoon. Battalion working party worked on the RESERVE LINE of SOUTH ST towards the old German Front Line. About 2.15 p.m. the remaining TOWER of LOOS PYLONS fell down. It took a long time to fall - only two girders are left standing up & the place will be very hard to recognise without these land marks. The enemy always used to register it on us the first - it is a wonder that these TOWERS stayed up for such a long time.	

6th BATTALION
THE
WELSH REGIMENT

Army Form C. 2118

WAR DIARY
or
INTELLIGENCE SUMMARY
(Erase heading not required.)

Instructions regarding War Diaries and Intelligence Summaries are contained in F.S. Regs., Part II. and the Staff Manual respectively. Title Pages will be prepared in manuscript.

Place	Date	Hour	Summary of Events and Information	Remarks and references to Appendices
MAROC (Sector) H.Qrs.	17/4/16		A wet day with a very cold wind. Nothing of importance occurred during the day. In the evening we relieved the 1st Gordons in the MAROC left subsection — the relief was carried out very quietly. It is certainly a great advantage when the men know the trenches well. There was the usual shelling of our lines today, NORTH and SOUTH MAROC also receiving of some attention.	

Army Form C. 2118

WAR DIARY
or
INTELLIGENCE SUMMARY
(Erase heading not required.)

Instructions regarding War Diaries and Intelligence Summaries are contained in F.S. Regs., Part II. and the Staff Manual respectively. Title Pages will be prepared in manuscript.

Place	Date	Hour	Summary of Events and Information	Remarks and references to Appendices
MAROC Left Section	18/4/16		A wet day. The usual shelling of our front & support lines — also SEVENTH AVENUE. NORTH MAROC was fired on with high velocity shells — there is absolutely no warning of these shells when they coming. At 2am one of our LEWIS guns fired on a working party in the TRIANGLE opposite SAP about M5c.1.8.1. At 2.45am. We blew up a mine near HARTS CRATER the enemy did not reply to our artillery fire etc. During the fall of LOOS TOWERS it is probably that the enemy can get direct observation on this road through NORTH MAROC to a point about M3b.2.4½. If observation this section from WINGLES. All the men in the battalion are provided with steel helmets which should reduce the number of casualties of head wounds. Owing to the rain the trenches got in a very bad state.	

Army Form C. 2118

WAR DIARY or INTELLIGENCE SUMMARY

Place	Date	Hour	Summary of Events and Information	Remarks and references to Appendices
MAROC (left sector)	19/4/16		A very wet day. Enemy was fairly quiet today. Battalion worked on improving front line, support line & saps. Owing to the wet weather several had falls occurred in the trenches — also there is a lot of water in places. Our Lewis guns caught three hostile working parties out last night — all of which had an exciting race for their parapet. The enemy was also firing a machine gun from the end of the sap on SOUTHERN CRASSIER during the night. A sniperscope (rifle) was fired in our sap there to cope with the hostile sniper opposite who becomes rather troublesome at times. The Padre came & visited the battalion in the afternoon. A peculiar incident happened this afternoon — an orderly died when on the way from Batn H.Qrs to his Company — probably heartfailure & now discovered that he died through a bullet wound in the shoulder.	

Army Form C. 2118

WAR DIARY
or
INTELLIGENCE SUMMARY
(Erase heading not required.)

8TH BATTALION,
THE
WELSH REGIMENT.

Place	Date	Hour	Summary of Events and Information	Remarks and references to Appendices
MAROC (Vermelles)	20/4/16		A wet morning – later on it cleared up nicely and the afternoon was warm and sunny. The Huns sent over light shells on MAROC starting at 6.15 a.m. this morning and kept on at intervals during the day. Our 6" howitzers fired 50 rounds on a suspected minehead at about M4c 8.4½. The shooting appeared to be very effective. The gap on the SOUTHERN CRASSIER was cleared a few minutes before the bombardment. In the evening we were relieved by the 2nd KRRs (2nd Brigade) and marched to PETIT SAINS where we took over billets from Loyal North Lancs.	

Army Form C. 2118

WAR DIARY
or
INTELLIGENCE SUMMARY
(Erase heading not required.)

Place	Date	Hour	Summary of Events and Information	Remarks and references to Appendices
PETIT SPINS (WILLO)	21/4/16		A very wet day. Nothing of importance happened today — some of the Battalion had baths in NOEUX-LES-MINES at the tamping baths near the 141st Field Ambulance. C Coy went on fatigue to MAROC.	

Army Form C. 2118

WAR DIARY
or
INTELLIGENCE SUMMARY
(Erase heading not required.)

Instructions regarding War Diaries and Intelligence Summaries are contained in F. S. Regs., Part II. and the Staff Manual respectively. Title Pages will be prepared in manuscript.

Place	Date	Hour	Summary of Events and Information	Remarks and references to Appendices
PETIT SAINS	22/4/16		A very wet day again — this is rotten weather for April. Remainder of the Battalion went to Baths in NOEUX-LES-MINES. There are no officers baths there unfortunately! Nothing of interest happened. Inspection of Rifles, equipment, smoke helmets emergency rations and socks.	

WAR DIARY
or
INTELLIGENCE SUMMARY

(Erase heading not required.)

Army Form C. 2118

Place	Date	Hour	Summary of Events and Information	Remarks and references to Appendices
PETIT SAINS	23/4/16		A quiet day - beautifully sunny weather. In the morning we had Church Parade in the open - on a field just below Headquarters Mess. The padre, Moneypenny took the service. He thus sent over several shells on the ridge towards Bracquemont which rather drew ones attention during the hymns. The Band particularly distinguished itself by playing some unknown tune to one of the well known Easter Hymns - no one knew it so the Band made a solo of it - to an appreciative audience. The padre in spite of the fact that he was lost also the evening the padre had no hymn books for the Voluntary service in the evening but luckily no one turned up. The rest of the day passed uneventfully.	

Army Form C. 2118

WAR DIARY
or
INTELLIGENCE SUMMARY

(Erase heading not required.)

Instructions regarding War Diaries and Intelligence Summaries are contained in F. S. Regs., Part II. and the Staff Manual respectively. Title Pages will be prepared in manuscript.

Place	Date	Hour	Summary of Events and Information	Remarks and references to Appendices
PETIT SAINS	24/3/16		A nice sunny day. The usual fatigue party of 100 men and 3 officers left at 8.15 am for MAROC where they worked until 1 pm. The men do not seem to mind this fatigue as they are conveyed there and back in G.S. Wagons. Nothing very interesting happened.	

WAR DIARY
or
INTELLIGENCE SUMMARY
(Erase heading not required.)

Army Form C. 2118

Place	Date	Hour	Summary of Events and Information	Remarks and references to Appendices
PETIT SAINS	25/9/16		A beautifully sunny day again. The fatigue party left at 8.15 am & had a very narrow escape from getting shelled on the way. Two enemy Observation Balloons were up - These observers can see all the country around here distinctly. The enemy blindly shelled the Mine & vicinity in the small village between PETIT SAINS and MAZINGARBE. A great deal of damage was done by these shells (10" & 8") on the Mine buildings & also the buildings on the road near the Railway Crossing. The C.O. had a narrow escape when riding back through the village to PETIT SAINS. An interpreter riding through had his horse's head half blown off by a shell but was unhurt himself.	

Army Form C. 2118

WAR DIARY
or
INTELLIGENCE SUMMARY
(Erase heading not required.)

Instructions regarding War Diaries and Intelligence Summaries are contained in F. S. Regs., Part II. and the Staff Manual respectively. Title Pages will be prepared in manuscript.

6th BATTALION, THE WELSH REGIMENT.

Place	Date	Hour	Summary of Events and Information	Remarks and references to Appendices
PETIT SAINS	26/4/16		A very sunny day. Nothing of importance occurred. There were no fatigues today. The people in PETIT SAINS seemed sorry that we were going back to the Trenches. In the evening we were paraded at 8 pm & marched to NORTH MAROC — on the way men artillery had a 'strafe' somewhere & there was some hostile retaliation but luckily no one was hit. We took over billets from the 9th Berks.	

1875 Wt. W5393/826 1,000,000 4/15 J.B.C. & A. A.D.S.S./Forms/C. 2118.

WAR DIARY
or
INTELLIGENCE SUMMARY
(Erase heading not required.)

Army Form C. 2118

Instructions regarding War Diaries and Intelligence Summaries are contained in F.S. Regs., Part II. and the Staff Manual respectively. Title Pages will be prepared in manuscript.

Place	Date	Hour	Summary of Events and Information	Remarks and references to Appendices
NORTH MAROC	29/4/16		'S.O.S' came through to us at about 5.30 am & everyone 'stood to' at once. The battalion marched away, (by companies, at once to SOUTH STREET near PICCADILLY & manned the reserve line. There was a big outburst of artillery fire about 5 pm. There was a big outburst of artillery fire about 5 pm. Right Battn. H.Qrs in LOOS. We 'stood down' about 8.30 am & marched back to NORTH MAROC. Battalion was then called out again & manned the RESERVE LINE from this time until about 1 pm. Heard about 10 pm that the enemy had made four raids on our line in the LOOS-HULLUCH sector (16th Division). Three of these raids were unsuccessful. The CHALK PIT was captured - our guns had to blow up the 4.5" Howitzer there before leaving. The enemy used gas which was blown back through MAZINGARBE - here the troops had to wear gas helmets for an hour. The enemy was driven out from these three points after having occupied our lines for about 2 hours. On the first signs of a counter attack the enemy at once left & went back to their lines. Their Brigade & the artillery expected a counter attitude in the afternoon as no news was received for some time.	

WAR DIARY
or
INTELLIGENCE SUMMARY

Army Form C. 2118

Place	Date	Hour	Summary of Events and Information	Remarks and references to Appendices
NORTH MAROC continued	27/4/16		The 16th Divisional report (wire) stated that the enemy left "many dead" behind but no definite news as to exact numbers has been received here yet. In the evening we had GAS, SOS, 2nd Welsh & immediately "stood to". This was at 7.16 pm & battalion waited for monitorious hillets until 7.35 when a message was received to "stand down". The night passed quietly although every one expected something to happen. Several small fatigues were furnished during the day. In the evening a large fatigue under the command of Capt. Wells worked on the Reserve Line in CARFAX ROAD.	

Army Form C. 2118.

WAR DIARY
or
INTELLIGENCE SUMMARY.
(Erase heading not required.)

Instructions regarding War Diaries and Intelligence Summaries are contained in F. S. Regs., Part II. and the Staff Manual respectively. Title pages will be prepared in manuscript.

Place	Date	Hour	Summary of Events and Information	Remarks and references to Appendices
NORTH MAROC	28/4/16		A nice sunny day. There was some desultory shelling of NORTH MAROC this morning by the hostile artillery. As the usual fatigue parties were found. In the evening the same fatigues paraded under Capt Tindly & went to work on the RESERVE LINE in BELFAST ROAD where battalion worked last night. At 8.45 pm there was an intense bombardment by all the batteries around here on the enemy lines where two raids were carried out. These raids were intended to happen last night but owing to the 16th Division "show" it was postponed until today. We noticed several "prematures" burst near the guns owing to faulty ammunition. The bombardment continued until 9.30 pm when it ceased. There was very little hostile retaliation or not much machine gun or rifle fire could be heard at the time.	

T2134. Wt. W708—776. 500000. 4/15. Sir J. C. & S.

Army Form C. 2118.

WAR DIARY
or
INTELLIGENCE SUMMARY.
(Erase heading not required.)

Instructions regarding War Diaries and Intelligence Summaries are contained in F. S. Regs., Part II. and the Staff Manual respectively. Title pages will be prepared in manuscript.

Place	Date	Hour	Summary of Events and Information	Remarks and references to Appendices
NORTH MAROC	29/4/16		A quiet day. The usual fatigues were done by the battalion. In the evening the battalion moved down to LOOS & took over the right sub section left sector (LOOS) from the 1st Pletina. Relief was completed by about 9.30 p.m. During the relief the Germans made a small bombing raid on Tri Street Sap — wounding two of our bombers. They were at once driven off & dispersed by machine gun fire.	

WAR DIARY
or
INTELLIGENCE SUMMARY.

Army Form C. 2118.

Place	Date	Hour	Summary of Events and Information	Remarks and references to Appendices
LOOS	30/4/16		A hot day. During the morning there was some shelling of our trenches by the enemy. At 10.10 + until 11.15 am two heavy minenwerfers bombarded our front line from M5d8.7 to M5d.6.1½ - considerable damage was done to our trenches. Hostile howitzers and "lip squeaks" also bombarded the portion of our line at the same time — on the whole our fellows had a rather hot time. During the afternoon the hostile minenwerfer dropped bombs between our lines & in their own wire – rather a suspicious thing. Meanwhile our trenches were being retaken. At 10.30 pm (about) the enemy commenced an intense bombardment of this portion of our line – hostile machine guns fired all the time on our parapets so that all sentries had to keep their heads down. This lasted about 5 minutes when the machine guns lifted a few feet off our parapet for about 2 minutes & then lowered again on our parapet. An enemy raiding party of about 50 men under one officer were then seen by as the machine gun lifted, by the sentry of the two machine guns on the right of the LENS ROAD who then heard shuffling of feet. He immediately fired at them	

Army Form C. 2118.

WAR DIARY
or
INTELLIGENCE SUMMARY.
(Erase heading not required.)

6th BATTALION
THE
WELSH REGIMENT.

Place	Date	Hour	Summary of Events and Information	Remarks and references to Appendices
LOOS	30/4/16		at close point blank range – the remainder of the machine gunners threw bombs. The Huns threw a large number of bombs in return which disabled all the Lewis gunners except Lance Corporal Jones who fired off 35 rounds when a bomb disabled the gun. Although he had been hit on the nose with a bomb which did not explode, he attempted to get away with the gun. He therefore climbed over the parados & pulled the gun after him. Unfortunately it caught on a wire & fell back into the trench. By this time 5 Germans and an officer were in the trench. Sergt Jones had been injured in both knees was unable to stand & was lying on his face in the trench. The German officer went up stunned him over & deliberately shot him through the stomach. Capt Truly then led a bombing party against them – large numbers of Mills bombs were thrown. On the party entered a bay a man was seen standing in the trench, when asked by Capt Truly who he was he replied in German. Capt Truly immediately shot him. The party had left by this time & they were only in the trench about 2 - 3 minutes. Two dead Germans were left behind 1 was wounded; the latter was found with an appearance his neck, and his two arms were tied together. He died about two	

WAR DIARY or INTELLIGENCE SUMMARY

Army Form C. 2118

Place	Date	Hour	Summary of Events and Information	Remarks and references to Appendices
LOOS.	30/4/16	3	home later - he absolutely refused to speak. The Lewis gun was found in the bank. Sergt Jones who was badly wounded was carried down to LOOS. An officers scouts patrol went out on the left of the LENS ROAD but was only able to stay out a short time - the machine guns were very active & played all over the ground in NO MAN'S LAND so that patrolling was distinctly unpleasant. The necessary information was gained however. When the patrol returned a German patrol was seen on the LENS ROAD - the patrol immediately opened fire & the Watch patrol ran back to their lines. At dawn Sergt Jones reached LOOS - the stretcher bearers had considerable difficulty in taking the stretcher down the trenches. The Doctor (Capt Smith) then said that Sergt Jones only chance was to be operated on at once & ordered three stretcher to take him either to MAROC or PHILOSOPHE. Three stretcher bearers, Ptes. 2343 S. Ma[...], 1249 P. Walker & 977 H. Piggott at once took him on a Jewker stretcher to MAROC. A machine gun fired on them once but they succeeded in getting to see alright. Sergt Jones however, died at Bethune about 12 hours later. Meanwhile will be reported by all. He was a fearless & very efficient sergeant who was very popular in his Battalion. [...] Pte J Rorano did very good during the bombardment on the morning	

T2134. Wt. W738—776. 500000. 4/15. Sir J. C. & S.

3rd Brigade &
1st Divisional Pioneers

BECAME 1st DIVISIONAL PIONEERS 15.5.16.

1/6th BATTALION THE WELCH REGIMENT :: MAY 1916

Became Pioneer Batt'n

Army Form C. 2118.

Vol XI

WAR DIARY or INTELLIGENCE SUMMARY.
(Erase heading not required.)

Instructions regarding War Diaries and Intelligence Summaries are contained in F. S. Regs., Part II. and the Staff Manual respectively. Title pages will be prepared in manuscript.

8.C
31 sheets

Place	Date	Hour	Summary of Events and Information	Remarks and references to Appendices
LOOS	1/5/16		A nice hot day. The Battalion was very busy all day repairing the wire damaged by the enemy trench mortars yesterday. During the day we discovered two more dead Huns lying between the lines. An officer's patrol went out & searched them & brought in identity discs, paybooks. A large wooden club studded with nails was also found on one man. The officer who went out was found just outside our wire - it had blood on the butt. Later, at 2.0 am, an officer's bomb patrol left our lines on the right of the line & attempted, by a bold & cunning ruse, to get some information. Pursued by M. Brigade this was obtained as well as some other information. Patrol had 4 rifle grenades thrown at it. Two machine guns opened fire but it returned safely to our lines at 2.30 a.m.	

Army Form C. 2118.

WAR DIARY
or
INTELLIGENCE SUMMARY.
(Erase heading not required.)

Place	Date	Hour	Summary of Events and Information	Remarks and references to Appendices
Loos	2/3/16		A fine day. During the morning Mine was sprung directly shelling of our lines by the enemy. During the afternoon the day passed fairly quietly. In the evening Battalion was relieved by 1st Gloster & then moved up to G.O.9.1	

6th BATTALION
THE
WELSH REGIMENT

WAR DIARY
or
INTELLIGENCE SUMMARY.

Army Form C. 2118.

Place	Date	Hour	Summary of Events and Information	Remarks and references to Appendices
O.G.1	3/7/16		A very hot day. S.O.S. message received at 1-10 am — we all got up but no one came across but. The enemy shelled our line in the usual places during the day. At 8.30 pm we noticed a large mine + camouflage on the S. Crassier it was a fine spectacle to witness. The enemy at once sent up red verelis(?) for artillery support however their artillery did not fire fully 5 minutes. A brisk bombardment was carried out on both sides until 9pm when it slackened. Several new verelis refused to go up straight. At 9-7 pm we had a message from 161st(?) Division that there was gas + heavy(?) as about 10-10 a message was received to say that this was a false alarm.	

Army Form C. 2118.

WAR DIARY
or
INTELLIGENCE SUMMARY.
(Erase heading not required.)

Instructions regarding War Diaries and Intelligence Summaries are contained in F. S. Regs., Part II. and the Staff Manual respectively. Title pages will be prepared in manuscript.

Place	Date	Hour	Summary of Events and Information	Remarks and references to Appendices
G.1	25/5/16		A fairly quiet day. Weather very hot. The enemys aeroplanes were very active during the morning no less than five were flying over our lines at the same time. Three fatigue parties worked for 173rd Coy R.E.	

Army Form C. 2118

WAR DIARY
or
INTELLIGENCE SUMMARY

(Erase heading not required.)

Instructions regarding War Diaries and Intelligence Summaries are contained in F. S. Regs., Part II. and the Staff Manual respectively. Title Pages will be prepared in manuscript.

Place	Date	Hour	Summary of Events and Information	Remarks and references to Appendices
	5/1/16		Nothing of importance happens today	

1875 Wt. W593/826 1,000,000 4/15 J.B.C. & A. A.D.S.S./Forms/C. 2118.

Army Form C. 2118

WAR DIARY
or
INTELLIGENCE SUMMARY
(Erase heading not required.)

Instructions regarding War Diaries and Intelligence Summaries are contained in F. S. Regs., Part II. and the Staff Manual respectively. Title Pages will be prepared in manuscript.

Place	Date	Hour	Summary of Events and Information	Remarks and references to Appendices
	6/8/16		Nothing of importance happened today. Weather has warm as usual.	

1875 Wt. W593/826 1,000,000 4/15 J.B.C. & A. A.D.S.S./Forms/C. 2118.

Army Form C. 2118

WAR DIARY
or
INTELLIGENCE SUMMARY
(Erase heading not required.)

Instructions regarding War Diaries and Intelligence Summaries are contained in F. S. Regs., Part II. and the Staff Manual respectively. Title Pages will be prepared in manuscript.

Place	Date	Hour	Summary of Events and Information	Remarks and references to Appendices
[Kebube?]	7/5/16		A nice day. The enemy sent over several shells on area a. Nothing else occurred.	

Army Form C. 2118

WAR DIARY
or
INTELLIGENCE SUMMARY
(Erase heading not required.)

Instructions regarding War Diaries and Intelligence Summaries are contained in F.S. Regs., Part II. and the Staff Manual respectively. Title Pages will be prepared in manuscript.

Place	Date	Hour	Summary of Events and Information	Remarks and references to Appendices
Robertia	8/5/16		Rather a wet day. Battalion on fatigue in the evening.	

Army Form C. 2118

WAR DIARY
or
INTELLIGENCE SUMMARY
(Erase heading not required.)

Instructions regarding War Diaries and Intelligence Summaries are contained in F. S. Regs., Part II and the Staff Manual respectively. Title Pages will be prepared in manuscript.

Place	Date	Hour	Summary of Events and Information	Remarks and references to Appendices
Lesboeufs	9/5/16		A fine day again. Nothing of importance occurred	

WAR DIARY
or
INTELLIGENCE SUMMARY

(Erase heading not required.)

Army Form C. 2118

Place	Date	Hour	Summary of Events and Information	Remarks and references to Appendices
Lahtin	10/5/16		Nothing of importance occurred.	

Army Form C. 2118

WAR DIARY
or
INTELLIGENCE SUMMARY

(Erase heading not required.)

Place	Date	Hour	Summary of Events and Information	Remarks and references to Appendices
Loos	1/6		A nice sunny day. During the evening the enemy has a big strafe on the roads running towards the line in this area. At large number of shells fell in Philosophe, Grenay, Maroc — a few number fell in the Pastries near the mine. The enemy next evening began to find out the positions of our batteries. An enemy attack opposite corridor on our lines at Hohenzollern Redoubt which was partly successful.	

Army Form C. 2118

WAR DIARY
or
INTELLIGENCE SUMMARY
(Erase heading not required.)

Instructions regarding War Diaries and Intelligence Summaries are contained in F. S. Regs., Part II. and the Staff Manual respectively. Title Pages will be prepared in manuscript.

Place	Date	Hour	Summary of Events and Information	Remarks and references to Appendices
La Bussie	17/5/15		Nothing of interest occurred	

THE WELSH REGIMENT.
No.........
Date.........

WAR DIARY
or
INTELLIGENCE SUMMARY

Army Form C. 2118

Place	Date	Hour	Summary of Events and Information	Remarks and references to Appendices
Le Sars	13/5/16		A nice sunny day - in the evening the Battalion moved up to S. Maroc (area "A") as Reserve Battalion. Some desultory shelling during the night but quiet on the whole.	

Army Form C. 2118

WAR DIARY
or
INTELLIGENCE SUMMARY
(Erase heading not required.)

Instructions regarding War Diaries and Intelligence Summaries are contained in F. S. Regs., Part II. and the Staff Manual respectively. Title Pages will be prepared in manuscript.

Place	Date	Hour	Summary of Events and Information	Remarks and references to Appendices
G.Manor.	14/5/16		Some heavy shelling of our Battery positions near the boundary at N.MARCE. A quiet day on the whole.	

WAR DIARY
or
INTELLIGENCE SUMMARY

(Erase heading not required.)

Army Form C. 2118

Place	Date	Hour	Summary of Events and Information	Remarks and references to Appendices
C MAROC	15/5/16		Anniversary day nothing of interest occurred.	

Army Form C. 2118

WAR DIARY
or
INTELLIGENCE SUMMARY
(Erase heading not required.)

Instructions regarding War Diaries and Intelligence Summaries are contained in F. S. Regs., Part II. and the Staff Manual respectively. Title Pages will be prepared in manuscript.

Place	Date	Hour	Summary of Events and Information	Remarks and references to Appendices
SAMRO	16/5/16		Nothing of interest happened during the day. In the evening the Battalion was relieved by the 2nd Welch about midnight who took over piecemeal the 3rd Brigade. Battalion marched by Companies to Les Brebis where C.S. Wagons took the men to Verchin.	

Army Form C. 2118

WAR DIARY
or
INTELLIGENCE SUMMARY
(Erase heading not required.)

Instructions regarding War Diaries and Intelligence Summaries are contained in F. S. Regs., Part II. and the Staff Manual respectively. Title Pages will be prepared in manuscript.

Place	Date	Hour	Summary of Events and Information	Remarks and references to Appendices
Houchin	5/16		Nothing of importance occurred. The C.O. inspected the Battalion in the morning.	

WAR DIARY
or
INTELLIGENCE SUMMARY

Army Form C. 2118

Place	Date	Hour	Summary of Events and Information	Remarks and references to Appendices
Houdain	15/5/16		Battalion parade in the morning. The C.R.E. visited the camp in the afternoon & gave a short lecture to the officers	

Army Form C. 2118

WAR DIARY
or
INTELLIGENCE SUMMARY

(Erase heading not required.)

Instructions regarding War Diaries and Intelligence Summaries are contained in F. S. Regs., Part II. and the Staff Manual respectively. Title Pages will be prepared in manuscript.

Place	Date	Hour	Summary of Events and Information	Remarks and references to Appendices
Nouvelle	19/5/16		Battalion moved up to March on the enemy. About 15 Officers and about half the N.C.O's of the Battalion were left at Donchin on an Instructing class	

8th BATTALION, THE WELSH REGIMENT.
No..........

Army Form C. 2118

WAR DIARY
or
INTELLIGENCE SUMMARY

(Erase heading not required.)

Instructions regarding War Diaries and Intelligence Summaries are contained in F. S. Regs., Part II. and the Staff Manual respectively. Title Pages will be prepared in manuscript.

Place	Date	Hour	Summary of Events and Information	Remarks and references to Appendices
	30/5/16		Battalion in Maroc works & trench Maintenance — remainder of Officers at demolition works en route — digging trenches near the Canal	

Army Form C. 2118

WAR DIARY
or
INTELLIGENCE SUMMARY
(*Erase heading not required.*)

Instructions regarding War Diaries and Intelligence Summaries are contained in F. S. Regs., Part II. and the Staff Manual respectively. Title Pages will be prepared in manuscript.

Place	Date	Hour	Summary of Events and Information	Remarks and references to Appendices
	31/5/16		Nothing of importance occurred.	

Army Form C. 2118

WAR DIARY
or
INTELLIGENCE SUMMARY

(Erase heading not required.)

Instructions regarding War Diaries and Intelligence Summaries are contained in F. S. Regs., Part II. and the Staff Manual respectively. Title Pages will be prepared in manuscript.

Place	Date	Hour	Summary of Events and Information	Remarks and references to Appendices
	22/5/16		C.O. arrived London with H.Q. staff early in the morning. Battalion took over Edgware Road & reveal other trenches in this sector.	

1875 Wt. W593/826 1,000,000 4/15 J.B.C. & A. A.D.S.S./Forms/C. 2118.

[Stamp: 6th Battalion THE WELSH REGIMENT]

Date	Hour	Summary of Events and Information	Remarks and references to Appendices
23/6/16		Nothing of importance occurred - usual work continued at Manor Hitchin	

Army Form C. 2118.

WAR DIARY
or
INTELLIGENCE SUMMARY.
(Erase heading not required.)

Instructions regarding War Diaries and Intelligence Summaries are contained in F.S. Regs., Part II. and the Staff Manual respectively. Title pages will be prepared in manuscript.

6th BATTALION.
THE
WELSH REGIMENT.

No.............
Date............

Place	Date	Hour	Summary of Events and Information	Remarks and references to Appendices
	24/5/16		Nothing of importance occurred. Fine weather.	

Army Form C. 2118.

WAR DIARY
or
INTELLIGENCE SUMMARY.
(Erase heading not required.)

Instructions regarding War Diaries and Intelligence Summaries are contained in F. S. Regs., Part II. and the Staff Manual respectively. Title pages will be prepared in manuscript.

Place	Date	Hour	Summary of Events and Information	Remarks and references to Appendices
	35. 5 16		Nothing of importance occurred. A rather wet day	

Army Form C. 2118.

WAR DIARY
or
INTELLIGENCE SUMMARY.
(Erase heading not required.)

Instructions regarding War Diaries and Intelligence Summaries are contained in F. S. Regs., Part II. and the Staff Manual respectively. Title pages will be prepared in manuscript.

Place	Date	Hour	Summary of Events and Information	Remarks and references to Appendices
	26/5/16		Nothing of importance occurred. A very wet day.	

WAR DIARY
or
INTELLIGENCE SUMMARY.
(Erase heading not required.)

Army Form C. 2118.

Place	Date	Hour	Summary of Events and Information	Remarks and references to Appendices
	27/5/16		A nice fine day. Blessed Louchin marched to Mount des Mines to see a mine blown up. It was a great success and was a fine spectacle to watch. A very small lip was formed by the blow in. Blows received orders to move up to MAROC and join Battalion.	

Army Form C. 2118.

WAR DIARY
or
INTELLIGENCE SUMMARY.
(Erase heading not required.)

Instructions regarding War Diaries and Intelligence Summaries are contained in F. S. Regs., Part II. and the Staff Manual respectively. Title pages will be prepared in manuscript.

Place	Date	Hour	Summary of Events and Information	Remarks and references to Appendices
	28/1/16		Gas winded up from trenches to Marre leaving the former at 6 a.m. Scuiring about 9 a.m. Gas gas party in the evening - also a large purry party on new trench being dug from Queen St. in the direction of Haymarket. Hostile Machine guns were very active and there were several casualties one of which proved fatal.	

8th BATTALION
THE
WELSH REGIMENT

Army Form C.2118.

WAR DIARY
or
INTELLIGENCE SUMMARY.
(Erase heading not required.)

Place	Date	Hour	Summary of Events and Information	Remarks and references to Appendices
	29/5/16		Nothing of interest during the day. Some shelling of hills occupied by the Battalion. In the evening another large party worked on the entanglements commenced last night — Officers & NCO's from different works on these entanglements. Machine gun fire was again active but only one NCO (Sgt Webb) was hit unfortunately fatally.	

Army Form C. 2118.

WAR DIARY
or
INTELLIGENCE SUMMARY.
(Erase heading not required.)

Instructions regarding War Diaries and Intelligence Summaries are contained in F. S. Regs., Part II. and the Staff Manual respectively. Title pages will be prepared in manuscript.

Place	Date	Hour	Summary of Events and Information	Remarks and references to Appendices
	30/5/16		Battalion working party worked on same trench and same entanglements. The wiring party was very lucky as there was no casualties from hostile machine gun and rifle fire. Hostile artillery again shelled MAROC during the day.	

WAR DIARY
or
INTELLIGENCE SUMMARY.
(Erase heading not required.)

Army Form C. 2118.

Place	Date	Hour	Summary of Events and Information	Remarks and references to Appendices
	31/5/16		Nothing of importance occurred during the day except for the usual shell fire on our billets in N. Maroc. In the evening Battalion fatigue parties were tapped the new trench and wiring parties completed the entanglements. There were no casualties	

R.C.C. Brabazon Lt.

WO95/1282   (2)

51/S.Wales Bords

Mar'19 – July'19

B.E.F.

1. DIVISION

3 BRIGADE

51 S.W.B.

1919 MAR. to 1919 JULY

Vol I

MARCH 1919.

WAR DIARY
— of —
51st Bn South Wales Borderers.

Vol. 1.

10/3/19 – 31/3/19.

ORIGINAL

Army Form C. 2118.

51st BN. SOUTH WALES BORDERERS.

Instructions regarding War Diaries and Intelligence Summaries are contained in F. S. Regs., Part II. and the Staff Manual respectively. Title pages will be prepared in manuscript.

WAR DIARY
51st BN. SOUTH WALES BORDERERS
INTELLIGENCE SUMMARY.
(Erase heading not required.)

Place	Date	Hour	Summary of Events and Information	Remarks and references to Appendices
STOWLANGTOFT (SUFFOLK)	10/8/19	08:00	51st BATTn. S. WALES BORD. under the command of Lieut-Colonel B.W. COLLIER, D.S.O. mobilised and proceeded by marchroute to THURSTON STATION.	App. I.
THURSTON	10/8/19	10.40	BATTn. entrained for port of embarkation under supervision of R.T.O. 23rd ARMY CORPS. STRENGTH on entrainment 31 Officers and 899 O.R.	THURSTON STATION & MOBZN. ORDER. App. II.
DOVER	10/8/19	17:30	BATTn. arrived at DOVER, detrained, and were accommodated in REST CAMP for night of 10/11 inst.	Rolls of Officers (offrs Embarked)
DOVER	11/8/19	14:00	BATTn. embarked H.M.T. PRINCESS ELIZABETH, followed on board by 52nd BATTn. R. SUSS. REGT.	
DUNKERKE	12/8/19	17:30	BATTn. debarked and accommodated in REST CAMP for night of 11/12th inst.	App.
DUNKERKE	12/8/19	12:00	BATTn. entrained to join ARMY of the RHINE at SAND SIDING, HAUTE REPAS. Re-entrained and crossed the battlefields to the SOUTH of ARMENTIERES. VIA LILLE to BATSIEUX.	
MERRIS	12/8/19	16:00		
BATSIEUX	12/8/19	21:00	HAUTE REPAS. Re-entrained. Night of 12/13 inst. spent in train.	App.
CHARLEROI	13/8/19	12:00	HAUTE REPAS. Re-entrained 1½ hour later. VIA NAMUR and HUY.	

ORIGINAL

Army Form C. 2118.

WAR DIARY
51st BN. SOUTH WALES BORDERERS.
INTELLIGENCE SUMMARY.
(Erase heading not required.)

Instructions regarding War Diaries and Intelligence Summaries are contained in F. S. Regs., Part II. and the Staff Manual respectively. Title pages will be prepared in manuscript.

Place	Date	Hour	Summary of Events and Information	Remarks and references to Appendices
HUY	12/3/19	21.50	HALTE REPAS. VIA LIEGE, AIX-LA-CHAPELLE to DUREN Night of 13/14 inst. spent in train.	ast
DUREN	14/3/19	09.00	HALTE REPAS. VIA EUSKIRCHEN TO MÜNSTER EIFEL.	
MUNSTEREIFEL	14/3/19	12.00	BATTⁿ were met at STA. by A/STAFF CAPT., 3ʳᵈ INF. BDE, detrained, and marched into billets at MÜNSTER EIFEL.	00A
MUNSTEREIFEL	15/3/19		DRAFT of 11 OFFICERS and 190 O.Rs. transferred from 2ⁿᵈ BATTⁿ S. WALES BORDS. Officers as below:-	
			LT. J. E. A. GIBBS. 2/LT A. N. GLOVER, M.C. 2/LT M. G. JONES	
			2/LT C. F. TUDGE. 2/LT J. DAVIES, 2/LT G. R. GRIMWOOD	
			2/LT W. N. DOUGLAS. 2/LT A. V. PRISTON 2/LT J. WILLIAMS.	
			2/LT B. G. DAVIES 2/LT D. T. JOHNS	ast
MUNSTEREIFEL	16/3/19		BATTⁿ "STAND TO" in BILLETS for inspection of billets by the Commanding Officer. 2 O.R. to HOSPITAL.	ast
MUNSTEREIFEL	17/3/19		Q.M.'s STORES taken over from 1ˢᵗ BATTⁿ S. WALES BORD, and workshops also taken over. 1 O.R. to BASE, 2 O.R. to HOSPITAL.	asp
MUNSTEREIFEL	18/3/19		TRANSPORT of 1ˢᵗ BATTⁿ S. WALES BORD. taken over. Strength two	

ORIGINAL

Army Form C. 2118.

WAR DIARY
51st BN. SOUTH WALES BORDERERS
~~INTELLIGENCE~~ SUMMARY.

Place	Date	Hour	Summary of Events and Information	Remarks and references to Appendices
			follow:- 10 Riding Horses 10 G.S. limbered Wagons	
			2 L.D. and 9 H.D Horses 4 Cookers and 2 Water Carts	
			5 Pack Horses 1 Maltese Cart	
			3 O.R. to HOSPITAL. 1 Officers' Mess Cart.	
			A programme of Coy. training came in force on this date	ASP
MUNSTEREIFEL	19/3/19		BATTN march to KIRCHHEIM via IVERSHEIM 14 to visit 1st BATTN	
			S. WALES BORDphries to return of 1st BATTN horse. All Orderly	
			Room Stores of 1st BATTN S. WALES BORD taken over with	
			exception of correspondence relating to individual Officers	
			and O.R. of unit handing over. 10.R. to HOSPITAL.	ASP
			EDUCATION classes restarted and in working order.	
MUNSTEREIFEL	20/3/19		REGT. CANTEEN (DRY) opened. 1 Offr to HOSPITAL, 3 & 5 Rate Halqrn	
MUNSTEREIFEL	21/3/19		BATTN provided GUARD of CORPORAL, H/CPL and SIX PTES. to	
			mount over 2nd ARMY COLLEGE at BONN. 2 O.R. to HOSPITAL.	ASP
MUNSTEREIFEL	22/3/19		2 O.R. to HOSPITAL.	ASP

ORIGINAL

Army Form C. 2118.

WAR DIARY
51st BN. SOUTH WALES BORDERERS.
INTELLIGENCE SUMMARY.

Instructions regarding War Diaries and Intelligence Summaries are contained in F. S. Regs., Part II. and the Staff Manual respectively. Title pages will be prepared in manuscript.

Place	Date	Hour	Summary of Events and Information	Remarks and references to Appendices
MUNSTEREIFEL	23/3/19		5.O.R. to HOSPITAL.	aut
MUNSTEREIFEL	24/3/19		Lt (A/Capt) J.R. MORRIS, M.C. reported for duty with the BATTⁿ from 115th T.M.B., 38th DIVISION	
			2 O.R. to HOSPITAL.	
			GUARD of 80.O.R. to 2nd Army College, COLOGNE.	aut
MUNSTEREIFEL	25/3/19		2 O.R. rejoined from HOSPITAL.	awa
			10.O.R. admitted to HOSPITAL.	
			5 D.Z. animals to ESSIG.	
			20.O.R. to DIVISIONAL Hd-Qrs.	aw R
MUNSTEREIFEL	27/3/19		Draft of 8 officers from 1st BATTⁿ S. Wales Bordrs:—	
			CAPT W.J. CRUTCH (R.W.Fus.) 2Lt W. DAVIES.	
			CAPT E.H. FRANCIS (Employed at DEM.B.CAMP) Lt A. HIBBERT	
			LIEUT B.S.W. MEREFIELD 2Lt R.W. LENICK (R.War.Regt)	
			LIEUT R.F. EASTHAM 2Lt W.F PIERCE (Traffic at Div. HdQrs)	
			and 172 O.R. 23 MULES taken on strength of transport.	
			20.O.R. to HOSPITAL & 2 O.R. to DIVISIONAL Hd-Qrs.	

ORIGINAL.

Army Form C. 2118.

WAR DIARY
51st BN. SOUTH WALES BORDERERS
INTELLIGENCE SUMMARY.
(Erase heading not required.)

Place	Date	Hour	Summary of Events and Information	Remarks and references to Appendices
(continued)			The u/m officers taken on strength of the BATT'n and detached as shewn:-	
			LIEUT J.M. HANSON (1st MONS REGT) Att 3rd Bde. Hr.Qrs.	
			" J.A. LONNON, S. Wales BORD (S.R.) Employed details 14/S WALES BORD.	
			T/ " J.H. HALL (Leave to U.K.) S. WALES BORD.	
			T/ " J.J. O'NEILL, M.C. (Leave to U.K.) S. WALES BORD	
			" 2LT E.R. JONES (2nd Mon Regt) (Leave to U.K.)	
			T/2LT S. HICKS, S. WALES BORD. (Leave to U.K.)	
			T/ L/PUT. F.TYLER, S. WALES BORD. (Sick in base Hospital)	
			T/2LT T.O. PHILLIPS, M.C., S. WALES BORD (do.	
			T/ LT G. H. RICHARDS, S. WALES BORD (Leave to U.K.)	
			do W.E. WILLIAMS, S. WALES BORD (do	
			T/2LT (A/CAPT) G. ESMOND, M.C., S. WALES BORD (att 53rd S.W.B)	
			T/2LT W.J. MILLARD, S. WALES BORD (att 53rd S. Wales Bord)	
			" T.C.P. BROMHAM, M.C., S. WALES BORD (do)	

ORIGINAL

Army Form C. 2118.

WAR DIARY
51st Bn. SOUTH WALES BORDERERS
INTELLIGENCE SUMMARY.
(Erase heading not required.)

Instructions regarding War Diaries and Intelligence Summaries are contained in F. S. Regs., Part II. and the Staff Manual respectively. Title pages will be prepared in manuscript.

Place	Date	Hour	Summary of Events and Information	Remarks and references to Appendices
MUNSTEREIFFA	28/2/19		BATT'N inspected by BRIGADIER-GENERAL COMMANDING 3rd INF'Y BDE.	
			9.O.R. as GUARD to 3rd Bde. Hd. Qrs.	
			3 O.R. to Bde. Hd. Qrs.	
			2 O.R. from HOSPITAL	
			" " COURSE.	
do.	29/2/19		10 O.R. to HOSPITAL	ask
			3 rejoined from leave to U.K.	
			11 O.R. proceeded on leave to U.K.	ask
do.	30/2/19		9 O.R. joined from 1st BATT'N, S. WALES BORD.	
			2 O.R. to HOSPITAL	ask
			5 O.R. to HOSPITAL	
do.	3/3/19		3 O.R. proceeded on leave to U.K.	
			1 Officer (2/Lt E.R. JONES) rejoined from leave to U.K.	ask

APPENDIX I

Copy of telegram received from War Office, London, 8th March 1919
===

K.9378 S.R.1.B. Train to convey your unit 29 Officers 635 other ranks
and all the baggage leaves Thurston 1040, Monday 10th inst. and
arrives Dover 1745 aaa Vans will be in position for loading baggage
0600 hours 10th aaa Battn. will be accommodated in Rest Camp, Dover,
for the night and embark on 11th inst. aaa Acknowledge aaa Addressed
51st S.W.B., Stowlangtoft, repeated Commandeth, London.

Certified true copy,

2nd April 1919

Capt. & Adjt.
51st Bn. South Wales Borderers

APPENDIX II.

Roll of Officers who embarked with 51st Bn. South Wales Borderers 11th March 1919.

Lieut-Colonel B.W.Collier D.S.O.	S.Wales Bord.
Major J.D.Kerr M.C.	Sher. For.(Notts & Derby Regt
Capt. C.V.Simpson	S.Staff. R.
Capt. H.H.W.Hurst	Ches. Regt.
" H.Pritchard M.C.	R.W.Fus.
" W.H.Tosdevine M.C.	S.Staff. R.
" H.Cottam M.C.	S.Wales Bord.
" T.R.Williams M.C.	R.W.Fus.
" W.T.Harris M.C.	S.Wales Bord.
" J.A.Wilson	Mons. Regt. (T.F.)
" E.M.Gibbon	S.Wales Bord. (S.R.)
Lieut. D.McKie	S.Wales Bord.
" H.F.Poulson	R.W.Fus.
" W.H.Lester	R.W.Fus.
" R.J.G.Cartmell	(Queen's Own (R.W.K. Regt.)
" W.C.Lush	S.Wales Bord.
2/Lieut. E.L.Palmer	Linc. Regt.
" A.R.P.Cannon	Glouc. Regt.
" G.S.Rate	R.W.Fus.
" J.M.Jones	S.Wales Bord.
" E.L.Jones	S.Wales Bord.
" I.G.Powell	S.Wales Bord.
" D.R.Windsor	S.Wales Bord.
" H.J.Edwards	S.Wales Bord.
" T.W.Thomas	R.W.Fus.
" H.T.Naish M.M.	R.W.Fus.
" A.E.Williams	R.W.Fus.
" G.H.Duckett	S.Wales Bord.
" R.L.Wynne	R.W.Fus.

Lieut. & Q.M. M.A.Godbeer

Capt. J.E.Turnley R.A.M.C.

ORIGINAL

Army Form C. 2118.

51st A.H.Q.a

WAR DIARY
51st BN. SOUTH WALES BORDERERS
INTELLIGENCE SUMMARY

(Erase heading not required.)

Instructions regarding War Diaries and Intelligence Summaries are contained in F. S. Regs., Part II. and the Staff Manual respectively. Title pages will be prepared in manuscript.

ORDERLY ROOM
2 MAY 1919
No. 227/196
51st Bn. South Wales

Place	Date	Hour	Summary of Events and Information	Remarks and references to Appendices
Munsterlager	April 1st 1919	—	Lt Col. A.J. REDDIE CMG DSO joined Battn.	
			Lt Col. B.W. COLLIER DSO proceeded to hospital.	
			9 OR to hospital	
Do	2nd		Lt Col. A.J. REDDIE CMG DSO assumes command of the Batt.	
			Major A.R. DOGMORE lectures on "Stalking African Big Game with a Camera" in the Recreation Room.	
			2/Lt T.O. PHILLIPS rejoins from hospital. 2 OR to Hospital.	
Do	3rd		2 OR demobilized. 9 OR from 101 Bn/S.	
			Small. 2/- 9 OR to hospital.	
Do	4th		Bonsa Commander inspects the Battn in Marching Order.	
			3 OR to hosp. 5 OR rejoined from hospital.	
			Proceeded on Army duration:— Capt W.T. CRUTCH, Capt T.R. Williams	
			2/Lt G.S. RATE 2/- A. HIBBERT.	
Do	5th		Lecture by Capt. G.G. NEEKS RAMC on "Work, Aims and Objects of the Royal Army Temperance Association"	W.T.

WAR DIARY
or
INTELLIGENCE SUMMARY.

Army Form C. 2118.

Place	Date	Hour	Summary of Events and Information	Remarks and references to Appendices
MUNSTEREIFEL	5th		Played 53rd S.W.B. Assoc. Football. 107s won easily. 5-1.	
do	6th		B.H. Guard rejoined. 1 O.R. to Hosp. 5 O.R. from Hosp. 2 O/fs (2/Lt SticksC.F Tudge) proceed to 53rd Bn B. — 2/Lt ANGLOVIER M.C. Proceed on leave to U.K. From 53rd Bn B – Capt. G. ESMOND M.C. 2/Lt N.I. NEYARD and 2/Lt T.C.R. BROMHAM M.C. Proceed for School = Pud. B.S.W. herefield, 2/Lt A.A. Naish N.M. 2/Lt H.J. EDWARDS. From 1st Bn B – 2/Lt I.R. GRIFFITHS (Hosp) & not joined R.S.M. Bridges joined Batts & takes over duties as SM. inst.	
do	7th		3 O.R. to Hospital. Lecture by HQ M/S & Junior Chaplain on "Venereal Disease and its prevention". 2/Lt W.N. DOUGLAS and N/G Jones proceeds on leave to U.K. 1 O.R. for Duties — 1 O.R. to hospital.	
do	8th		From Hosp.: – Capt. A.C.S. DAVIES. From Hosp. – 2/Lt W.E. COOPER. 3 O.R. from Hosp. 2 O.R. to Hosp. 2/Lt G.R. GRIMWOOD & PRISTON on leave to U.K.	

WAR DIARY or INTELLIGENCE SUMMARY

Army Form C. 2118.

Place	Date	Hour	Summary of Events and Information	Remarks and references to Appendices
Wunsdorf.	9th		R/Jd from Perry - 2/Lt GA RICHARDS & W.E WILLIAMS. 1 OR from hospital.	
do	10th		Franz leave - 2/Lt R.H. DAWSON with effect from 7.4.19. Demonstration in Light Lewis guns at NITTERSCHLICK, all Coy Offrs attended. To leave :- 2/Lt T.J. WILLIAMS. 1 OR to hospital.	
do	11th		Lieut T.R.MORRIS M.C. & 8 OR to 3rd TMB, also 2/Lt L.O DAVIES. Capt W.T. HARRIS M.C. on course at 2 Army Agric College, BONN. R. Coy advanced party performed. 2 OR to hospital.	
do	12th		1 OR to UK to rejoin regular Unit. 6 DICKIE & 2/Lt E.I. JONES also 2/Lt T.J. O'NEILL M.C. & T.T. HALL rejoined from our played 52nd Buffs at Soccer and 53rd Sub. Rugby. - Won the former 6-1 and lost the latter 33-6. 10R Reported. Capt H.C.S DAVIES M.C.	WS

WAR DIARY
INTELLIGENCE SUMMARY.
(Erase heading not required.)

Army Form C. 2118.

Place	Date	Hour	Summary of Events and Information	Remarks and references to Appendices
MUNSTEREIFEL	13th	—	Lieut J A O'NNON & Lieut. 3 OR from Hosp.	
do	14th	—	Lieut J E A GIBBS proceeded to Senob.	
do	15th	—	~~2/Lt A.T. WIGARE~~ Lt R.J. EASTMAN proceeded to Senob. 1 G.O.R. Dental'd.	
do	16th	—	6 OR to Hosp.	
do	17th	—	6 OR to Hosp. 1 OR Senob'd.	
			1 Coy banners Early performed in Garrison Room.	
do	18th	—	1 OR to Hosp. 1 OR Senob'd.	
			Good Friday — Church services only — 2/Lt R W EVICK to ou Bn Guards	
			7 men leave — 2/Lt B J AYERS. 2 OR to Hosp. 2 to Senob.	
do	19th	—	Supplied a Brigade Guard of 9 OR.	
			1 OR to Hosp. -B Coy played 104 Coy Train at Soccer	
			and won — 3–1.	
do	20th	—	Lt G PAINER & Lt T O PHILLIPS NC proceed to Senob.	
			2 OR to 3th N L T M B. 3 OR to Hosp. 3 OR to Senob.	
do	21st	—	2 OR for Senob'd. 2 OR to Hosp. 1 OR from Hosp.	
do	22nd	—	2 OR from Hosp. 1 OR to Hosp. 2 OR for Senob.	

WAR DIARY or INTELLIGENCE SUMMARY

Army Form C. 2118.

Place	Date	Hour	Summary of Events and Information	Remarks and references to Appendices
Munsterlager	23rd		Lecture by Lt. Col. Cannon D.S.O. on "MESOPOTAMIA"; the Key of the Future. Played 63rd S.W.B. at Soccer and won.	
	24th		1 OR to leave. 1 OR from hosp. 4 OR to hosp. Pres. Guard reinforced by 1 NCO & 3 men.	
	25th		2/Lt F.M. JONES to 52nd SWB. 7 ORs + 200 OR rein. on trip by RAYNE. Peacock. Heaver. 7 ORs + 200 OR to COBLENZ.	
			3 OR from hosp. Major Ja Frasse DSO Dent Lainé. Jones Royal Scots present. 3 OR of Battalion Concert in recreation Room.	
	26th		2/Lt McGowen to 52nd SWB. — Bde Guard repaired.	
	27th		2/Lt A.W. GLOVER MC from leave. 2 OR to hosp 3 OR from hosp.	
	28th		2/Lt G.R. GRIM(WOOD) from leave. 1 OR to hospital.	
	29th		2/Lt G.R. GRIMWOOD to 4th Bn SWB. - 3 OR from hosp.	
			2 OR to hosp. 2 OR + 50 OR to Corps Composite Guard. IV Corps HQ.	
	30th		G. O.C.-in-C., British Army of the Rhine, Sir Wm ROBERTSON GCB, KCVO, DSO, ADC.	

Army Form C. 2118.

WAR DIARY
or
INTELLIGENCE SUMMARY.
(Erase heading not required.)

Instructions regarding War Diaries and Intelligence Summaries are contained in F. S. Regs., Part II. and the Staff Manual respectively. Title pages will be prepared in manuscript.

Place	Date	Hour	Summary of Events and Information	Remarks and references to Appendices
Wunstorf	30		inspected 3rd Western Infantry Brigade, in F.S. Marching Order. Later 53rd Ind.B. at soccer and from 4-1. 2 sd for lunch. 2/L WINNARD to leave t OR to hosp.	ASR

51st Bn. South Wales Borderers.

Roll of Officers - 30/4/19.

Lieut.-Colonel	A.J. Reddie, C.M.G., D.S.O.	Commanding.
Major	J.A. Frazer D.S.O., D.C.M.	Leave
Major	J.D. Kerr M.C.	
Captain	C.V. Simpson	Adjutant.
Lt. & Q.M.	M.A. Godbeer	
Lieut.	W.H. Lester	

Captain	H.H. Hurst.	Commanding "A" Company.
"	H. Pritchard M.C.	
Lieut.	F. Tyler	Hospital.
"	A.R.P. Cannon	
2/Lieut.	G.H. Duckett	Education Officer.
"	W.L. Wynne	" "
"	W.E. Williams	
"	W.E. Cooper M.C.	
"	R.H. Dawson	Corps Guard.
"	B.G. Davies.	
"	D.T. Johns	2/Army Leave Train.
"	G.H. Richards.	

Captain	W.H. Tosdevine M.C.	Commanding "B" Company.
Lieut.	H. Cottam. M.C.	
"	R.J.G. Cartmell	No.4 Sub Area
"	J.J. O'Neill	Corps Guard
2/Lieut.	J. Davies	
"	W.J. Millard	Leave
"	A.N. Glover M.C.	
Lieut.	H.F. Poulson	
"	R.A. Faro	

Captain	W.T. Harries M.C.	Course.
Lieut.	G. Esmond M.C.	Commanding "C" Company.
"	W.F. Pierce	Div. H.Q.
"	J.M. Hanson	Bde. H.Q.
2/Lieut.	W. Davies	T.M.B.
"	E.R. Jones.	
"	I.G. Powell	
Lieut.	D.R. Windsor.	
2/Lieut.	W.N. Douglas.	
2/Lieut.	A.V. Priston.	
"	T.W. Thomas	

Captain	J.A. Wilson.	Commanding "D" Company.
"	E.H. Francis.	2nd Army.
Lieut.	E.M. Gibbon M.C.	
"	W.C. Lush	
"	L.A. Lonnon.	Assistant Adjutant.
"	J.R. Morris M.C.	T.M.B.
"	J.H. Hall	
2/Lieut.	A.E. Williams	
"	T.J. Williams	
"	T.C.R. Bromham M.C.	
"	J.R. Griffiths.	Hospital.
"	B.J. Ayers.	

CONFIDENTIAL

War Diary

Of The

51st Battn

South Wales

Borderers.

From Mar 1st To Mar 31st

1912

Volume

No 3.

WAR DIARY
or
INTELLIGENCE SUMMARY.

Army Form C. 2118.

Place	Date	Hour	Summary of Events and Information	Remarks and references to Appendices
MUNSTEREIFEL	1/5/19		Training as usual. Lt. Lalonnon & 2/Lt. W.W. Douglas & T.J. Williams M.S. rejoined from leave.	
do	2/5/19		2/Lt. T.J. Williams left the unit to report to the 6th Bn. S. Wales Bord. M.	
do	3/5/19		The Bn. was inspected by Commander Everard R.N. on the Staff of British Delegation during Peace. 2r. W.S.H. to U.K. on leave.	
do	4/5/19		Church Parade for C.of E., N.C's & R.C's.	M
do	5/5/19		Training as usual. In the evening a concert was given in the recreation Room by the Women's Theatre Coy.	M
do	6/5/19		Training as usual. The Women Theatre Coy gave another performance in the Rgt. Recreation Room, their efforts were much appreciated by all ranks of the Bn.	
do	7/5/19		Training as usual. The Piquets the whole Bn. were thoroughly rehearsed Rugby & Soccer trial games took place during the evening	M
do	8/5/19		Training as usual. In the evening a Rugby football match was played versus the 53rd S. Wales. Bord. ending after a good game in a victory for the 53rd Bn. by 1 goal 1 try to Nil. Trial nearly of peace terms.	

Army Form C. 2118.

WAR DIARY
or
INTELLIGENCE SUMMARY.
(Erase heading not required.)

Instructions regarding War Diaries and Intelligence Summaries are contained in F.S. Regs., Part II. and the Staff Manual respectively. Title pages will be prepared in manuscript.

Place	Date	Hour	Summary of Events and Information	Remarks and references to Appendices
MÜNSTEREIFEL	8/5/19		which were submitted to the German authorities received at the Bn. HQ	
- do -			means of the COLOGNE POST.	AAz
- do -	9/5/19		Training as usual. Rugby Assoc. practices went ahead.	AAz
- do -	10/5/19		Usual Sat. programme, Kit Inspection, Pay &c. In the afternoon the Bn. Assoc.	
			team played the 52nd Bn. Scots Bords. at ARLOFF. the result being a draw 1-1.	AAz
- do -	11/5/19		Church Parade for C of E, R.C. and N.C. O/c 'B' O/R per Coy went to SECHTEM, where	
			an amalgamated team of the 53rd & 51st Middx. Borderers play the 6th Bn. Welsh Regt.	
			at Rugby, the same ending in a win for the latter by 8 tries 24 pts to nil.	AAz
- do -	12/5/19		Training as usual. The Bn. Cinema was first shown tonight, all ranks stand	
			a very enjoyable evening.	AAz
- do -	13/5/19		Training as usual.	AAz
- do -	14/5/19		Training as usual. The Bn. Assoc. Football team played the 3rd Inf. Bde. a	
			won by 10 goals - nil.	AAz
- do -	15/5/19		Training as usual	AAz
- do -	16/5/19		Training as usual.	AAz
- do -	17/5/19		Training as usual. The Bn. concert party gave an excellent.	AAz

Army Form C. 2118.

WAR DIARY
or
INTELLIGENCE SUMMARY.
(Erase heading not required.)

Instructions regarding War Diaries and Intelligence Summaries are contained in F. S. Regs., Part II. and the Staff Manual respectively. Title pages will be prepared in manuscript.

Place	Date	Hour	Summary of Events and Information	Remarks and references to Appendices
MÜNSTEREIFEL	17/3/19		Show in the Recreation Room.	MR
- do -	18/3/19.		Coy Pay, Kit inspection &c. Afternoon Recreation. In the evening the Bn. played the 53rd S/D/B. after a very scrappy game won by 5 - 1.	MR
- do -	19/3/19		Drill, Musketry, P.T. Games etc.	MR
- do -	20/3/19		Programme of training carried out as usual.	MR
- do -	21/3/19		Training in the morning. In the afternoon games & practice for Bn. Sports.	MR
- do -	22/3/19		Training as usual.	MR
- do -	23/3/19		Musketry, P.T. Drill &c.	MR
- do -	24/3/19		Pay, Kit Inspection &c. The Bn. Assoc. Team played the 52nd S/D/B - won by 6 goals to nil. (5 - 2). Hereby winning the Brigade Championship.	MR
- do -	25/3/19		Church parade & Coy's & R.C. as usual. The N.C.O's had a Brigade Parade service at 3rd Inf. Bde. H.Q.	MR
- do -	26/3/19		Coy Parade as usual. Recreational Training as per organisation.	MR
- do -	27/3/19		P.T. Training carried out as usual.	MR
- do -	28/3/19		Training as usual. A draft of 95 private soldiers proceeded to the 53rd R. The Welch Regt., after an inspection of the draft by the B.G.C. 3rd	MR

Army Form C. 2118.

WAR DIARY
or
INTELLIGENCE SUMMARY.
(Erase heading not required.)

Instructions regarding War Diaries and Intelligence Summaries are contained in F. S. Regs., Part II. and the Staff Manual respectively. Title pages will be prepared in manuscript.

Place	Date	Hour	Summary of Events and Information	Remarks and references to Appendices
MÜNSTEREIFEL	28/3/19		Infantry Brigade. Hg. were marched down to the Station by the Band & Drums for entrainment.	
- do -	29/3/19		"B" Coy paraded as to move, marched off at 0940 hrs. Had a very successful day. Remaining Coys. paraded as usual.	
- do -	30/3/19		The Bn. less "B" Coy did a practice move. On arrival at its destination a kit inspection was held. Bn. returned to MÜNSTEREIFEL at 1640 hr.	
- do -	31/3/19		Kit Inspection, interior economy, etc.	

G.J. Ritchie

51st Bn. South Wales Borderers

Roll of Officers   31st May 1919

Lieut-Colonel A.J.Roddie C.M.G.,D.S.O.	Commanding
Major J.A.Fraser D.S.O.,D.C.M.	2nd in Command
Captain C.V.Simpson	Adjutant
Lt. & Q.M.Godbeer	Quartermaster
Lieut. W.H.Lester	Signal Officer
Major J.D.Kerr M.C.	Comdg. "A" Coy.
Capt. H.H.W.Hurst	
" H.Pritchard M.C.	Education Officer
Lieut. F.Tyler	Hospital
" A.R.P.Cannon	
2/Lieut. G.H.Duckett	Education Officer
" R.L.Wynne	" "
" W.E.Williams	
" W.E.Cooper M.C.	
" R.H.Dawson	Corps Guard
" B.G.Davies	
" D.T.Johns	2/Army Leave Train
" G.H.Richards	
Capt. W.H.Tosdevine M.C.	Comdg. "B" Coy.
Lieut. H.Cottam M.C.	
" R.J.G.Cartmell	No. 4 Sub-Area
" J.J.O'Neill M.C.	Corps Guard
" H.F.Poulson	
" R.A.Faro	Education Officer
2/Lieut. J.Davies	Leave
" W.J.Millard	
" A.N.Glover M.C.	
Lieut. G.Esmond M.C.	Leave
" J.H.Hall	Comdg. "C" Coy.
" W.F.Pierce	Div. H.Q.
" J.M.Hanson	Brigade H.Q.
2/Lieut. E.R.Jones	
" I.G.Powell	Transport Officer
Lieut. D.R.Windsor	
2/Lieut. W.N.Douglas	
" A.V.Priston	
" T.W.Thomas	
Capt. J.A.Wilson	Comdg. "D" Coy.
" B.H.Francis	2nd Army
Lieut. E.M.Gibbon M.C.	
" W.C.Lush	
" L.A.Lonnon	Asst. Adjutant
" J.R.Morris M.C.	3rd L.T.M.Battery
2/Lieut. A.E.Williams	
" T.C.R.Bromham M.C.	Leave
" B.J.Ayers	

War Diary

of the

51st Bn.

South Wales Borderers.

From June 1st 1919   To June 30th 1919.

Volume No.

4

Army Form C. 2118.

WAR DIARY
51st BN. SOUTH WALES BORDERERS.
INTELLIGENCE SUMMARY.
(Erase heading not required.)

Instructions regarding War Diaries and Intelligence Summaries are contained in F. S. Regs., Part II. and the Staff Manual respectively. Title pages will be prepared in manuscript.

Place	Date	Hour	Summary of Events and Information	Remarks and references to Appendices
MUNSTEREIFEL	1/6/19		Church Parade as usual.	
- do -	2/6/19		Inter Coy. parades altered however since so Whit hour 7 is not carried out. Skinny to test of the day.	
- do -	3/6/19		Brigade Parade at IVERSHEIM for the King's Birthday, in the afternoon the Bn. held sports. There were very successful but the weather very poor.	
- do -	4/6/19		Training as usual.	
- do -	5/6/19		Approx'y 292 Officers & O/Rs went for a "Trip on the RHINE" this tour was much enjoyed by all ranks.	
- do -	6/6/19		Training & Trek preparation.	
- do -	7/6/19		Coy. interior economy, &c. In the afternoon the Bn. Tug of War Team defeated a team by the 3rd Infantry Brigade.	
- do -	8/6/19		Church Parades as usual.	
- do -	9/6/19		Whit Monday a holiday so granted. Many officers & other ranks visited the Sports of the 53rd S. Wales Bnd.	
- do -	10/6/19		Training as usual.	
- do -	11/6/19		Training as usual. In the afternoon the Bn. Heavy & Light	

WAR DIARY
51st BN. SOUTH WALES BORDERERS.
INTELLIGENCE SUMMARY.

Army Form C. 2118.

(Erase heading not required.)

Place	Date	Hour	Summary of Events and Information	Remarks and references to Appendices
MUNSTEREIFEL	11/6/19		Light Tug of War team pulled the 52nd South Wales Borderers on their ground at ARLOFF. After a good struggle the Bn was successful in both cases.	
- do -	12/6/19		Training as usual.	M.
- do -	13/6/19		Training as per programme. The G.O.C. Western Division inspected the Bn. area during the morning	M.
- do -	14/6/19		Usual Saturday routine pay &c.	M.
- do -	15/6/19		C of E, N.C. & R.C. services as usual	M.
- do -	16/6/19		Training as per programme. B. Coy commenced firing 9 M.C.	M.
- do -	17/6/19		Training as usual. Orders received from 3rd Bde for move	M.
- do -	18/6/19		Preparing to move. Packing surplus kit &c.	M. M.O.T.O Odr
RHINBACH	19/6/19		Bn moved to RHINBACH & billeted for the night	M.N.No 2.
QUISDORF	20/6/19		Bn continued move & reached Quisdorf where it billeted	M.
do	21/6/19		Interior economy, inspection of billets &c.	M.
- do	22/6/19		C of E, R.C. & N.C. Service as usual	M.
- do	23/6/19		Coy Training. "D" Coy commenced firing 9 M.C.	M.

Army Form C. 2118.

WAR DIARY
or
INTELLIGENCE SUMMARY.
(Erase heading not required.)

Instructions regarding War Diaries and Intelligence
Summaries are contained in F. S. Regs., Part II.
and the Staff Manual respectively. Title pages
will be prepared in manuscript.

Place	Date	Hour	Summary of Events and Information	Remarks and references to Appendices
DUISDORF	24/6/19		Weather warm but no continuation of M.C. Coy practiced on short route march.	Mh
Duisdorf	25/6/19		C Coy commenced S.M.C.	Mh
- do -	26/6/19		A Coy commence S.M.C. C Coy continue S.M.C.	Mh
- do -	27/6/19		A Coy continue range practice.	Mh
- do -	28/6/19		Major J.A.FRASER. D.S.O. DCM assumes command of Bn for one Lt Col. A.T. REDDIE CMG D.S.O. also proceeded to the United Kingdom for 1 month leave. C.B.E. & R.C. parades as usual.	Mh Mh
- do -	29/6/19		2 Platoons of B & C Coy find part of S.M.C. & Ramming Corps at airfield of	Mh
- do -	30/6/19		Coy Commanders collecting stores in preparation for march to RHEINBACH	

G. Fraser Major.
Comm.g 1/51st South Wales Borderers

51st Bn. South Wales Borderers

Roll of Officers   30th June 1919

Lieut-Colonel A.J.Reddie C.M.G.,D.S.O.	Leave
Major J.A.Fraser D.S.O.,D.C.M.	Commanding
Capt. C.V.Simpson	Adjutant
Lieut. J.Radcliffe	Quartermaster
Lieut. L.A.Lennon	Assistant Adjutant
2/Lieut. I.G.Powell	Transport Officer
2/Lieut. E.R.Jones	Signal Officer
2/Lieut. B.J.Ayers	Musketry and Lewis Gun Officer
Major J.D.Kerr M.C.	Leave
Lieut. A.R.P.Cannon	Commanding "A" Coy.
Lieut. F.Tyler	Hospital
2/Lieut. W.E.Williams	
2/Lieut. W.E.Cooper M.C.	
2/Lieut. R.H.Dawson	
2/Lieut. B.G.Davies	
2/Lieut. D.T.Johns	Hospital
2/Lieut. G.H.Richards	
Capt. W.H.Tosdevine M.C.	Commanding "B" Coy.
Lieut. H.Cottan M.C.	Leave
Lieut. J.J.H.O'Neill M.C.	
2/Lieut. J.Davies	
2/Lieut. A.N.Glover M.C.	
Lieut. G.Esmond M.C.	Commanding "C" Coy.
Lieut. W.F.Pierce	Division H.Q.
Lieut. J.M.Hanson	Brigade H.Q.
Lieut. D.R.Windsor	Leave
2/Lieut. W.N.Douglas	
2/Lieut. A.V.Priston	Hospital
2/Lieut. T.W.Thomas	~~Hospital~~ Leave.
Capt. J.A.Wilson	Leave
Lieut. E.M.Gibbon M.C.	Commanding "D" Coy.
Capt. E.H.Francis	R.A.O.D.
Lieut. W.C.Lush	
Lieut. J.H.Hall	Course, MONTJOIE
2/Lieut. A.E.Williams	Leave
2/Lieut. T.C.R.Bromham M.C.	

EDUCATION INSTRUCTORS

Capt. H.Pritchard M.C.	Leave
Lieut. R.A.Faño	
2/Lieut. G.H.Duckett	
2/Lieut. R.L.Wynne	

J.A. Fraser Major,
Commanding 51st Bn. South Wales Borderers

51st Bn. South Wales Borderers

OPERATION ORDER NO. 2 *was diary* 29/6/19

Ref:- Maps Germany
1:100000 Sheets 1L & 2L

SECRET

Copy No. 16

Move
1. The battalion will return to its former billeting area at MUNSTEREIFEL on the 1st and 2nd July staging for the night at RHEINBACH.
Moves will take place as shown in the attached table.
<u>Dress</u>:- Marching order less packs. Haversacks to be worn on the back and to contain towel, holdall and soap. Mess tin and steel helmet to be slung outside. Waterproof sheets will not be carried.

Headquarters Personnel
2. The same personnel will march with Headquarters at the head of the column as on the march to the present area. Personnel of "D" Coy. at present on H.Q. will rejoin their company at the first halt.

Stragglers Party
3. "A" Coy will detail one section under an Officer to act as stragglers party throughout the march. This party will march in rear of the Transport.

Transport
4. The following transport will be with companies.
   Pack Animal
   Lewis Gun Limber
   Cooker

Advance Party
5. (a) <u>For RHEINBACH</u> will consist of:-
   2/Lieut: E.R.Jones
   1 N.C.O. per company
   A representative from transport
The Signal Officer will arrange for bicycles for this party(less transport representative)
Party will assemble at "C" Coy. Officers' Mess at 0515 hours on the 1st July and will report at the Burgomeisters office RHEINBACH at 0700 hours.

(b) <u>For MUNSTEREIFEL</u> will consist of 1 Officer and 5 N.C.O.s from the "B" Coy detachment now stationed there and the Battalion Interpreter. They will report at the Burgomeisters office at 0700 hours on July 2nd.
Companies etc, will occupy the same billets at MUNSTEREIFEL and RHEINBACH as previously.

Baggage
6. (a) The following baggage will be stacked outside the guard room DUISDORF by 1800 hours tomorrow, 30th inst.
   Packs of other ranks
   1 Blanket per man
   Rifles, steel helmets and S.B.R.s of leave men.
   All stores which will not be required in RHEINBACH.
The Transport Officer will arrange to convoy such baggage from "D" Coy. H.Q. to the dump by 1st Line Transport.
(b) The following baggage will be stacked in a separate dump(at least 25 yds clear of the above) by 0630 hours on 1st July.
   1 blanket per man
   Officers valises and packs(the latter separate)
   All other stores which <u>will</u> be required at RHEINBACH.

P.T.O.

-2-

All orders contained in Operation Order No. 1 dated 17/6/19 and Addenda thereto dated 18/6/19 regarding rolling & labelling of blankets and marking of packs etc. will be adhered to.
No kit beyond the scale laid down will be placed in the pack.

Water   7.   Water bottles and water carts will be filled before marching off.

Loading Parties
         8.   The following loading parties will report to the Quartermaster at the times stated to proceed with lorries.

```
        A Coy.   4 men    )
        B  "     2  "     )   1700 hours
        C  '     1 N.C.O. and 3 men )   30/6/19
        D  "     4 men    )


        A Coy.           4 men )
        B  "             2  "  )   0650 hours
        C  "     1 N.C.O.2  "  )   1/7/19
        D  "             4  "  )
```

The above will be selected from N.C.O.s and other men unable to carry out the march. Companies will report to this office by 1200 hours on 30/6/19 the names of any such N.C.O.s and men stating cause of unfitness. Arrangements will then be made for their conveyance.

Billets   9.   Billets at DUISDORF, LESSENICH and RHEINBACH will be left scrupulously clean. Certificates will be handed to the Adjutant at the first halt on each days march to the effect that all such billets have been inspected and found satisfactory.

Vehicles   10.   All Transport Vehicles will be thoroughly cleaned before each days march.

Rations of H.Q.
Personnel   11.   The rations of H.Q. and Transport will be drawn as follows:-

         1st July.   H.Q. and drums with "D" Coy.
                     Transport with "C" Coy.
                     (less breakfast rations which will be cooked as at present)
         2nd July   H.Q. and Drums with "B" Coy.
                     Transport with "A" Coy.

        12.   Attention is drawn to Battalion Order No.147/10 dated 25/6/19.

        13.   ACKNOWLEDGE

                                         Capt. & Adjt,
                                         51st Bn. S.Wales Bords.

```
Copy No. 1   A Coy.              10.  Education Officer
         2   B  "                11.  3rd Inf. Brigade
         3   C  "                12.  Commanding Officer
         4   D  "                13.  Adjutant
         5   Q.M.                14.  2/Lt. A.N.Glover
         6   T.O.                15.  Medical Officer
         7   Signal Officer      16.  War Diary
         8   L.G.O.              17.  File
         9   R.S.M.              18.  Spare
```

MARCH TABLE TO ACCOMPANY 31st BN. SOUTH WALES BORDERERS OPERATION ORDER NO.2   29/6/19

Date	From	To	Starting Point	Order of March	Route	Remarks
1/7/19	DUISDORF	RHEINBACH	"C" Coy. Officers Mess at 0725	Drums D B A C	BUSCHOVEN - PEPPENHOVEN	(1) 100 yds distance will be maintained between companies. 100 yds between rear Coy. and Transport
2/7/19	RHEINBACH	MUNSTEREIFEL	POINT WHERE RAILWAY CROSSES RHEINBACH - OBERDREES ROAD at 0511 hours	Drums B C D A	ESSIG X ROADS ODENDORF - FLAMERSHEIM - KIRSPENICH	(2) Baggage wagons will accompany 1st Line Transport. (3) Watches will be synchronised at Bn. H.Q. at 0630 hrs on 1st July and 0515 on 2nd July.

CONFIDENTIAL.

To:-   Headquarters,

         3rd Western Infantry Brigade.

Herewith War Diary for the period 1st to 31st JULY 1919, completed and forwarded.

Munstereifel,
1/8/19.

                                    J.A. Fraser Major,
                        Commanding, 51st Bn South Wales Borderers.

War Diary

of the

51st Bn.

South Wales Borderers.

From 1st July To 31st July

1919

Volume No.

5

51st Sqdn. Army Form C. 2118.

WAR DIARY
or
INTELLIGENCE SUMMARY.
(Erase heading not required.)

Place	Date	Hour	Summary of Events and Information	Remarks and references to Appendices
RHEINBACH	1/7/19		Bn. moved from billeting area at DUISDORF & arrived at RHEINBACH after a good march at 1100 hours. On the march the salute was taken by the Brigade Commander, Divisional Commander & Corps Commander. Great satisfaction was expressed at the turn-out of the Bn.	
MÜNSTEREIFEL	2/7/19		Bn. moved from RHEINBACH to its old billeting area at MÜNSTEREIFEL, arriving there after a long march at 1200 hours.	
Münstereifel	3/7/19		Usual Coy training. All Best Shots went for a 30 yds range.	
— do —	4/7/19		The day was devoted to close order drill saluting S.B.R. inspection &c.	
— do —	5/7/19		Usual Sat. morning programme. Also inspection by Interior economy &c.	
— do —	6/7/19		Church Parade for C of E R.C. & N.C. as usual.	
— do —	7/7/19		Bn. Parade according to training programme.	
— do —	8/7/19		Musketry on the 200 yds range. Lecture was given to the Bn on Mercury	
— do —	9/7/19		A. C. & B. Coy's Musketry & General Training. D Coy 200 yds range.	
— do —	10/7/19		This day was observed as a General Holiday to celebrate Peace. Several of the Bn. went on a trip up the RHINE	
— do —	11/7/19		Training as usual. Official Notification was received that the	

Army Form C. 2118.

WAR DIARY
or
INTELLIGENCE SUMMARY.
(Erase heading not required.)

Instructions regarding War Diaries and Intelligence Summaries are contained in F. S. Regs, Part II. and the Staff Manual respectively. Title pages will be prepared in manuscript.

Place	Date	Hour	Summary of Events and Information	Remarks and references to Appendices
Munsterlager	11/7/19		Command of the 3rd Western Brigade was assumed by Brig. Genl. J.G. Rowley CB CMG DSO vice Maj. Genl. T.A. Cubitt CB CMG DSO.	
- do -	12/7/19		Training as usual. Kit inspection day & several M.Gs sent to Cologne.	
- do -	13/7/19		A continued Church Service for C.B.Es M.Cs was held on the 53rd Div. Recreation Ground E. of IVERSHEIM on a celebration thanksgiving to peace.	
- do -	14/7/19		G.M.C. Pt. 2 was commenced by B. Coy, other Coys. trained as usual.	
- do -	15/7/19		"C" Coy commenced G.M.C. Pt. 2.	
- do -	16/7/19		Training in the morning as usual. Lena Ashwell Concert party performed in the Cinema Hall & went much enjoyed. The Major Genl. Comdg. 1st Western Division visited the Bn. during the day.	
- do -	17/7/19		A Coy commenced G.M.C. Pt. 2. Four Officers & four NCOs attended a Chemistry & Platoon drill at PIERZHEIM.	
- do -	18/7/19		Men of "B" Coy who did not fire G.M.C. Pt. 2 commenced on the Brigade Range	
- do -	19/7/19		The Comd. Offr. Officer inspected A Coy, armoury Coys. Kit inspection &c.	
- do -	20/7/19		Church Service for N.C. C.of E. R.C. as usual.	

WAR DIARY
or
INTELLIGENCE SUMMARY.
(Erase heading not required.)

Army Form C. 2118.

Place	Date	Hour	Summary of Events and Information	Remarks and references to Appendices
Nowshera	21/7/19		A Coy completed Pt II G.M.C. Other Coys training as usual	
— do —	22/7/19		Completion Pt II G.M.C. by "B" Coy.	
— do —	23/7/19		A Coy commence G.M.C. Pt III, training to the morning as usual	
— do —	24/7/19		C & D Coys commence G.M.C. Pt III. Other Coys usual programme	
— do —	25/7/19		First day of Brigade Sports, excellent weather, all events keenly enjoyed today	
— do —	26/7/19		Second day of Brigade Sports. The weather was not so good as the first day but the events proved very interesting & very hotly contested.	
— do —	27/7/19		Church Parade as usual. The Adjutant, Capt. C.V. Simpson returned from leave to U.K.	
— do —	28/7/19		Training as usual.	
— do —	29/7/19		G.M.C. training as usual. The Bn Cricket Team defeated the 65th Bde R.F.A. hereby qualifying to the Final of the Divisional Cup.	
— do —	30/7/19		Training as usual. Finals of Bde Boxing took place in the afternoon	
— do —	31/7/19		G.M.C. training as usual	

Major

51st Bn. South Wales Borderers

Nominal Roll of Officers Month ending 31st July 1919

Lieut.-Colonel A.J.Reddie C.M.G.,D.S.O.	~~Commanding~~ leave to UK
Major J.A.Fraser D.S.O.,D.C.M.	~~2nd in~~ Commanding
Capt. C.V.Simpson	Adjutant
Lieut. L.A.Lomon	Assistant Adjutant
Lieut. J.Radcliffe	Quartermaster
2/Lieut. B.J.Ayers	Musketry Officer
2/Lieut. E.R.Jones	Signal Officer
Capt. J.D.Kerr M.C.	Commanding "A" Company
Lieut. A.R.P.Cannon	
2/Lieut. W.H.Williams	Leave to U.K.
" W.E.Cooper M.C.	
" R.H.Dawson	Leave to U.K.
" B.G.Davies	
" D.T.Johns	Hospital
" G.H.Richards	
Capt. W.H.Tosdevine M.C.	Leave to U.K.
Lieut. H.Cottam M.C.	Commanding "B" Coy.
" J.J.H.O'Neill M.C.	
2/Lieut. J.Davies	Course, COLOGNE
" A.N.Glover M.C.	
Capt. G.Esmond M.C.	Commanding "C" Coy.
Lieut. W.F.Pierce	Divisional Traffic Officer
" J.M.Hanson	Brigade H.Q.
2/Lieut. T.G.Powell	
Lieut. D.R.Windsor	
2/Lieut. W.N.Douglas	Course, BONN
" A.V.Priston	Hospital
" T.W.Thomas	
Capt. J.A.Wilson	Commanding "D" Coy.
" D.H.Francis	R.A.O.D.,COLOGNE
Lieut. E.M.Gibbon M.C.	
" W.G.Lush	
" J.H.Hall	
2/Lieut. A.E.Williams	
" T.C.R.Bromham M.C.	
Capt. H.Pritchard M.C.	Education Instructor
Lieut. R.A.Faro	do.
2/Lieut. G.H.Duckett	do.
" R.L.Wynne	do.

31st July 1919

J.A.Fraser Major,
Commanding 51st Bn. South Wales Borderers

WO95/1282 ③
52/S.Wales Bords
Mar '19 - July '19

BEF

1 Division

3 Brigade

52 S.W.B.

1919 Mar to 1919 July

To:- Headquarters,
    3rd. Infantry Brigade.
    ....

    Herewith A.F. C.2118 (War Dairy) for period from
1/5/1919 to 31/5/1919 please.

Kirspenich.   Lieut Colonel.
1/6/1919.   Commanding 52nd. Battn S.W. Borderers.

52 Lowestoft

Army Form C. 2118.

WESTERN DIV

WAR DIARY
or
INTELLIGENCE SUMMARY.
(Erase heading not required.)

Instructions regarding War Diaries and Intelligence Summaries are contained in F.S. Regs., Part II. and the Staff Manual respectively. Title pages will be prepared in manuscript.

Hour, Date, Place	Summary of Events and Information	Remarks and references to Appendices
6am 22nd/3rd/1919 COLCHESTER	Left COLCHESTER at 6 am arrived DOVER 12-19. Left DOVER per S.S. ANTRIM at 13.45 o'clock arrived DUNKIRK about 14.00 o'clock. Strength of BATTⁿ 24 Officers and 896 other ranks.	
23-3-19 DUNKIRK	Entrained at Sand Siding DUNKIRK at 14.55 am proceeded via MERRIS, ARMENTIERES, LILLE.	
24-3-19 in train AMRITSAR No 39.	Arrived at BAISIEUX at 03.55 o'clock and TOURNAI at 07.00, where No 67969 Pte Bushing No 67969 Pte Boardman "B" Coy. were left behind, reached GHISLENCHIEN at 15.30, SUD QUAI CHARLEROI at 16.35 and HUY at 22.40 o'clock.	
25th March 1919 in train and WITTERSCHLICK.	Arrived HERBERTSTAL at 08.00 o'clock and at WITTERSCHLICK at 11.50 o'clock, took over billets from 2nd Battⁿ ROYAL SUSSEX REGT for "A" & "B" Companies at WITTERSCHLICK, "C" Company up HEIDGEN, and for "D" Company at WOLMESHOVEN.	
26/3/19 WITTERSCHLICK	Taking over equipment etc from 2nd Battⁿ ROYAL SUSSEX REGT.	
27/3/19 -do-	Companies carried out physical training and 1½ hours ROUTE MARCH. Pte BUSH and BOARDMAN rejoined.	

Army Form C. 2118.

WAR DIARY
or
INTELLIGENCE SUMMARY.
(Erase heading not required.)

Instructions regarding War Diaries and Intelligence Summaries are contained in F. S. Regs., Part II. and the Staff Manual respectively. Title pages will be prepared in manuscript.

Hour, Date, Place	Summary of Events and Information	Remarks and references to Appendices
Wittenchich 28-3-19	Companies at training	
29-3-19	stood at Wittenchich.	
30-3-19	Church Parades: Roman Catholic an 10.15 o'clock and Church of England an 11.30 o'clock.	
Wittenchich	Left Wittenchich. Strength of Battalion 24 officers and 902 Other Ranks.	
11.15 — Arloff	Arrived Arloff. Left's Coys billetted in Kirspenich — 540 — I billetted in Arloff and the Factory. Draft of 1.0 p.m. and 108 Other Ranks from 1st Batt were unable or in supplements as	

ARLOFF.

KIRSPENICH
2nd April 1919.

G. Morgan Lieut
Commandg 52nd Bn S.W. Borderers

[Stamp: 52ND BATTN. SOUTH WALES BORDERERS No. 2 APR 1919 ORDERLY ROOM]

WAR DIARY or INTELLIGENCE SUMMARY.

Army Form C. 2118.

57 nd Bn South Wales Borderers

Place	Date	Hour	Summary of Events and Information	Remarks and references to Appendices
KINMEL PARK	1/4/19		Allotted A & B, 1st Battalion to companies as under: A Coy 27, B 27, C 30, D 34. Transport posted to B Company, which made Battalion up to 25 Officers and 1010 other ranks.	J.C.
	2/4/19		Battalion inspected by Brigadier General T.A. CUBITT, C.B., C.M.G., D.S.O.	J.C.
	3/4/19		Companies at training	J.C.
	4/4/19		do	J.C.
	5/4/19		Battalion inspected by Lieut. General Sir W.P. BRAITHWAITE, K.C.B.	J.C.
	6/4/19		Battalion attended Church of England Service at 11.30 hours	J.C.
	7/4/19		Companies at training. Lectures at 14.30 hours by A.D.M.S. and Senior Chaplain. Subject Venereal Disease.	J.C.
	8/4/19		Companies at training	J.C.
	9/4/19		Battalion Route March.	J.C.
	10/4/19		Companies at training. Dress State 23 Officers	J.C.
	11/4/19		A/C. See Appx 3. Gods, Ox 1 Gods.	J.C.
	12/4/19		Companies at training	J.C.

Army Form C. 2118.

WAR DIARY
or
INTELLIGENCE SUMMARY.

52nd Bde: S.W. Borderers

(Erase heading not required.)

Instructions regarding War Diaries and Intelligence Summaries are contained in F. S. Regs., Part II. and the Staff Manual respectively. Title pages will be prepared in manuscript.

Place	Date	Hour	Summary of Events and Information	Remarks and references to Appendices
MAISNIL AU BOIS A.P.L.D.F.E.	12/4/16		Companies at Training. Cricket match 52nd Br Suffs against 5/1 Suffs. B/1 MUNSTERFIELD Score 5/1 Suffs 5/1 Suffs 57/Suffs/Suffs/Suffs/1 Bn/. Inspection board on 18.30 hours by A.P.L.D.F.E.	H.C.
	13/4/16		C of E service not held owing to rain.	H.C.
	14/4/16		Companies at Training. Conference for all officers at MUNSTERFIELD at 11.00 hours.	H.C.
	15/4/16		Companies at Training.	H.C.
	16/4/16		Battalion ceremonial parade. Soccer Match 52nd Br 57 52nd Bn Suffs Score 52nd Br Suffs 5 Goals, 57 Br Rifle/Brid/2nd.	H.C.
	17/4/16		Companies at Training.	H.C.
	18/4/16		Good Friday. Voluntary Service held for nonconformists. Companies at Training.	H.C.
	19/4/16		Companies at Training.	H.C.
	20/4/16		Holy Communion and Voluntary Service held, Easter Sunday.	H.C.
	21/4/16		Companies at Training.	H.C.
	22/4/16		— do —	H.C.
	23/4/16		Battalion Route March and practising Artillery formation. Soccer match with 51st Br. Score 57 or Br 9 Goals, 52 Br 1 Goal.	H.C.
	24/4/16		Companies at Training.	H.C.

__WAR DIARY__ _of_ 52nd Bn S.W.Borderers   Army Form C. 2118.

INTELLIGENCE SUMMARY.
(Erase heading not required.)

Place	Date	Hour	Summary of Events and Information	Remarks and references to Appendices
KIRCHENICH ARLOFF	23/4/19		Companies on training. Nine Officers and 233 Other ranks for trip on RHINE from BONN to COBLENTZ leaving ARLOFF at 0900 hours and return from BONN at 1920 hours. Lt Col L.I.G. MORGAN OWEN CMG, DSO was in charge of the train.	J.C.
--	26/4/19		Companies in training.	J.C.
--	27/4/19	13:15	Church Service held for C of E and United Patrol. Fire in a barn and house at ARLOFF which the battalion parades for extinguished.	J.C.
--	28/4/19		Companies in training. Four Officers and 50 Others attended the London Divisional Rugby meeting at KALK near COLOGNE.	J.C.
--	29/4/19		Companies in training. Four Officers and 50 Others attended the London Divisional Rugby meeting at KALK near COLOGNE.	J.C.
--	30/4/19	11:30	Brigade inspected by General Sir W.R. ROBERTSON G.C.B., K.C.V.O., D.S.O.	J.C.

Kirspenich
for May 1919

G.I. Morgan Owen
LIEUT.-COLONEL,
COMMANDING 52nd BATTN. S. W. BORDERERS.

WAR DIARY 57/Br Supplovers.

Army Form C. 2118.

INTELLIGENCE SUMMARY.

(Erase heading not required.)

Place	Date	Hour	Summary of Events and Information	Remarks and references to Appendices
KIRSPENICH r ARLOFF	1/5/19		Companies at training.	J.C.
—	2/5/19		— Do —	J.C.
—	3/5/19		— Do — . In afternoon Soccer match north Brigade Head Quarters. Score 52nd Br. 8 Goals, Bde 2 Goals.	J.C.
—	4/5/19		Church services held for C. of E. R.C.'s & Nonconformists.	J.C.
—	5/5/19		Companies at training.	J.C.
—	6/5/19		— Do —	J.C.
—	7/5/19		Battalion Route march, afternoon Soccer match Officers v Sergts. Score Officers 4 Goals, Sergeants 1 Goal.	J.C.
—	8/5/19		Companies at training.	J.C.
—	9/5/19		— Do —	J.C.
—	10/5/19		— Do — afternoon Soccer match north 57th Br. Groups. Score 57th Br. 1 Goal, 52nd Br. 1 Goal.	J.C.
—	11/5/19		Church services held for C. of E., R.C.'s & Nonconformists.	J.C.
—	12/5/19		Companies at training.	J.C.
—	13/5/19		— Do —, Cinema display at ARLOFF	J.C.

1500 Lumps

WAR DIARY 37/B S.W. Borderers

Army Form C. 2118.

INTELLIGENCE SUMMARY.
(Erase heading not required.)

Place	Date	Hour	Summary of Events and Information	Remarks and references to Appendices
KIRSPENICH & ARLOFF	14.5.19		Battalion Route March, afternoon Soccer match with 53rd Bn. Score 53rd Bn 4 Goals, 37th Bn 2 Goals.	A.C.
" "	15.5.19		Companies in training, and two platoons digging on new rifle ranges or Musketerigel.	A.C.
" "	16.5.19		do — — once lecture by Canon Maynard Subject Ancient Rome.	A.C.
" "	17.5.19		Companies in training.	A.C.
" "	18.5.19		Service held for Coys, R.C. & Nonconformists, afternoon Root & Shoot Officers & Sergeants on 30 yards range.	A.C.
" "	19.5.19		Companies in training.	A.C.
" "	20.5.19		do	A.C.
" "	21.5.19		Companies in training and 2 platoons digging on new ranges at MUNSTEREIFEL. Two lectures by Brigadier General STONE 10:30 & 14:30 hours Subject "Economics of reconstruction". Afternoon D Coy's Sports and Soccer match with Brigade Head Quarters. Score 37th Bn 5 Goals, Brigade H.Q. Nil	A.C.

WAR DIARY of 62nd Bn. S.W.Borderers

INTELLIGENCE SUMMARY.

Army Form C. 2118.

Place	Date	Hour	Summary of Events and Information	Remarks and references to Appendices
KIRSPENICH & ARLOFF	22/5/19		Companies at training; Two Platoons working on new range at MUNSTEREIFEL. "C" Company Sports during evening.	J.C.
	23/5/19		— do — "D" Company Sports during evening	J.C.
	24/5/19		Companies at training. One Platoon working on new range. Engin Officers and Sgts & O/Ranks sent for trek on Rhine from BONN to COBLENTZ.	J.C.
	25/5/19		Soccer match with 57th Bn. Score 57th Bn 5 Goals, 62nd Bn 2 Goals. Service held Church of England & Roman Catholics at KIRSPENICH. General service for non-conformists at Borgwile/Keent Quarters. Pool Shoot for Officers & N.C.O.s during afternoon. Soccer match Officers v Sergeants. Score Officers nil Sergeants two. Band of Western Divisional String Orchestra.	J.C.
To 75 yd	26/5/19		Companies at training. Two Platoons working on new range	J.C.
	27/5/19		— do —	
			"A" Company Sports; Canwea as ARLOFF; Soccer match Sergeants v "D" Company during evening. Score Sergeants 1 Goal, "D" Company 4 Goals.	J.C.

Army Form C. 2118.

53/98r 2nd Borderers

WAR DIARY
or
INTELLIGENCE SUMMARY.
(Erase heading not required.)

Instructions regarding War Diaries and Intelligence Summaries are contained in F. S. Regs., Part II. and the Staff Manual respectively. Title pages will be prepared in manuscript.

Place	Date	Hour	Summary of Events and Information	Remarks and references to Appendices
KIRSPENICH				
A-R LOFF	28/5/19		Battalion March out as Flying Column. Soccer match with 53rd 98r at MUNSTEREIFEL. Score 53rd 98r 2 goals, 53rd Br 3 goals.	A.C.
	29/5/19		Companies in training. Two Platoons working on new range.	A.C.
	30/5/19		Do — Do — Do —	
	31/5/19		Companies in training. One platoon working on new range. Organised games afternoon & evening.	A.C.

G. Morgan- [illegible]
LIEUT.-COLONEL,
COMMANDING 52nd & 98th S. W. BORDERERS.

KIRSPENICH
1st June 1919

Army Form C. 2118.

53rd Bn South Wales Borderers

WAR DIARY
or
INTELLIGENCE SUMMARY.
(Erase heading not required.)

Place	Date	Hour	Summary of Events and Information	Remarks and references to Appendices
ARLOFF and KIRSPENICH	1/6/19		Service held for nonconformists & Roman Catholics.	—
	2/6/19		Prot. Short. all ranks afternoon. Companies at training. One company at work on rifle ranges. A & B Companies tested in anti-gas measures.	—
	3/6/19		King's Birthday. Brigade paraded at 9.00 a.m. in Recreation ground of 53rd Battn. Subordinates, area of IVERSHEIM. General holiday after parade.	—
	4-5/6/19		Companies at training. Front full of Eng & W.O. League. 53rd Batt. v. Brigade HQ Coy. Result 6 Olchwigs 53rd Rh 2 Polos. 3rd Vols HQ Coys Kill. 1 four margin. 53rd Bn v Rhib Rue 1 goal nil.	—
	5-6-19	15.00	Companies at training. One company at work on new ranges. Flue Band Concert Party at ARLOFF.	—
	6-6-19		Companies at training. One company on new ranges. 6 Officers & 93 Officers and troops on Rhine from BONN to COBLENZ.	—
	7/6/19		Companies at training. 6 & O & 100 infantry tested in anti-gas measures. Lecture by Rev M.A. Phillips at ARLOFF subject:- Wild life in meadow, stream and wood.	—

Army Form C. 2118.

WAR DIARY 53rd Bn South Wales Borderers
or
INTELLIGENCE SUMMARY.
(Erase heading not required.)

Instructions regarding War Diaries and Intelligence Summaries are contained in F.S. Regs., Part II. and the Staff Manual respectively. Title pages will be prepared in manuscript.

Place	Date	Hour	Summary of Events and Information	Remarks and references to Appendices
ARLOFF and KIRSPENICH	4/6/19		(cont'd) Eng of war League held. 52nd Bn & 53rd Bn Results: Enterweiher 53rd Bn 3 Pulls, 53rd Bn Pd. Lightweight 52nd Bn 3 Pulls. 53rd Bn Nil.	J.C.
—	8/6/19		Whit Sunday. Services held for to offr RCs & honconformists	J.C.
—	9/6/19	1010	To 6440 Pte J Reeves 16 Coy accidentally drowned whilst bathing	J.C.
—	10/6/19		Whit Monday. General Holiday	J.C.
—	11/6/19		Companies in training. One company working on new ranges	J.C.
—			The body of Pte J Reeves received from a drowning found Drumgerven	J.C.
—			Companies in training. Eng of war League held 51st Bn v 53rd Bn Results: Enterweiher 51st Bn 3 Pulls, 53rd Bn Nil. Lightweight 51st Bn 3 Pulls. 53rd Bn 1 Pull.	J.C.
—	12/6/19		Companies in training. One company on new ranges	J.C.
—		11:30	Funeral of Pte J Reeves at Buskirchen Cemetery	J.C.
—	13/6/19		Companies in training. One company on new ranges Divisional General visited the Battalion.	J.C.
—	14/6/19		Companies at training. One company on new ranges	J.C.
—	15/6/19		Capt. H.R. Honeyman. Corner of Enquiry held on death of Pte J Reeves. also Memorial Service held.	J.C.
—			at 18.00 hours at ARLOFF for its late Pte J Reeves 16 Coy.	J.C.
—	16/6/19		Companies in training. One company on new ranges	J.C.
—	17/6/19			J.C.

WAR DIARY

52nd Bn South Wales Borderers

Army Form C. 2118.

INTELLIGENCE SUMMARY

(Erase heading not required.)

Instructions regarding War Diaries and Intelligence Summaries are contained in F.S. Regs., Part II. and the Staff Manual respectively. Title pages will be prepared in manuscript.

Place	Date	Hour	Summary of Events and Information	Remarks and references to Appendices
KIRSPENICH and ARLOFF	18-6-19		Companies at training and preparing for move to OBR DREES and NIEDER DREES.	A.C.
OBR DREES and NDR DREES	19-6-19	15.00	Left KIRSPENICH by march route and arrived in OBR DREES and NDR DREES at 17.45 hours. "A" & "B" Companies billeted in OBR DREES, "C" & "D" Coys in NIEDER DREES.	A.C.
ENDENICH	21-6-19	04.30	Left OBR DREES and marched to ENDENICH near BONN arriving at 11.30 hours. Whole battalion billeted in ENDENICH.	A.C.
—	23-6-19		Companies cleaning up and opening up billets.	A.C.
—	24-6-19		Coys Service held in ENDENICH, and R.C. Service in GIELSDORF.	A.C.
—	25-6-19		Battalion Route March.	A.C.
—	26-6-19		Route march by Companies and arm and saluting drill.	A.C.
—	25-6-19		Companies carry out close order arm and saluting drill.	A.C.
—	26-6-19		Companies carry out Route marching and close order drill.	A.C.
—	27-6-19		Companies carry out close order arms drill and Lewis Gun training, inspection of billets.	A.C.
—	28-6-19		Companies at training, inspection of billets.	A.C.
—	29-6-19		Coys C, R.B. and Nonconformist services held in ENDENICH.	A.C.
—	30-6-19		Companies at training and preparing for return march to OBR DREES and NIEDER DREES on 1st July 1919.	A.C.

G. Morgan MW
LIEUT. COLONEL
COMMANDING 52nd BATTN. S. W. BORDERERS.

Army Form C. 2118.

WAR DIARY 52/ Br South Wales Borderers

INTELLIGENCE SUMMARY

(Erase heading not required.)

Instructions regarding War Diaries and Intelligence Summaries are contained in F.S. Regs., Part II. and the Staff Manual respectively. Title pages will be prepared in manuscript.

Place	Date	Hour	Summary of Events and Information	Remarks and references to Appendices
ENDENICH	2/7/19	07.20	Left ENDENICH by march route for OBR DREES and NIEDER DREES reached destination at 11.35 hours. 'A' & 'B' Coys were billeted at OBR DREES, and 'C' & 'D' Coys at NIEDER DREES.	FC
OBR DREES	3/7/19	06.20	Left for ARLOFF and KIRSPENICH by march route, arrived destination at 09.20 hours, all companies returned to their old billets.	FC
NOR DREES				FC
ARLOFF	3/7/19		Companies cleaning up and opening up billets.	FC
KIRSPENICH	4/7/19		Organised games afternoon	FC
"	5/7/19		Companies at training, organised games afternoon	FC
"	6/7/19		do — do —	APT
"	7/7/19		C.of E. & R.C. Church Parades. Companies at training. Parties left for Victory March PARIS and for CATTERAI & new battlefield.	APT
"	8/7/19		(Volunteer heads of Battalion sports and Tug-of-war. Companies at training. Basket ball match v 51st SWB. Result lost.	APT
"	9/7/19		Return on War Savings at 1030 hrs.	APT
"	10/7/19		Companies at training. C'ly sent one platoon to SATZVEY on IX C/pr Guard.	APT
"	11/7/19		Brigade Peace Holiday. Battalion Sports.	APT
"	12/7/19		Companies at training. Baker's bread party proposed at AKLOFF 1230 hrs. Battalion Holiday. 200 OR to Cologne Races.	APT

Copy

5/2nd Bn South Wales Borderers Army Form C. 2118.

WAR DIARY
INTELLIGENCE SUMMARY.
(Erase heading not required.)

Instructions regarding War Diaries and Intelligence Summaries are contained in F. S. Regs., Part II. and the Staff Manual respectively. Title pages will be prepared in manuscript.

Place	Date	Hour	Summary of Events and Information	Remarks and references to Appendices
ARLOFF & KIRSPENICH	13/7/19		Brigade United Church Parade (Near Rauxigny) + R.C. parade. Battn had played at R.E.s parade.	A.P.J
	14/7/19		Conferences at Training. Organised games afternoon. Dirt arena (Bocken)	A.P.S.
	15/7/19		Do — Horse jumps erected.	A.P.J
	16/7/19		Do	A.P.J
	17/7/19		Do — Cricket match v 61st DWR. lost 28 & 40 runs	A.P.J
	18/7/19		Do	A.P.J
	19/7/19		General Holiday.	A.P.J
	20/7/19		C.of E. R.C. & Non Conformist Church parades.	A.P.J
	21/7/19		Major Gen. T.O. Marden only Western Div: visited Battn & Platoon training. Organised games afternoon.	A.P.J
	22/7/19		Conferences at training. Organised games — our Brigade boxing tournament afternoon.	A.P.J
	23/7/19		Do	A.P.J
	24/7/19		Do	A.P.J
	25/7/19		Divisional sports — GIERSBERG MUNSTEREIFEL	X
	26/7/19		Do	X
	27/7/19		Coys P.E. & Non-competitive games held.	X
	28/7/19		Champions in Training. Arrears of Divisional Ancedon during evening.	X

Army Form C. 2118.

WAR DIARY

INTELLIGENCE / SUMMARY.

52nd Bn. South Wales Borderers

(Erase heading not required.)

Instructions regarding War Diaries and Intelligence Summaries are contained in F. S. Regs., Part II. and the Staff Manual respectively. Title pages will be prepared in manuscript.

Place	Date	Hour	Summary of Events and Information	Remarks and references to Appendices
ARLOFF and KIRSPENICH	29-7-19			
—	30-7-19		Companies in training. Organized games afternoon.	KIRSPENICH J.C.
			Companies in training. In afternoon Boxing, Border Ball and Tug of War contests bn 53rd Bde ground in Münstereifel, 52nd Bn won the boxing and Tug-of-War, but lost the Basket Ball 26.53.28.	J.C.
—	31-7-19		Companies in training. Sports afternoon Tug of war (Contesting) one Border Ball match bn. 52nd Bn. 52nd Bn won Tug of war & pulls 16 Bn., but lost Border Ball 57=2 scoring 24 points & 52nd 4 points.	J.C.

Kirspenich
1st August 1919

A. Mynn-Lean
LIEUT.-COLONEL
COMMANDING 52nd BATTN. S. W. BORDERERS.

WO95/1282 ④
53/S. WALES BORDS
Mar '19 – July '19

BEF

1 DIVISION

3 BRIGADE

53 S.W.B

1919 MAR to 1919 JULY

Army Form C. 2118.

53rd Bn., S.W. BORDERERS.

WAR DIARY
INTELLIGENCE SUMMARY.
(Erase heading not required.)

Instructions regarding War Diaries and Intelligence Summaries are contained in F.S. Regs., Part II. and the Staff Manual respectively. Title pages will be prepared in manuscript.

Place	Date	Hour	Summary of Events and Information	Remarks and references to Appendices
DUNKIRK.	1919 Mch. 22.	13.00.	Battalion disembarked :- 41 Officers and 824 other ranks. Accommodated for night 22/23rd at No. 3 Rest Camp.	
"	" 23.	12.00.	Battalion entrained. Proceeded via BERGUES, ESQUELBEC, MORRIS, BAILLEUL, ARMENTIERES, PERENCHIES, LILLE, BAISIEUX, CHARLEROI, NAMUR, LIEGE, VERVIERS, AIX-LA-CHAPELLE, DUREN, EUSKIRCHEN, to MUNSTEREIFEL. Halte Pages en route at MORRIS, BAISIEUX, CHARLEROI and VERVIERS. Light fall of snow.	
MUNSTEREIFEL.	" 25.	08.20.	Battalion detrained, same strength, and accommodated in billets.	
"	" 26.		C.O. met 10th Corps Commander.	
"	" 27.		G.O.C., 3rd Infantry Brigade, and Staff, visited C.O. Snow during night. "A" and "D" Companies removed in Billets at IVERSHIEM, under Major H.M. LONG. 3 Officers and 58 other ranks arrived from 1st Bn. S.W.B. and 8 Officers and 155 other ranks from 2nd Bn. S.W.B., and were equally distributed among Companies and platoons. Instructions issued as to duties towards civilians, and rights of Army of Occupation. Day and Night guards, and Picquet, posted.	
"	"28.		C.O. presided at Military Court on civilians. Transport vehicles, horses, and stores, taken over from 1st Bn. Gloucestershire Rgt. Orders issued as to the use of German money and purchase of German goods, and as to fraternization and bounds.	
"	"29.		G.O.C., 3rd Infy. Bde. called on C.O. and arranged inspection of Battalion. Very cold. M.O. (Capt. P.G. Simpson) returned to England. Arrangements made for Lewis Gun Course, 30 yards Range, School and Signal Office. Stiff Caps. issued to Companies, on payment. Adjutant proceeded to Euskirchen for cash to pay Battalion. (15.00 - 18.00). 2/Lt. F.E. HARLOW selected to attend 2nd Army P.T. & R. Course on 2-4-1919. Capt. C.K.CARROLL, R.A.M.C., assumed New Training Programme issued. Workshops started. Medical Charge. Cold. Rain.	
"	"30.	14.00 - 16.00.	C.O. and Adjutant inspected vicinity, and took photographs. Church Parade at 11.30. Chaplain attached for duty.	
"	"31.	1000.	G.O.C. 3rd Infy. Bde. inspected and addressed Battalion, and afterwards gave instructions to all Officers as to system of training. Orders received for demobilization.	
"		1430.	G.O.C. inspected Billets and Cook-houses at MUNSTEREIFEL and IVERSHIEM. Orders received that Officers over 35, or who joined Colours before 1916, are eligible for demobilization. Bun Classes arranged for Officers and N.C.Os. 5 men detailed for course in water duties. Fine and Sunny.	

Army Form C. 2118.

WAR DIARY
or
INTELLIGENCE SUMMARY.
(Erase heading not required.)

53rd., BN., SOUTH WALES BORDERERS.

Instructions regarding War Diaries and Intelligence Summaries are contained in F. S. Regs., Part II. and the Staff Manual respectively. Title pages will be prepared in manuscript.

Place	Date 1919.	Hour	Summary of Events and Information	Remarks and references to Appendices
Munstereifel.	Apl. 1st.	1100 1200	Commanding Officer and Adjutant inspected billets, cookers, etc., at MUNSTEREIFEL. 14.00 hour C.O. and Transport Officer inspected Transport, animals and vehicles. Battalion Dry Canteen opened. Orders issued as to War Savings.	
	2nd.	0945	Batta.Route March in fighting Order and steel Helmets to ARLOFF. Lecture at 14.30 hours by Major Dugmore on "Beaver and Caribou".	
	3rd.	0900	Orders received for inspection tomorrow by Corps Commander, and issued to Companies. All Transport cleaned and painted. C.O., dealt with 5 Civilian cases. C.O. attended C.O's., Conference. At 16.30 hours C.O. and Adjutant, selected Parade Ground for inspection. Weekly cash received from EUSKERCHEN, Marks 14,000.	
	4th.	1130	Inspection by Corps Commander. 12.30 hours C.O. dealt with one civilian case, Fined 1,000 M. Concert at 18.00 hours by 141st. F.A. Troupe. Issued ammunition 100 & 120 rounds S.A.A. per man. Accident to Transport Driver at IVERSHEIM.	
	5th.		Orders received that Officers who joined Colours before 1.1.1917 are demobilisable. Football Match at 14.30 hours, 51st. V 53rd.,S.W.B. C.O. and Adjutant inspected Transport at 17.00 hours.	
	6th.		Church Parade 09.30 hours. C.O. and Adjutant rode over Country E. of Munstereifel and selected training Areas.	
	7th.		C.O. admitted to Hospital. Major.H.M.Long assumes Command. "X" & "Y" forms rendered to Bde. as to Officers for Army of Occupation. Football Match at EUSKERCHEN 53rd.SWB V lX Corps Headquarters Score 23 pts to 3pt. 30 Yards Range started.	
	8th. 9th. 10th.		2 Officers arrived from 6th.Bn.SWB. Conference with D.A.D.O.S at 15.00 hours. Route March to EICHERSHAID and Schwaz. Arrangements made with Burgomeister for sale of dripping and swill. Cash obtained from Field Cashier, EUSKERCHEN, 31.000 Marks.	
	11th.		Major Long and Adjut., inspected 30 yard Range and training ground at IVERSHEIM. Company Commanders' Conference. 11.00 hour to 12.00 hours re Sports etc. 3 Civilian cases dealt with by Mjr.Long. Non.Com. Chaplain reported for duty.	
	12th.		Major Long, & Adjt., visited "B" & "C" Company's areas. Football Match 51st. V 53rd.,SWB. 37 - Nil. Captain Middall M.O. arrived.	
	13th. 14th.		Church Parades in morning. Lieut.L.A.Hows demobilized. Conference of C.O's. and Education Officers at 10.00 hours and 10.30 hours. Address by Divnl. Commander 11.00 hours. Orders received to wear stell Helmets on guard, route marches and range. Lewis Gun Training begun.	
	15th.		Lieut. J.F.Rees.M.C., 2/Lt.A.C.Bingham and 2/Lt. R.O.Hughes demobilized.	

Army Form C. 2118.

WAR DIARY
or
INTELLIGENCE SUMMARY.
(Erase heading not required.)

53rd. BATTN., SOUTH WALES BORDERERS.

Instructions regarding War Diaries and Intelligence Summaries are contained in F.S. Regs., Part II. and the Staff Manual respectively. Title pages will be prepared in manuscript.

Place	Date 1919.	Hour	Summary of Events and Information	Remarks and references to Appendices
MUNSTEREIFEL	Apl. 16th.		Wet morning. No. Route march. Major Long and Musketry Officer attended board on ranges.	
	17th.		"D" Coy Fired. 3 Platoons on 30 yard Range. Rain 12.00 hours until 17.00 hours. Supply Officer inspected Transport harness.	
	18th.		Good Friday. Church parades in the morning.	
	19th.		Adjutant proceeded to BORNHELM to defend accused at F.G.C.M. Signallers selected for Training.	
	20th.		Easter Sunday. Fine and warm.	
	21st.		Easter Monday. Work as usual. G.O.C. orders conference of C.O. and O.C. Coys' tomorrow.	
	22nd.		G.O.C. Conference with C.O., Adjt., and O's C.Coys' re training programme etc. G.O.C. inspected Unit registers and demobilization returns.	
	23rd.		Route March and tactical exercise 09.30 hours to 12.50 hours. Lecture 14.30 hours by Canon Parfitt, on "Bagdad" - The plot that failed".	
	24th.		Two Officers reported from 6th. Bn. SWB. orders issued as to care of ammunition & Lewis Guns. 2/Lieut. J.M. Lloyd attached for Education duty.	
	25th.		G.O.C. called at 11.00 hours. 8 Officers & 200 O.R's., went to BONN for Rhine excursion 2/Lieut. Wynn reported from 26th. R.W.F's.	
	26th.		Inspected Transport and Company dining rooms. Conference of O's.C.Coy's. at 12.00 hours. Special vigilance ordered by 3rd. Inf., Bde., at, 21.45 hours and action taken. Football Match 52 V 53 S.W.B.	
	27th.		New training programme and routine orders issued. Brigade Sports Meeting at 14.30 hours.	
	28th.		Programmes for Summer Training and Gas Training issued.	
	29th.		Lieut. H.T. Dale appointed Educational Officer to 2nd. Infantry Brigade. Orders for inspection tomorrow by G.O.C. in C., Rhine Army.	
	30th.		Inspection of Brigade, at IVERSHEIM by Genl. Sir W. Robertson, G.O.C.in C., British Army of the Rhine, at 11.30 hours. Orders issued for inlying piquets and special vigilance tomorrow, 1st. May, owing to German Labour demonstrations.	

Munstereifel.
3rd. May, 1919.

P.W.Wilkinson. Colonel.
Commanding, 53rd. Bn., S.W. Borderers.

WAR DIARY
or
INTELLIGENCE SUMMARY.

(Erase heading not required)

53rd.,BN.,SOUTH WALES BORDERERS.

Army Form C. 2118.

Place	Date	Hour	Summary of Events and Information	Remarks and references to Appendices
MUNSTEREIFEL.	May 1919. 1st.		German Labour Day. No demonstration. Col.O.De.L.Williams,CMG.,DSO., assumed Command of Bn. Value of Mark descends to 61 per £1 Sterling.	
	2nd.		C.O. & Major Long inspected training grounds etc. at MUNSTEREIFEL & IVERSHEIM.	
	3rd.		Officers & Runners selected for course at EUSKIRCHEN in pigeon duties. Lt.A.V.Curtice selected for Birkamstead Course.	
	4th.		Sunday. Football Match & practice in afternoon.	
	5th.		C.O.inspected Billets at MUNSTEREIFEL 11.00 hours. C.O. inspected "D" Coy., at IVERSHEIM 14.30.	
	6th.		11.00 C.O. inspected "A" Coy., at IVERSHEIM.	
	7th.		Route March towards EIFELBERG 09.00 - 12.30. Half holiday.	
	8th.		14.30. C.O. inspected "B" Coy.,at MUNSTEREIFEL. Stretcher bearers classes started. Adjutant mounted Guard at IVERSHEIM.	
	9th.		14.30. C.O. inspected "C" Coy., at MUNSTEREIFEL. C.O. & Adjt., dined at IVERSHEIM.	
	10th.		"D"Coy.,moved to MUNSTEREIFEL. "B" Coy.,moved to IVERSHEIM. Steel helmets fitted with badges and painted. Conference of C.O's with Divisional Commander at Bde.H.Q. at 12.15 hours. Brig.-Genl. attended dinner & concert.	
	11th.		Sunday. Football Match. 6th.Welsh V 53 S.W.B., away. 8pts.- Nil.	
	12th.		Site for "A" & "B" Coys', camp selected at MUNSTEREIFEL. A.D.M.S. inspected kitchens, sanitation etc.	
	13th.		C.O. inspected L.G. Sections at training, and L.G. demonstration sections. Adjt., visited STOTSHEIM to prepare scheme for tactical exercise tomorrow.	
	14th.		Route March to RHEDER. Night outpost exercise between BILLIG & STOTZHEIM. Afterwards Battn.,attended Assoc.,Match at ARLOFF between 52 & 53 S.W.B. 4 Goals 2.	
	15th.		Lewis Gun Demonstration for Officers and Lewis Gun Section commanders 10.30 - 11.45 hours.	
	16th.		Adjt., lectured to "D" Coy., on guards etc., C.O. visited "A" & "B" Coys. at IVERSHEIM 14.00.	
	17th.		Adjt., took further German evidence in case of Pte.Davies.	
	18th.		Court of Inquiry held on 3 absentees off pass. Arrangements made for Officers' Riding School.	
	19th.		Adjt., proceded to SCHONAU to select site for day outpost scheme. Major.V.B.Ramsden,D.S.O.,M.C., reported for duty as 2nd.in.C. Ridding Class started. Adjt., lectured to "B" Coy.	
	20th.		Route March to SCHONAU in marching order. Day outpost scheme.	
	21st.		C.O. & Mjr.Ramsden visited IVERSHEIM. Orders issued re use of bullet & bayonet courses & ranges.	
	22nd.		Divnl.Comdr. visited 3rd.Bde. Adjt.lectured to "A"Coy., at IVERSHEIM.	

Army Form C. 2118.

WAR DIARY
or
INTELLIGENCE SUMMARY.

53rd. BN., SOUTH WALES BORDERERS.

(Erase heading not required)

Instructions regarding War Diaries and Intelligence Summaries are contained in F.S. Regs., Part II. and the Staff Manual respectively. Title pages will be prepared in manuscript.

Place	Date May 1919.	Hour	Summary of Events and Information	Remarks and references to Appendices
MUNSTEREIFEL	23rd.		C.O. visited IVERSHEIM 14.00 hours.	
	24th.		8 Officers & 250 O.R. to BONN for RHINE Trip to COBLENTZ. C.O., at COLOGNE. F.G.C.M., on Cpl. Evans & Pte. Davies.	
	25th.		Conference of O's.C. Coys., re Training, hours, etc., 11.00 - 12.30 hours.	
	26th.	10.30.	Major Ramsden & Adjt., to IVERSHEIM, with Demonstration platoon. A.A.Q.M.G., C.O., to IVERSHEIM called. Concert by Divnl. Orchestra at 19.00.	
	27th.		Lecture by Mr. Kirwan on " In Shakespeares Country". Halfday.	
	28th.		Route March to NOTHEN with exercises in advance, f1ank & rear guards.	
	29th.		3 Classes arranged for Officers, all N.C.O's and Junior N.C.O's commencing 2.6.19. Adjt., visited IVERSHEIM.	
	30th.		C.O., visited "A" & "B" Coys., at IVERSHEIM. Football Match 17.00. MUNSTEREIFEL V IVERSHEIM.	
	31st.		Officers & N.C.O's attended Demonstration in Drill, guards, field work etc., by Platoon of "D" Coy. Final Platoon Assoc., Match, Drums V No.1 "A" Coy., 2 goals each.	

Munstereifel.
3rd. May, 1919.

Colonel,
Commanding, 53rd., Battn., South Wales Borderers.

Army Form C. 2118.

WAR DIARY
or
INTELLIGENCE SUMMARY.

53rd., Battn., SOUTH WALES BORDERERS.

(Erase heading not required.)

Instructions regarding War Diaries and Intelligence Summaries are contained in F.S. Regs., Part II. and the Staff Manual respectively. Title pages will be prepared in manuscript.

Place	Date June.	Hour	Summary of Events and Information	Remarks and references to Appendices
ALFTER.	26th.		Signallers detailed for Divisional Course.	
	27th.		N.C.O's absent from Battalion Class 17.50 hours. N.C.O's absent from Class placed under Arrest. Senior N.C.O., of each Coy., remanded for F.G.C.M. War Savings Association formed.	
	28th.		Col. Williams CMG., DSO., returned to England. Lt. Col. Corfe, DSO assumed Command. Major H.P. Williams reported for duty as 2nd.in.C.	
	29th.		Brig. Genl. addressed our Officers., C.O. saw all officers afterwards. Orders received for return to MUNSTEREIFEL AREA.	
	30th.		Divnl. Comdr., visited C.O., addressed N.C.O's at 14.30 hours, Preparation for move. C.O., addressed N.C.O's at 14.30 hours, and O's.C.Companies at 15.00 hour.	

Rolfe
Lieut. Colonel,
Commanding, 53rd., Battn., S.W., Borderers.

MUNSTEREIFEL.
2nd. July, 1919.

WAR DIARY or INTELLIGENCE SUMMARY

(Erase heading not required.)

Army Form C. 2118.

53rd., Battn., SOUTH WALES BORDERERS.

Instructions regarding War Diaries and Intelligence Summaries are contained in F.S. Regs., Part II. and the Staff Manual respectively. Title pages will be prepared in manuscript.

Place	Date	Hour	Summary of Events and Information	Remarks and references to Appendices
MUNSTEREIFEL.	June 1st		Sunday.	
	2nd.		"B" Company's Flying Column test at IVERSHEIM. C.O. & Adjt. visited "A" Company.	
	3rd.		King's Birthday parade at IVERSHEIM. Holiday afterwards. Rain.	
	4th.		Weather doubtful, no Route March. Lena Ashwell's concert. Man accidentally shot in leg by a Lewis Gun at IVERSHEIM.	
	5th.		C.O. dealt with 15 civilian cases. Court of Inquiry on shooting accident at IVERSHEIM.	
	6th.		Guard:- 2 Officers & 54 Other Ranks sent to Corps Comdr's. residence at SATZVEY. Major RAMSDEN ordered back to ENGLAND.	
	7th.		Major V.B. RAMSDEN returned to England. Bde.Tug of War 53 V 52 S.W.B.	
	8th.		Re-Enlisted men sent to 51st. Welsh.	
	9th.		Whitmonday. Holiday. Battn. Sports. Brig., Genl., Cubitt,CB.,CMG.,DSO., presented prizes.	
	10th.		C.O. at IVERSHEIM. Adjt., at N.C.O's Class. Lecture by Brigade Major for Officers. Lecture by Adjt., for N.C.O's on protection.	
	11th.		Flying Column test for "A", "B", "D" Coys., and Transport at IVERSHEIM.	
	12th.		C.O., at IVERSHEIM. Adjt., at N.C.O's Class. Lecture by Adjt., to N.C.O's on night operations.	
	13th.		Inspection of training by Major.General Strictland, G.O.C. in C., Western Division, Lecture for Officers on Aircraft 14.00 hours.	
	14th.		Adjt., on N.C.O's examination. Kit Inspection for Drummers. 8 F.G.C.M.,cases promulgated.	
	15th.		Mule Race, Cross Country Race, and Football Competition in Battn. Sports, 18.00 hours. "B" Company won Championship.	
	16th.		2nd.N.C.O's Class opened, Adjt.& RSM. Adjt.,lectured N.C.O's 14.00 on discipline & duties.	
	17th.		Orders for advance to ALFTER received 09.15 hours. N.C.O's Class cancelled. Orders issued to Coys.	
	18th.		Stores assembled at IVERSHEIM under guard. Requisitioned Stores assembled at MUNSTEREIFEL & IVERSHEIM, and placed i/c Burgomaster.	
	19th.		Battalion(less "A" Coy.) marched to RHEENBACH. Billetted overnight.	
	20th.		Battalion(less "A" Coy.) marched to ALFTER. "C" Company on Detachment at GIELSDORF.	
	21st.		C.O., visited Billets, Transport, and Training Ground.	
ALFTER.	22nd.		Sunday. At ALFTER.	
	23rd.		C.O., at demonstration packing Lewis Gun Limber. Adjt., visited "B" & "D" Coys. C.O., to TROISDORF 14.00 hours. "B" Coy. concert.	
	24th.		C.O. & Adjt., visited Coys.	
	25th.		Route March DRANSDORF, ENDENICH, ROTTGEN, WITTERSCHLICK, DUISDORF, ALFTER. Germans agreed to sign peace.	

WAR DIARY
or
INTELLIGENCE SUMMARY
(Erase heading not required.)

Army Form C. 2118.

53RD. BATTN. SOUTH WALES BORDERERS.

Instructions regarding War Diaries and Intelligence Summaries are contained in F.S. Regs., Part II. and the Staff Manual respectively. Title pages will be prepared in manuscript.

Place	Date	Hour	Summary of Events and Information	Remarks and references to Appendices
	1.7.19.		Battalion moved to Rheinbach, and billeted overnight.	
	2.7.19.		" " Munstereifel and Iversheim.	
	3.7.19.		Court Martial of 5 N.C.O's, and 1 man at Bernheim. Conference of O's.C. Coys.	
	4.7.19.		G.O. and Adjutant at Iversheim. 14.30 G.O. and Adjt. at Brigade Headquarters.	
	5.7.19.		Guards and picquots reduced to 2 sections by night, and 1 N.C.O. and 2 men by day. Last Post 22.30.	
	6.7.19.		Major General Cubitt addressed N.C.O's. Brigadier General Morley assumed Command of 3rd.Bde. Sports Conference.	
	7.7.19.		Lieut. R.Thomas, and 5 O.R. to Cambrai. 4 N.C.O's to Paris for Victory March.	
	8.7.19.		G.O. and Adjutant at Iversheim, A. & B. Coys.	
	9.7.19.		G.O. and Adjutant visited A. B. & C. Coys.	
	10.7.19.		Peace Holiday. Sports, and Rhine Trip.	
	11.7.19.		G.O. inspected "C" Company at Training. Lewis Gun limber poled for demonstration. Conference of O's.C. Coys. at 14.00 hours. Brigade Sports Conference at 15.00 hours. G.O. held Summary Court on 6 civilians.	
	12.7.19.		G.O. at Brigade Sports Conference 10.00. G.O. visited Transport Lines, "C" and "D" Coy Cookhouses. 4 Officers, 150 Other Ranks, Cologne Races.	
	13.7.19.		Brigade Combined Thanksgiving Peace Church Service at Iversheim. C.O. at Brigade Sports Conference at 15.00 hours.	
	14.7.19.		G.O. inspected all Coys at work. Farewell dinner to Adjutant, evening.	
	15.7.19.		G.O. and Adjutant selected site for "A" Company Camp at Iversheim.	
	16.7.19.		Capt. Canton departed. Lieut. A.A.McKay took over duties of Acting Adjutant.	
	17.7.19.		Adjutant, 4 Company Officers, 4 Company Sergt.Majors', went to 2nd.Brigade Western Divn. Platoon Competition, Florsheim. Battalion boxing afternoon.	
	18.7.19.		C.O. visited all Company Stores, and "A" Company's Camp. Evening, Battn.Boxing Competition.	
	19.7.19.		C.O. at After. Judging 2nd.Brigade Sports.	
	20.7.19.		C.O. inspected Transport, Afternoon, Brigade Sports Conference.	
	21.7.19.		C.O. visited "A" and "B" Companies, Iversheim. C.B., O.M.G., Dining Hall.	
	22.7.19.		Divisional General (Major General T.O.MADEN, C.B.,O.M.G.) visited the Battalion. Inspected "A" and "B" Companies at work, and visited Cookhouses. Afternoon, Brigade Boxing Tournament.	
	23.7.19.		G.O. and Adjutant visited "A" and "C" Companies on Iversheim Train Area. Afternoon, Brigade Sports Conference.	

Army Form C. 2118.

WAR DIARY
or
INTELLIGENCE SUMMARY
(Erase heading not required.)

Sheet No. 2.

53RD. Batt. SOUTH WALES BORDERERS.

Instructions regarding War Diaries and Intelligence Summaries are contained in F. S. Regs., Part II. and the Staff Manual respectively. Title pages will be prepared in manuscript.

Place	Date	Hour	Summary of Events and Information	Remarks and references to Appendices
	24.7.19.		Morning - O.O. at a G.C.M. at Flerzheim. Evening - C.O. and Adjutant on Brigade Sports Ground arranging Athletic Sports details.	
	25.7.19.		3rd. Western Brigade Infantry Sports, and Horse Show.	
	26.7.19.		3rd. Western Brigade Infantry Sports, and Horse Show. The Battalion won the Brigade Commanders Cup for the Unit scoring the most points. The result being :- 53rd. S.W.B. - 27 points. 52nd. S.W.B. - 20 points. 51st. S.W.B. - 15 points.	
	27.7.19.		C.O. visited Transport Lines, and Coolhouses "C" and "D" Companies.	
	28.7.19.		C.O. inspected "A" Company at work.	
	29.7.19.		C.O. visited "B" Company on area. Afternoon, Battalion v. 51st. Bn. S.W.B. at Basket Ball, Result: 53rd. S.W.B. 6., 51st. S.W.B. 1. Evening, Battalion v. 51st. S.W.B. Tug-of-War, 51st. S.W.B. won Catchweights, 53rd. S.W.B. won 100 Stone Team.	
	30.7.19.		Finals, Brigade Boxing Tournament. Result: 1st - 52nd.S.W.B., 2nd. - 53rd. S.W.B. 3rd. - 51st. S.W.B. Battalion v. 52nd.S.W.B. at Tug-of-War (Catchweights and 100 Stone Team). 52nd.Battalion won both events. Battalion v. 52nd.S.W.B. at Basket Ball, Result: 53rd.S.W.B. - 18 points, 52nd.S.W.B. - 2 points.	
	31.7.19.		C.O. visited Training Areas. Afternoon,Company Commanders' Conference.	

Ralphe Lt. Col.
Cmdg. 53rd. Bn., S. W. Borderers.

WO95/1282 (5)
3 INF BDE
LIGHT T.M.B
AUG '16

1st Division.
3rd Infantry Brigade.
———

3rd BRIGADE LIGHT TRENCH MORTAR BATTERY

AUGUST 1 9 1 6 :::

Army Form C. 2118.

WAR DIARY
or
INTELLIGENCE SUMMARY 3RD TRENCH MORTAR BATTERY

(Erase heading not required.)

Place	Date August	Hour	Summary of Events and Information	Remarks and references to Appendices
Millencourt	1-10	—	Training	
"	11	10.45am	Conference at Divsn. of Stokes Mortar Officers 1st 2nd & 3rd Divs.	
"	12-15		Training	
"	16	9-10am	Marched to Bécourt Wood. Bivouced (Divisional Reserve)	
Bécourt Wood	17-19		Divisional Reserve.	
"	20	1pm	Moved up via Mametz Wood and relieved 1st & 2nd Bde T.M. in line left of High Wood. Four guns in Clarkes Trench. One gun firing on N.W. corner of High Wood, one trained beyond head of O.P. off Clarkes Trench. Two kept for counter attack. Two guns in Intermediate Trench both firing on the section of trench occupied by enemy.	
"	21		Same positions as on 20th.	
"	22		Same positions as on 20th & 21st.	
In action	23		Two guns kept for counter-attack in Clarkes Trench taken out by the Divic by order of the Brigadier. Remaining guns in Clarkes positions guns in Intermediate Trench doing good work. One gun in Clarkes Trench received a direct hit. Another gun brought up to replace	

Army Form C. 2118.

5.

WAR DIARY or INTELLIGENCE SUMMARY

3RD TRENCH MORTAR BATTERY

(Erase heading not required.)

Place	Date August	Hour	Summary of Events and Information	Remarks and references to Appendices
In action	24		Two guns in Blackies Trench removed to Strong Post 300yds in front of Blackies Trench. One gun trained on N.W. Corner of High Wood, other gun trained to traverse in front of Strong Post. One gun out of action in Intermediate Trench. Two more brought up. Thirty rounds fired in action on this trench.	
"	25	5.45pm	Opened with Artillery, a hurricane bombardment for 5 minutes with the three guns, immediately afterwards the 2nd R.M.F. attempted to take the enemy position. After the attack only one gun was able to fire owing to positions of guns blown in and casualties.	
"	26		Two guns came forward in Strong Post off Blackies Trench. Reported to fire little, as much work of fortifying this safety piece by us. Good targets of course were engaged.	
		6.30pm	The S.W.B's attacked the Stalke guns opened a bombardment in conjunction with the Artillery. As the S.W.B's gained his strench we lengthened range. Two Germans were seen to be blown about 16 ft in the air by a Stokes Bomb explosion.	
"	27	3pm	Guns in same position as on 26th. Handed over positions of guns to 46th T.M.B. Proceeded to billets in Albert.	

Army Form C. 2118.

6

WAR DIARY
or
INTELLIGENCE SUMMARY

(Erase heading not required.)

3RD TRENCH MORTAR BATTERY

Instructions regarding War Diaries and Intelligence Summaries are contained in F. S. Regs., Part II. and the Staff Manual respectively. Title Pages will be prepared in manuscript.

Place	Date	Hour	Summary of Events and Information	Remarks and references to Appendices
Albert	28 to 31		Training.	

A.P. Ellis Capt.
Comdg. 3 T.M.B.

1/9/16.

WO95/1282 (6)
3 INF BDE
LIGHT T.M.B.
July '17 – Jan '19

1st Division

3rd L.T.M. Battery

3rd Infantry Brigade

From 1st July, To 31st December 1917

WAR DIARY.

3rd. L. T. M. Battery.

3rd. INFANTRY BRIGADE.

1st. Division.

JULY. 1917.

Army Form C. 2118.

WAR DIARY
or
INTELLIGENCE SUMMARY

July 1917
3rd Trench Mortar Battery.

(Erase heading not required.)

Instructions regarding War Diaries and Intelligence Summaries are contained in F.S. Regs., Part II. and the Staff Manual respectively. Title Pages will be prepared in manuscript.

Place	Date	Hour	Summary of Events and Information	Remarks and references to Appendices
COXYDE BAINS	July 1st		The Battery is billetted in a boarding house, some 20 yards from the shore. Officers are staying in a hotel overlooking the sea. This place is about 7000 from the line. Morning activity	JELW
	2nd		Ordinary training carried on with	
	3rd & 4th		These days have been devoted to the building of new enemy emplacements in our sub-sector. 15610 Pte Brown has been appointed Sanitaire L/Sg (L/Cpl with).	JELW
	5th		30309 Pte Dillon proceeded this morning on 1 months leave (time expires) Ordinary training cont.	JELW
	6th		Between 7pm & 8pm 5in shells were dropped in the vicinity of the COXYDE – COXYDE BAINS road but no horses were hit. Cpl Shorpe attd from parent unit finished his	JALW
	7th		Shifer & returned to duty with his battalion (2/RMF). Remaining today as a name 10702 Corporal Flynn (2/RMF) joined the Battery to replace Pte Shorpe. 2/Lt R.W.Canning returned today off leave	JELW
	8th		The whole morning was spent in making emplacements in our training area	JELW
	9th & 10th		This morning live firing has been carried out. The guns were fired from new emplacements, guns yesterday at an object floating in the sea, with excellent result. Considerable hostile shelling of COXYDE BAINS the whole day.	JELW
	11th		Hostile shelling especially violent between the hours of 1am & 2am this morning. No further shelling today. Shelling yesterday was in conjunction with an enemy attack at 7.45 pm on our trenches in NIEUPORT area. 10023 L/Cpl Durning admitted hospital today.	JELW
	12th, 13th & 14th		Training as usual. Battling on 13th & 14th. An interesting cricket match on the same was played on the 13th. A very close game which resulted in the Welch Borders beating the Gloucesters Hundred by 6 runs.	JELW
GHYVELDE	15th		We were relieved today by the 199th T.M.B. & moved to GHYVELDE at 11 am arriving at 4pm. 24 lorries were dropped on Railhead in the afternoon, one of which destroyed	JELW
CAPPELLE	16th		Left GHYVELDE this morning at 7.30am. arriving at CAPPELLE at 2.30pm.	JELW

Army Form C. 2118.

WAR DIARY or INTELLIGENCE SUMMARY

July 1917. (Sheet 2)

(Erase heading not required.)

Instructions regarding War Diaries and Intelligence Summaries are contained in F.S. Regs., Part II and the Staff Manual respectively. Title Pages will be prepared in manuscript.

Place	Date	Hour	Summary of Events and Information	Remarks and references to Appendices
CAPPELLE	July 17th	—	Battery stood to all day for move which was eventually cancelled.	JBdu
CHATEAU DE PONT DE PETITE SYNTHE	18th		At 7pm. orders to make room for a new draft. Battery was moved to CHATEAU du PONT de PETITE SYNTHE, a distance of 4 kilometres.	JBdu
	19th		Left Chateau at 2pm. arrived in camp at 6pm.	JBdu
LE CLIPON CAMP	20th		Training in the morning & bathing in the afternoon.	
	21st		Training & cleaning of guns in the morning.	
	22nd		Usual training, bathing for all men in afternoon.	
	23rd		Training. New form of training provided in the "Obstacle Course", which proved a fairly good stumbling block to all ranks. Running the Ramp was fairly difficult. This is one of the most interesting forms of our work here. Men much enjoy it.	stiff
	24th		Continued training with Obstacle Course in afternoon. Men went on leave today, & afternoon provided tool Evening.	
	25th		Usual training. We practised carrying loads on Yukon packs and succeeded in convincing the majority of the battery of the superiority of this method over the old one.	
	26th		Usual training with bathing and football in the afternoon.	
	27th		Ordinary training. We received our ammunition sled today, adding materially to our comfort. Two gun's complete were sent to the IV Army School today for training of gun re-inforcements. S.S.M. F. No. 203 Pr. O'Shea M., 2nd R.M.F. today promulgated. 90 lifts FP. No. 1. (14 days monthly)	
	28th		Usual training. New scheme of feeding sections commenced today; will be watched with interest.	
	29th		Usual Sunday work. 1st Bde Race meeting in afternoon attracted most officers. M.9.Coy reports all ready "Broke" consequent upon failure of "Satan". Rather tragic!	
	30th		Not of much moment. Light on Bde. drill supplemented by firing tomorrow. A physical and expert gave two our hour's.	
	31st		In the afternoon orders were in general fighting. Very interesting though difficult work. Excellent ranges - firing but accuracy obviously wanting	

WAR DIARY.

3rd. L. T. M. Battery.

3rd. INFANTRY BRIGADE.

1st. DIVISION.

AUGUST. 1917.

3rd T.M. Battn.

August 1917

Army Form C. 2118.

WAR DIARY
or
INTELLIGENCE SUMMARY.
(Erase heading not required.)

Place	Date	Hour	Summary of Events and Information	Remarks and references to Appendices
LE CLIPON CAMP	1st	Wed.	Very wet day. Toredown training impossible. Cleaning guns. Checking stores.	
	2nd	Thur	Still raining heavily. Packing of Yukon packs practiced. 10 or 30 oz. 3" Stokes Shells were drawn. C.O.s conference at Bgde H.Q. to discuss training.	
	3rd	Fri	Still more rain. Wall was first visited tested. Men were also tested with loads of various kinds. C.O. handed to B.O.C. his scheme for "Battery in Action." Staff Capt visited the Battn.	
	4th	Sat.	Weather still hopeless for outdoor work. Handcarts were experimented with, with a view to ascertaining their most suitable loads. Shot work much with loaded handcarts on the dunes.	
	5th	Sun	Church services as usual in the morning. Practice on scaling wall.	
	6th	Mon	Live firing on the beach. Much fog rendering observation difficult. Good results were obtained. 16 duds - due mainly to faulty fuzes. Bylast course run in the afternoon.	
	7th	Tues	Usual training	
	8th	Wed	" "	
	9th	Thur	Practice in loading Model pontoon in morning. Unloading in afternoon.	
	10th	Fri	Live firing on line of trenches on beach. Range good. Out of 150 shells fired there were no blinds at 6" inst.	
	11th	Sat	Blades. R M L sections practiced deployment from pontoon with their Battn	
	12th	Sun.	Usual church services.	
	13th	Mon.	Practice loading & unloading Model pontoon.	

Army Form C. 2118.

WAR DIARY
or
INTELLIGENCE SUMMARY.
(Erase heading not required.)

3rd L.M. Battery

Instructions regarding War Diaries and Intelligence Summaries are contained in F.S. Regs., Part II. and the Staff Manual respectively. Title pages will be prepared in manuscript.

Place	Date	Hour	Summary of Events and Information	Remarks and references to Appendices
	14th	Thur	Yesterday's programme repeated for C-in-C's inspection	
	15th	Wed	Ordinary routine	
	16th	Thurs	Live firing this morning. Watched by G.O.C.	
	17th	Fri	Another good live firing practice carried out today.	
	18th	Sat	Ordinary training	
	19th	Sun	Church services.	
	20th	Mon	Route march in forenoon. Soccer match in afternoon. Lost to 1 M.E. 0-2.	
	21st	Tues	Rehearsal of Divisional Ceremonial parade. Night firing – poor results – 28 hits out of 80 rounds fired	
	22nd	Wed	General training	
	23rd	Thurs	Practice in loading Model pontoon cancelled. Heavy rain.	
	24th	Fri	Another rehearsal of Ceremonial parade. Marred by rain.	
	25th	Sat	Ceremonial parade on beach. Presentation of Medal ribbons. A/B Sn Snugler received D.C.M. March past the Army Comdr.	
	26th	Sun	Usual Sunday routine	
	27th	Mon	Practice in loading turnloading Model pontoon. Two men went on leave.	
	28th	Tues	General training	
	29th	Wed	Live firing in morning – a good practice.	
	30th	Thurs	Train from Lamar Park expected tomorrow. Conference training programmes. 6 AB's are attached to this unit.	
	31st	Fri	Naval party landed at mid-day.	

M/S. Bradley, Capt.
O.C. 3rd L.M.B.

WAR DIARY.

3rd. L. T. M. Battery.

3rd. INFANTRY BRIGADE.

1st. DIVISION.

SEPTEMBER. 1917.

WAR DIARY
INTELLIGENCE SUMMARY

Army Form C. 2118.
Sheet T
3rd Trench Mortar Battery

Place	Date	Hour	Summary of Events and Information	Remarks and references to Appendices
	Sept 1st			
	3rd		A demonstration of rifle firing was given to the attached Naval party from H.M.S. Lord Clive. A second demonstration given to Naval Party.	JELW
	4th 5th 6th		Route March. Q.M.S. Curtis & Pte Allert saved a gunner from drowning in the afternoon. Lieut. J.E.L. Warren went on leave to Paris. Usual training. Three monitors left about midday.	JELW JELW JELW JELW
	7th		Another party from new monitor "Sir John Moore" attached to us.	JELW
	8th		Demonstration given by the M. Gunners & ourselves to the Naval Party. Cricket Match v the Navy in the morning. Naval party in afternoon. Detachment of Naval Party left Warne attached Captain W.J. Bradley went on leave to England.	JELW
	9th		Officers from Paris.	JELW
	10th		Loading model pontoon in the morning. Cricket Match v 3/RWF HQ's in the afternoon. Series:- Brigade 45. T.M.B. 40.	JELW
	11th		Rifle firing with live firing in the morning. Cricket Match v Welch Sergt's Mess. Score:- Welch 12. T.M.B. 44.	JELW
	12th		Brigade Field Day. Practise in exploiting a successful landing.	JELW
	13th		Practise on WALL, otherwise ordinary parades.	JELW
	14th		Brigade Field Day. Same general idea as on the 12th.	JELW
	15th		Live Firing. Practise in rapid shifting of barrage from enemy wire to his front line communication trench & support line. Good results obtained.	JELW
	17th		Practise in loading Model Pontoon.	JELW
	18th		Brigade Field Day. Practise in attack on 3rd objective after a landing.	JELW
	19th		Live Firing. Armature almost caused by placing two shells down the barrel at once. Lieut E.A. Zavio proceeded on leave to Paris.	JELW

Army Form. C. 2118.

WAR DIARY
or
INTELLIGENCE SUMMARY

(Erase heading not required.) 3rd Trench Mortar Battery

Instructions regarding War Diaries and Intelligence Summaries are contained in F. S. Regs., Part II. and the Staff Manual respectively. Title Pages will be prepared in manuscript.

Sheet 1

Place	Date	Hour	Summary of Events and Information	Remarks and references to Appendices
Clifton Camp	Sept. 20th		Live Firing Scheme. A practice barrage on enemy wire front line prior to a bombing raid.	J.B. Lieut.
	21st		Collecting on the beach with one gun for action. As a result several unfit necessary alteration to Range Table have been made.	J.B. Lieut.
	22nd		Ordinary Training. Kit Inspection. Captn. J. Bradley returned off leave.	J.B. Lieut.
	24th		Forty reinforcements from battalions reported for special training.	J.B. Lieut.
	25th		2/Lieut E.A. Jarvis returned off leave. Cricket Match v 2/T.M.B. Scores:- 2/T.M.B. 16 3/T.M.B. 47.	J.B. Lieut.
	26th 27th		Special Training of reinforcements. Played return Cricket Match with 2/T.M.B. Scores:- 2/T.M.B. 17. 3/T.M.B. 26.	J.B. Lieut.
	28th		Live Firing Practice with reinforcements. Played 2/Welsh at Cricket. Well 17- 3/T.M.B. 14.	J.B. Lieut.
	29th		Route March for Battery, lecture & gun drill for reinforcements.	J.B. Lieut.
	30th		Ordinary Training.	J.B. Lieut.

WAR DIARY.

3rd. L. T. M. Battery.

3rd. INFANTRY BRIGADE.

1st, DIVISION.

OCTOBER. 1917.

WAR DIARY
INTELLIGENCE SUMMARY.
(Erase heading not required.)

Army Form C. 2118.

3rd Trench Mortar Battery

October 1917

Place	Date	Hour	Summary of Events and Information	Remarks and references to Appendices
Etaples Camp	1 to 4		During these four days of the month continued the training of the Reinforcements, both officers and men, in addition to training the Battery proper. These Reinforcements to take the places of officers & men of the Battery in case of casualties, they would also be used for carrying parties to the gun emplacements, if we have to go through trench warfare again.	
	5		Practised firing Live Shells. No 5 Bombs. Instructed Reinforcements on making "T-Bay – Emplacements" & in making large circular gun emplacements for Trench Mortars.	
	7		Live firing of Stokes. Practice in rapid shifts of barrage from enemy wire to his front line.	
	8		Lecture on "Cleaning Gun Portions." "Gun Portions"	
	9		Officers Sunday Lecture & look again at the wire.	
	10		Ordinary Sunday routine.	
	11		Gunnery training	
	12		Route march for Battery – Reinforcements ordinary training	
	13		Bayonet fighting and battery drill – Live firing.	
	14/15		2nd Lieut E.A. Jarvis went on leave (12-10-17 to 22-10-17). Practised the Advance with Stokes guns.	
	16		Practised throwing hills Live Bombs.	
			Live firing of Stokes – Practice in Bracketting. H.S.L. Inspection. Ordinary Saturday routine. Battery went a route march. Lectures to Reinforcements on the supply of Ammunition in the trenches & the proper method of laying guns & ammunition clean in the line. Lectures on map Reading and the Prismatic Compass. We making has important it is for both N.C.Os and men to know all about that Compass, which by firing of the rank & file also last Jayfstoning of the Reinforcements (many Officers a day or two back...	

Army Form C. 2118.

WAR DIARY
INTELLIGENCE SUMMARY.
(Erase heading not required.)

October 1917 (continued)   3rd Trench Mortar Battery

Place	Date	Hour	Summary of Events and Information	Remarks and references to Appendices
St Idesbald Camp	17.		First Firing - Whilst firing live shells, we had a premature which wounded one of the Reinforcement officers and wounded three men of the Battery. None of the cases was very bad, but the officer & two of the men had to be admitted to hospital. The accident is considered was due to a faulty cartridge & to an inexperienced officer in the shell which caused the premature (ignition of the fuse).	
	18.		Ordinary training	
	19.		Made preparations for leaving St Idesbald Camp.	
Zeggers Cappel	20.		Left St Idesbald Camp at 9.30. Arrived Zeggers CAPPEL at 5 p.m. 2nd Lt E.H.Canning left for an interview in his going to the Royal Flying Corps, at Staples.	
	21.		Left ZEGGERS-CAPPEL Area at 9 am, arrived RUBROUCK at 11-30 A.M. Shoun Battery was in very good billets, took on as for an officers and men as can suit.	
Rubrouck	23.		Baths. Practised loading guns and ammunition on pack ponies, and gave a demonstration at Royal H.Q. 2nd L.E.H.Canning returned from a successful R.F.C. interview at Staples.	
	24.		Made preparations for leaving Rubrouck.	
	25.		Left RUBROUCK. Arrived in billets near HOUTKERQUE, after a long march. The last two kilometers we had to pull over roads through very thick mud.	
Houtkerque	26.		Billet was a farm the yard of which is like the trenches in winter, plenty of mud and smell. Harroun left the Battery at 11 p.m. for England, on his way to America as Instructor in the States gun to the U.S.A. Army.	
	27.		2nd Lt Symonds, 1st S.W.B. came for the first time to the Battery, to be instructed in the Stokes 3 inch trench mortar - trained technically of the parts of the gun, & was shewn how to take a battery in & out.	
	28.		2nd Lt V/th Underhay, 1st Leicesters, reported his arrival, to be attached to the Battery.

Army Form C. 2118.

WAR DIARY
or
INTELLIGENCE SUMMARY.
(Erase heading not required.)

October 1917 (continued)
3rd Trench Mortar Battery

Place	Date	Hour	Summary of Events and Information	Remarks and references to Appendices
	29		Instructed 2nd Lt Symonds and 2nd Lt Underhay in Gun Drill and showed them other forms of training in Stokes Mortar, including a lecture on the "Parts of the Mortar".	
	30		Continued training of 2nd Lt Symonds & 2nd Lt Underhay. Lectures on "Gun Drill" & the "Stokes Shell".	
Hondeghem	x28		2nd Lt K. Williams, 2nd Welch Regiment, attached 3rd T.M.B., was taken on the strength of the Battery (in place of J.E.L Warren, 2nd Welch) vide B.R.O. 30-10-17	
	30		2/Lt Jackie (Nº 2001), 1st Glosters attached a/oyr Eylpe from 30-10-17	
	31		Continued training of Reinforcement Officers (Lts Symonds & Underhay) - Gave them the Battery to drill in Gun Drill, as practice.	

WAR DIARY.

3rd. L. T. M. Battery.

3rd. INFANTRY BRIGADE.

1st. DIVISION.

NOVEMBER.1917.

WAR DIARY / INTELLIGENCE SUMMARY

Army Form C. 2118

for November 1917

3rd Trench Mortar Battery

Place	Date 1917	Hour	Summary of Events and Information	Remarks and references to Appendices
Locre	1 Thurs		Route March (full marching order) Afternoon Lt W.V. Phillips sat at a Field General court martial, held at the 2nd Bn H.Q.	
	2 Fri		Inspection by Major General Hickbold. New Stokes Battery Road cart in anticipation of an issue on the 2nd instant. Rifle drill. Practised loading pack mules with parts of Stokes mortar. Men also practised carrying Legs, Howitzer + Base Plate on Yukon Packs; during this latter practice we tried carrying the parts on a man in slings formed by the straps of the equipment. This method of carrying the parts of the mortar, particularly in the case of the Howitzer, seems especially practical, though muddy trenches + shell holes.	
	3 Sat		Gun drill + practice of changing wilt + without clinometer. Gun Practice today. Shell on pack ponies. Trying several methods: found the best method was to place the shell in shell packets + lash them on to the four hooks on the saddle. Pony will possibly be able to carry 16 Stokes Shells by this method. Usual Church Parade.	
	4 Sun			
	5 Mon		Fatigue party under Sgt. Brown returned Stokes Ammunition to Brigade. Day devoted to general cleaning up and checking stores, preparatory to moving forward to Dambre Camp.	
	6 Tues		Left billets, near HOUTKERQUE at 8.30 a.m. with Road-Cart, by Route March for DAMBRE CAMP. A long + tiring journey. Battery arrived at destination at 4 p.m. Lt Phillips left at 7.30 a.m. on bicycle billeting for the battery + reported to Lt. Evans, Camp commandant, Office at 7.30am. Battery left at 9.30 p.m. for BRAKE CAMP: on arrival at midnight all stores, food etc were taken that night to DAMBRE CAMP. Arrived at BRAKE CAMP at 11 p.m.	
	7 Wed		Left BRAKE CAMP for DAMBRE CAMP. Captain Bradley + Lt Phillips went up to CHEDDAR FARM (H.Qrs of the 188th Bde.), there they met the O.C. 188th T.M.B. They discussed the employment of Trench Mortars in the Piave, + the O.C. 188th T.M.B. told them that they found it impossible to use Trench mortars in the front system of the line, owing to the nature of the ground. Being impossible to dig in + set up a gun on account of shell hole.	

Sheet II

Army Form C. 2118.

WAR DIARY for November 1917 (continued)

INTELLIGENCE SUMMARY.

3rd Trench Mortar Battery

Place	Date	Hour	Summary of Events and Information	Remarks and references to Appendices
	8 Thurs		Left DAMBRE CAMP at 10.30 a.m. by route march, for IRISH FARM CAMP, arriving there at 1.30 p.m. 2nd Lt Phillips & 2nd Lt Williams & the Scouts & section of the Battery tried to get up to SOURCE FARM, to fire at certain Pill Boxes, pointed out to them on the map at TOURMANT FARM. The guide, supplied by the 2nd Welch, lost 2nd Lt Phillips' party & also the Company Party with Stokes Mortars, who had joined 2nd Lt Phillips' party at the 2nd Welch H.Q. at ALBATROSS FARM. The place where the party was lost was YETTA HOUSES. 2nd Lt Phillips viewing from the nature of the ground, was absolutely impossible it was to set up the mortars, thought it best as the party had lost their way, & were thus in an unknown there & ordered his section to return to IRISH FARM. 2nd Lt Phillips & 2nd Lt Williams took up the S.W.B. section of the Battery to make another attempt to dig in the mortars at SOURCE FARM. After wandering round the Country for eight hours, partly owing to a misunderstanding about the guides, the party reached their destination. As 2nd Lt Phillips correctly judged, the ground made it quite impossible to set up & fire the mortars. If an attempt had been made to do so, the Pill Boxes would have made very in & no firing could have taken place. 2nd Lt Phillips reconnoitred the ground both at SOURCE FARM itself & further back at the Pill Boxes; 500 yards in rear of the FARM. The ground near the Pill Boxes was marshy thou soft, & besides this difficulty, was out of Range, this being beyond the capability of the Stokes mortars. Shortly after the German barrage had died down somewhat, twelve? men were wounded as can albien?	
	9 Fri			
	10 Sat			
	11 Sun		2nd Lt Woodhays took up 32 men as a Carrying Party of S.A.A., for the machine Guns Company in the line. They marched at destination (YETTA HOUSES & Cemetery) safely, on the way to TPA he had to release the party of three machine guns, belonging to the 3rd m.g.C. he found there & brought them back.	
	12 Mon 13 Tues		Left IRISH FARM for DAMBRE CAMP. Rifle Inspection & cleaning. Hair cuts in morning. In afternoon went to Baths at BRAKE CAMP, but owing to the water supply being cut off, the men could not have a bath.	

Sheet III

Army Form C. 2118.

WAR DIARY for November 1917

3rd Trench Mortar Battery

INTELLIGENCE SUMMARY.

Instructions regarding War Diaries and Intelligence Summaries are contained in F.S. Regs., Part II. and the Staff Manual respectively. Title pages will be prepared in manuscript.

(Erase heading not required.)

Place	Date	Hour	Summary of Events and Information	Remarks and references to Appendices
Brake Camp	14 Nov	Wed	Went to Bath at BRAKE CAMP at 9 AM, followed by Rifle Inspection & Physical Drill.	
	15	Thurs	Early morning parade for Physical drill, Battery Rifle Inspection. Camp Improvement - Box Respirator Inspection, Battery pathways etc.	
	16	Fri	Camp Improvement - Battery in making further improvements to Camp.	
	17	Sat	Men busy again in making further improvements to Camp.	
	18	Sun	Usual Church Parade in the morning. In the aft. afternoon Battery marched from DAMBRE CAMP to DIRTY BUCKET CAMP. The Riffles attended Court of Inquiry at GWALIA FARM, to inquire into the accident which occurred to Driver Brown of the Canadian R.E.s. Also general clean up of Battery & of Huts.	
Dirty Bucket Camp	19	Mon	A party of 1 N.C.O. + 150 O.R. detailed for fatigues at the new refilling point - the party reporting to O.C. brigade from H.2 at 8 AM. Remainder of Battery to Camp Improvements.	
	20	Tues	As on Tuesday, a party of 1 N.C.O. + 15 were detailed for work at the Refilling Point. The remainder of the Battery engaged in making further improvements to Camp.	
	21	Wed	Rifle Drill, Steady drill & Physical drill with morning. In the afternoon Battery went to Brownwell Battle for bathing & change of underclothing. Captain Bradley attended conference of C.O's. at Brigade H.Q. during the morning.	
	22	Thurs	Battery left DIRTY BUCKET CAMP by Route march for SCHOOLS CAMP arriving at 1:30 pm.	
	23	Fri	Rifle Inspection, Physical drill, Steady (Guns + Horns + Stores - Inspection of Box Respirators, 10 Officers + 11 O.R. reported Battery from "B" Echelon.	
	24	Sat	Usual Church Parade.	
	25	Sun	Rifle Inspection, Arms drill, Gun drill & Bayonet Fighting.	
	26	Mon	Battery left SCHOOLS CAMP by Route march for PICCADILLY CAMP arriving there at 3.15 pm.	
	27	Tues		
	28	Wed		
Piccadilly Camp	29	Thurs	Morning + afternoon Battery were engaged in making improvements to Camp.	
	30	Fri	A party of 20 N.C.Os + men under Captain W.J. Bradley attended Brigade H.Q. for the instruction of filling dugouts by the Light Trench Mortars. Remainder of Battery were engaged making further improvements to Camp, & 2 Refilling parties & Stretchers & Stokes Tobies written on by & also Stokes Tobies written on by Battery as artillery unit.	

WAR DIARY.

3rd. L. T. M. Battery.

3rd. INFANTRY BRIGADE.

1st. DIVISION.

DECEMBER. 1917.

Army Form C. 2118.

WAR DIARY for December 1917

INTELLIGENCE SUMMARY. 3rd Trench Mortar Battery

Instructions regarding War Diaries and Intelligence Summaries are contained in F.S. Regs., Part II. and the Staff Manual respectively. Title pages will be prepared in manuscript.

(Erase heading not required.)

Place	Date Dec.	Hour	Summary of Events and Information	Remarks and references to Appendices
	1	Sat	Rifle Inspection. Battery drill & lectures by C.O. in the morning. Afternoon spent in Camp improvements. An officer from the 1st S.W.B. + an officer + 3 men from the 1st Gloster attached to the 3rd Trench Mortar Battery for Course on Stokes Mortars.	
near PROVEN	2	Sun	Men attended usual Church Parades.	
	3	Mon	Rifle Inspection. Arms drill & Battery drill. Cleaning Arms etc. Men engaged on improvements to Camp.	
Piccadilly Camp	4	Tues	Rifle Inspection. Battery drill. Cleaning up and improvement of Camp. Lt. Phillips went to WOESTEN to take over billets for Battery which was to follow next day.	
	5	Wed	Battery left Piccadilly Camp at 10-30 a.m. by Route march for WOESTEN, arriving there at 2 p.m.	
Woesten	6	Thurs	Battery prepared to move. Lt Jenner & the Battery Sgt Major went to Canal Bank to reconnoitre for suitable billets, but were unsuccessful, the Battery therefore remained at WOESTEN.	
Woesten	7	Fri	Lt Phillips + 3 other officers (Lt Jenner, 2Lt Williams + 2Lt Clarke) with the section went forward to erect shelters in which to billet the section whilst engaged in track laying. Captain Proctor left WOESTEN VILLAGE for Army Co. about one and half miles away, put off WOESTEN-ELVERDINGE Road near Woesten	

A834 Wt. W4973 M687 750,000 8/16 D.D. & L. Ltd. Forms/C2118/13.

Army Form C. 2118.

WAR DIARY for December 1917
INTELLIGENCE SUMMARY. 3rd Trench Mortar Battery

(Erase heading not required)

Instructions regarding War Diaries and Intelligence Summaries are contained in F. S. Regs., Part II. and the Staff Manual respectively. Title pages will be prepared in manuscript.

Place	Date	Hour	Summary of Events and Information	Remarks and references to Appendices
Wolster near	8	Sat	Three sections under 2/Lt Williams & 2/Lt Clarke went up to start on the work of Trench digging. The Munster section under Lt Jarvis finished the shelter in the Forward Sector of the Track.	
	9	Sun	Three sections were engaged in completing repairs to shelter in the Forward area.	
	10	Mon	Sections under 2/Lt Williams & 2/Lt Clarke were engaged in Trench digging. About 90 Duck Boards were drawn from CORMORAN DUMP. 40 Boards were carried to the Pill Box on the forward area, 30 of same being laid on the Track, this side of the BROENBECK RIVER.	
Het Sas Canal Bank	11	Tues.	The remainder of the Battery, under Captain Bradly, moved forward to Canal Bank HET SAS. Glosters & Welch sections drew 90 Trench Boards from CORMORAN DUMP. 25 Boards were laid on Track. 50 yards of Track were repaired.	
	12	Wed.	160 yards of IBIS TRACK were relaid by the Munster & S.W.B Sections, from the BROENBECK westwards. Slight damage to CIGOGNES (late HEMEL) & and 74 Trench Boards were carried to the forward area	
	13	Thurs.	100 yards of track were relaid by Munster & S.W.B Sections on IBIS TRACK, west end of the BROENBECK. The Gloster & Welsh sections were engaged in clearing	
	14	Fri	& repairing (where necessary) the dugouts + shelters at Canal Bank (HET SAS). 100 yards of track laid by the Munster + S.W.B Sections, & 76 Boards carried to the forward area.	
	15	Sat	80 yards of track were laid by the Munster + S.W.B sections. The Gloster + Welsh Sections	

Army Form C. 2118.

WAR DIARY for December 1917
or
INTELLIGENCE SUMMARY. 3rd Tunnel Battery

(Erase heading not required.)

Instructions regarding War Diaries and Intelligence Summaries are contained in F.S. Regs., Part II. and the Staff Manual respectively. Title pages will be prepared in manuscript.

Place	Date	Hour	Summary of Events and Information	Remarks and references to Appendices
Canal Bank SAS HET	15	Sat	Weather 2/Lt Clarke & 2/Lt Williams went up to relieve the Tunnellers & S.W.B section.	
	16	Sun	130 yards of IBIS TRACK laid.	
	17	Mon	150 yards of track laid.	
	18	Tues	120 " " " "	
	19	Wed	Tunnel & S.W.B Sections relieved Lysters & Welsh sections. 200 yards of track laid. Captain W.J. Pooley left Canal Bank to proceed on leave to England, on C.O.'s leave.	
	20	Thurs	120 WPL yards of track laid.	IBIS TRACK 800 yards complete. 80 yards non laid.
	21	Fri	180 " " " "	IBIS TRACK recommenced.
	22	Sat	on IBIS TRACK + 100 hundred on CIGOGNES TRACK.	
	23	Sun	160 yards of track laid	
	24	Mon	160 " " " "	
Canal Bank HET SAS	25	Tues	210 " " " " Christmas Day. No track laid but patrolled	
	26	Wed	130 yards of track laid	
	27	Thurs	140 " " " " The S.W.B & R.W.F Sections relieved the Lysters & Welsh sections	
	28	Fri	140 yards of track laid	
	29	Sat	144 " " " "	Court Martial of Cpl Flynn (2nd R.W.F) promulgated.
	30	Sun	170 " " " "	
	31	Mon	180 " " " " Lyster & Welsh sections relieved the Tunnel & Bodmin sections	

W.J. Phillips LC
31/12/17 O/C 3rd T.M.B

1st Division

War Diaries 3rd Infantry Bde.

3rd Trench Mortar Battery.

From 1st January, TO 31st January 1919
~~December 1918~~
_____

Army Form C. 2118.

WAR DIARY

or

INTELLIGENCE SUMMARY.

(Erase heading not required.)

for January 1918. 3rd Trench Mortar Battery

Place	Date	Hour	Summary of Events and Information	Remarks and references to Appendices
Canal Bank (Hut 100)	1918 January 1st Tuesday		Double Track laid. The Summary of Evidence taken in the case of Pte Sweeney	
	2nd Wed		The ground was in a very bad condition as the enemy has had great difficulty in taking up the old boards on the IBIS TRACK	
	3 Thur		170 yards of Double Track laid.	
	4 Friday		Work greatly retarded owing to the condition of the ground.	
	5 Sat		Track repairs owing to boards being hit by shells in several places. The road at BOIS 14 repaired, and new trench road prepared for cookers to be taken up to BOIS 14.	
	6 Sun		104 yds of Double Track laid and also 108 Pd props. S.O.R. proceeded to 2nd Army School for course in Stokes Light Trench Mortars	
	7 Mon		Bridging and Tracks continued. Bridging at Railway Crossing completed.	
	8 Tues		Capt. Bradley and Lt. Williams went up to see what work was necessary for the tracks (CIGOGNES & IBIS) forward of the BRONBECK	

Army Form C. 2118.

WAR DIARY for January 1918

INTELLIGENCE SUMMARY.
(Erase heading not required.)

Instructions regarding War Diaries and Intelligence Summaries are contained in F. S. Regs., Part II. and the Staff Manual respectively. Title pages will be prepared in manuscript.

Place	Date January	Hour	Summary of Events and Information	Remarks and references to Appendices
CANAL BANK (HET SAS)	9	Wed	30 logs laid and 140 yds of Double Track	
	10	Thurs.	70 Prefab. C.'s and 60 yds of Single Track.	
	11	Friday	Ground levelled for duckboards for the advance track. Bridging complete.	
	12	Sat.	10 frames of Bridging completed and pieces. Bridge at 20.B.1.9 repaired. Three Bridges suffered from the effects of Shell fire.	
	13	Sun	Ground in a very bad condition, and work proceeded very slowly.	
	14	Mon	Three forward Dumps were constructed, and Duckboards were unloaded and prepared ready for Carrying Parties.	
	15	Tues.	On the night of the 15th Carrying Parties laid 700 yds of Duckboards from LONELY MILL towards the BROENBEEK. The ground was very bad owing to the heavy rain, and the men had great difficulty in getting along, however excellent work was done, and men worked very well.	

Army Form C. 2118.

WAR DIARY for January. 1918

INTELLIGENCE SUMMARY
(Erase heading not required.)

Instructions regarding War Diaries and Intelligence Summaries are contained in F. S. Regs., Part II. and the Staff Manual respectively. Title pages will be prepared in manuscript.

Place	Date	Hour	Summary of Events and Information	Remarks and references to Appendices
CANAL-BANK. (HEL) S4	16	Wed	Repairs to tracks owing to floods, and were cleared out the water from the dugouts and pillbox.	
	17	Thurs.	110 yards of advance track laid as part of renewing track where destroyed by shell fire. 1 Bis Track. repairs in four places.	
	18	Friday	102 Duckboards carried to Pillbox at about 15. C. o. 9. 40 Duckboards laid on new Track.	
	19	Sat	300 Duckboards carried from CORMORAN Dump to forward area.	
	20	Sun	Forward track repaired and tracks. Six Dumps completed & boards carried.	
	21	Mon	4 Bridges were constructed. Corduroy Road in rear of BOIS 14 repairs 400 yds of advance track laid on the right of IC 20 a.	
	22	Tues.	50 yards of single track laid near NEY FARM, and portion of track relaid LONELY MILL track was completed. by 8 o'clock tonight	
	23	Wed	Forward track relaid. 130 yds of track laid from BOIS 14	

Army Form C. 2118.

WAR DIARY for January, 1918
INTELLIGENCE SUMMARY.
(Erase heading not required.)

Instructions regarding War Diaries and Intelligence Summaries are contained in F.S. Regs., Part II. and the Staff Manual respectively. Title pages will be prepared in manuscript.

Place	Date	Hour	Summary of Events and Information	Remarks and references to Appendices
IRISH FARM CAMP	24 Thurs		The whole of the advanced head is now completed and fit for use. The head has been raised and propped. 150 yards of head laid in rear of WOOD. 14.	
	25 Fri Sat(day)		Battery moved by route march to IRISH FARM CAMP arriving here at 11.30 A.M	
	26 Sat		Battery were engaged in sandbagging huts and generally improving camp.	
	27 Sun		35 men and 2 N.C.O.s paraded for fatigues at MOUSE TRAP FARM. in conjunction with 2nd Welsh Regt.	
	28 Mon		Same parties as on the 27th for fatigues. The 2/R.W. Fusiliers were this day returned to their Battalion	
	29 Tues		29 men and 2 N.C.O's were on fatigue at MOUSE TRAP FARM. The remainder of the Battery were engaged in camp improvements	
	30 Wed		Battery moved by route march to billets near LION BELGE (522a) arriving there 1 p.m.	
	31 Thurs		Battery worked on camp improvement, also cleaned equipment	

Allanadale Lt. Col
O.C. 2/1 m.g.
31/1/1918

Army Form C. 2118.

WAR DIARY or INTELLIGENCE SUMMARY. 3RD TRENCH MORTAR BATTERY

February 1918

(Erase heading not required.)

Place	Date	Hour	Summary of Events and Information	Remarks and references to Appendices
NEAR. LION. BELGE	Feb 1st Friday		Battery commenced course of special training, and the morning was spent in (1) Lecture on general description of gun and ammunition (2) Demonstration of firing without knowledge (3) Lecture on gun Drill (4) Physical Training. In the afternoon practising rigging and mounting gun.	
	2nd Sat		Morning inspection and Squad Drill. Description of both kinds of Fuses (Pistol Head + Allways) Gun Drill. Judging Distance. Afternoon was spent in construction of Range Cards. Regulating firing, Drummers and Base Registration Drill. Lt. Williams proceeded to U.K. on leave with 14.2.19. 2/Lt. H.G. Clark and 3 O.R. proceeded to XIX Corps School for Stokes howitzer Course	
	3rd Sun		Church Parades.	
	4th Mon		Morning inspection and Squad Drill. Uses and construction of Range Cards. Continued work laying by (N.C.O) O.R practising histires with Pistol Head and Allways. Practise fire without knowledge, and steps in coming into action. Lecture on firing (4 hrs) on unseen targets and S.O.S fires. Afternoon Recreational Training. In the evening a combined concert of 1st, 2nd, 3rd T.M. B's was held.	

Army Form C. 2118.

WAR DIARY
or
INTELLIGENCE SUMMARY

for February 1918

(Erase heading not required.)

Instructions regarding War Diaries and Intelligence Summaries are contained in F. S. Regs., Part II. and the Staff Manual respectively. Title pages will be prepared in manuscript.

Place	Date	Hour	Summary of Events and Information	Remarks and references to Appendices
Lion BELGE	5th Tuesday		Morning. Firing dummy without homsting. laying guns by heap. on objects in and out of trees, and testing by firing dummy. Gun drill in gas masks. Lecture on L.T.M's in defence. Afternoon football.	
	6th Wed		Morning: Inspection. laying by Compass (Short lecture and tactical work). Traversing lecture on Shell-hole emplacements. Gun Drill. Afternoon: Demonstration by one Gun Team to C.O's	
	7th Thurs		Last morning lecture given in billets on points on before and after firing also during firing. Lecture on L.T.M's in attack. Gun drill in gas masks. N.C.O's engaged in heap work.	
	8th Friday		Men were engaged in Gun drill, Traversing. Spade in action. N.C.O's engaged in heap making and Compass work for two hours. Lecture given to N.C.O's and men on L.T.M's in Attack	
Siege Camp	9th Sat		Battery moved by route march to SIEGE CAMP arriving there at 1.30 P.M.	

D. D. & L., London, E.C. (A8049) Wt. W1771/M.31 750,000 5/17 Sch. 93 Forms/C2118/14

Army Form C. 2118.

WAR DIARY or INTELLIGENCE SUMMARY.

(Erase heading not required.)

Instructions regarding War Diaries and Intelligence Summaries are contained in F. S. Regs., Part II. and the Staff Manual respectively. Title pages will be prepared in manuscript.

for February 1919

Place	Date	Hour	Summary of Events and Information	Remarks and references to Appendices
SIEGE CAMP	Feb 10th		Church Parade	
	11th		Rifle Inspection in Physical Drill. after which men were engaged in thoroughly cleaning and overhauling equipment. Lt Jarvis proceeded to U.K. on leave	
	12th		Morning work consisted of bayonet exercise, Company lewis gun drill & an examination of Lewis Gun. 5 N.C.O's attended a lecture in the afternoon given by R.F.C. officer	
	13th		Kit Inspection in Huts. Rifle. Lecture on S.O.S lines as S.O.S action. Speed in Action Types of Entanglements. lecture on Carrying of Ammunition as tactical	
	14		In accordance with Brigade Orders, Battalion went for route march in fighting marching order	
	15		Friday Bayonet fighting. Arms Drill, Lecture on Trenching. Practice in judging elevations & fire to give good range without mountings. N.C.O setting guns by	

Army Form C. 2118.

WAR DIARY
or
INTELLIGENCE SUMMARY.
(Erase heading not required.)

for February 1919

Instructions regarding War Diaries and Intelligence Summaries are contained in F. S. Regs., Part II. and the Staff Manual respectively. Title pages will be prepared in manuscript.

Place	Date Feby	Hour	Summary of Events and Information	Remarks and references to Appendices
Siege Camp	16	Sat.	Physical Training. Gun Drill. Fatigues Aisbine. Letters on "Care of Mules". Battery attended Concert in conjunction with 2nd Welch and 14. M. G. Cy	
	17	Sun	Church Parade	
	18	Mon	Lecture on Tent Discipline. Practice in Shell hole entrenchments; Setting gun by compass. Gun Drill and Box Respirator Drill. 2/Lt [illiams returns from leave	
	19	Tues	Battery were engaged in Gun Drill. Gun Drill and Physical Training. Battery Stores were checked and equipment classes by Officers. Armer Battery from Camer at 𝒯15 Corps School	
	20	1030 Friday	Battery moved by route march to Billets at CANAL BANK arriving here at 10.45 AM	
Canal Bank	21	Thurs	24 men and 1 N.C.O handed over [illiams as horses to Turco Farm for work on Salvage Dump. Remainder of Battery were engaged in Salvage work at CANAL BANK	

(A8604) W. D. & L., London, E.C. Wt. W1771/M231 750,000 5/17 **Sch. 52** Forms/C2118/14

Army Form C. 2118.

WAR DIARY for January 1918
or
INTELLIGENCE SUMMARY.
(Erase heading not required.)

Instructions regarding War Diaries and Intelligence Summaries are contained in F. S. Regs., Part II. and the Staff Manual respectively. Title pages will be prepared in manuscript.

Place	Date Feby	Hour	Summary of Events and Information	Remarks and references to Appendices
CANAL BANK	22nd	Friday	Fatigues were carried out by 24 men and one N.C.O at Salvage Dump, TURCO FARM. Men remaining in Camp were engaged in Salvage work in Battery Area	
	23rd	Sat	A party of 24 men and N.C.O were employed at Salvage Dump near Battery billets. Williams and 1st Cavalry went to Forward Area to reconnoitre T.M. emplacements	
	24th	Sun	24 men and 1 N.C.O were at work on Salvage Dump, TURCO FARM: the remainder of the Battery employed in repairing Dugouts at CANAL BANK	
	25th	Mon	Battery were engaged on work at TURCO FARM and repairing Dugouts at Canal Bank.	Ditto
	26th Tues		Ditto	Ditto
	27th Wed		"	"
	28th Thurs		Capt Bradley proceeded on 6 months leave to England. Battery engaged on Salvage work at TURCO FARM and repairing Dugouts at CANAL BANK	Ditto

Sgnd Kirkland Lt
37th M. Battery

WAR DIARY of 3rd T.M. Battery for March 1918

INTELLIGENCE SUMMARY.

(Erase heading not required.)

Army Form C. 2118.

Place	Date	Hour	Summary of Events and Information	Remarks and references to Appendices
CANAL BANK	March 1. Fri.		Battery attended Divisional Baths in the morning. The remainder of the day was spent on Fatigues (repairs to Dug outs at CANAL BANK.	
	2. Sat.		24 Men and 1 N.C.O. on Fatigues at Salvage Dump, TURCO FARM, under Divisional Salvage Officer. Remainder of Battery on Fatigues at CANAL BANK under Area Commandant.	
	3. Sun.		Lt Jarvis & party of N.C.O's and men proceeded to Front Line to take over posts from 1st T.M.B. Lt Williams attended Conference at Brigade H.Q.	
HILL TOP FARM	4. Mon.		Battery moved to HILL TOP FARM. Reliefs of T.M. posts complete.	
	5. Tues.		1 Officer and 22 O.R. with guns in line. The remainder of the Battery were engaged on Fatigues in Billet Area.	
	6. Wed.		As on 5th. Lt Williams & 2/Lt Clarke visited BURNS HOUSES.	
	7. Thurs.		— do — 2/Lt Clarke visited POELCAPPELLE.	
	8. Fri.		— do —	
	9. Sat.		— do —	

WAR DIARY of 3rd T.M. Battery for March 1918

INTELLIGENCE SUMMARY.

Army Form C. 2118.

Place	Date	Hour	Summary of Events and Information	Remarks and references to Appendices
CANAL BANK HILL TOP FARM (CANAL BANK)	March 10	Sun.	1 Officer + 22 O.R. with guns in the line. Lt Williams + 2/Lt Clarke visited posts at POELCAPPELLE. 2/Lt Clarke visited H. Qrs. 1st Gloster Regt.	
	11	Mon.	1 Officer + 24 O.R. with guns in the line. 2/Lt Clarke visited H. Qrs. 1st Gloster Regt.	
	12	Tues.	As on the 11th	
	13	Wed.	1 Officer + 24 O.R. with guns in the line.	
	14	Thurs	— do —	
	15	Fri.	— do — Lt Williams visited all posts at night by the 2nd T.M.B.	
	16	Sat.	Battery were relieved and moved to CANAL BANK.	
	17	Sun	Men engaged in cleaning + overhauling equipment + rifles	
	18	Mon	1 N.C.O + 24 men were on Salvage Work at dump at BATTLE. Remainder of Battery on improvements to Billets. (CANAL BANK)	

WAR DIARY of 3rd T.M. Battery for March 1918.
or
INTELLIGENCE SUMMARY.

Army Form C. 2118.

(Erase heading not required.)

Instructions regarding War Diaries and Intelligence Summaries are contained in F. S. Regs., Part II. and the Staff Manual respectively. Title pages will be prepared in manuscript.

Place	Date	Hour	Summary of Events and Information	Remarks and references to Appendices
CANAL BANK	Mch 19 Tues.		As on the 18th Lt. C. Saunders joined the Battery	
	20 Wed.		— do — Lt. C. Saunders assumed command of Battery from this date.	
	21 Thur.		— do —	
	22 Fri.		1 N.C.O & 24 O.R. on Salvage work at TURCO FARM Remainder of Battery on improvements to Billets at CANAL BANK	
	23 Sat.		— do —	
	24 Sun.		— do — Men not engaged on fatigues attend Church Parade.	
	25 Mon.		— do —	
	26 Tues.		— do — Lt. Jarvis conducted carrying party in the vicinity of MARINE VIEW.	
	27 Wed.		— do — Capt. Saunders visited all the posts in the front line. 2/Lt. Clark conducted carrying party in the vicinity of PHEASANT TRENCH.	

WAR DIARY of 3rd T.M. Battery Army Form C. 2118.
or
INTELLIGENCE SUMMARY. for March 1918

(Erase heading not required.)

Place	Date	Hour	Summary of Events and Information	Remarks and references to Appendices
HILL TOP	Mch 28	Thurs.	Battery Hd Qrs moved to HILL TOP. Relieved 2nd T.M.B. in the Line.	
	29	Fri.	1 Officer + 25 O.R. with guns in the Line. Remainder of Battery engaged on cleaning Bullets, equipment, rifles &c. L.Q. Jarvis visited all the posts in the front line.	
	30	Sat.	1 Officer + 25 O.R. in the Line. Remainder of Battery on Camp improvements.	
	31	Sun.	— do — . Capt Saunders visited all the posts in the front line.	

G.J. Saunders
CAPTAIN,
COMD 3RD TRENCH MORTAR BATY.

Army Form C. 2118.

WAR DIARY of 3rd T.M. Battery for April 1918.

INTELLIGENCE SUMMARY.

(Erase heading not required)

Instructions regarding War Diaries and Intelligence Summaries are contained in F.S. Regs., Part II. and the Staff Manual respectively. Title pages will be prepared in manuscript.

Place	Date	Hour	Summary of Events and Information	Remarks and references to Appendices
HILL TOP	1918 April 1 Mon.		1 Officer and 25 O.R in line with guns the remainder of the Battery at HILL TOP at work improving drainage.	
	2 Tues		ditto	
	3 Wed.		ditto Lt. James visited POELCAPPELLE posts	
	4 Thurs		ditto	
	5 Fri.		ditto Lt Williams visited all the posts in front line.	
HOSPITAL FARM	6 Sat		Battery were relieved in line & moved to HOSPITAL FARM.	
	7 Sun		Battery engaged in preparing for move.	
	8 Mon		Battery paraded at 2.30 a.m & marched to PESEL HOEK, where after loading Omnibus Train, they entrained for CHOQUES and BETHUNE, arriving at latter place at 3.30 p.m.	
BETHUNE	9 Tues		Lt Clarke + 1. N.C.O. visited H.Qrs. 32nd T.M.B with a view to taking over positions from that Battery	
	10 Wed		Lts Williams + James + 1 N.C.O of T.M.B. left returned to SAILLY-LA-BOURSE to relieve 32nd T.M.B, but with 86 guns went to BETHUNE as relief had been postponed for 24 hours.	

War Diary for April 1918 of 3rd T.M. B.y.

Place	Date Hour	Summary of events and information	Remarks

BETHUNE	1918 11 Thurs	As on the 10th 2/Lts Williams & Jarvis and party went to SAILLY-LA-BOURSE but again had to return owing to further postponement of relief. On the night of the 11/12th at 7 p.m. the Battery received orders to take up a defensive position along the CANAL BANK as follows:—
		4 guns at CANAL BANK, BETHUNE between E.5.d.5.1 and E.5.d.1.5 under Lt. Williams.
		4 guns at CANAL BANK, LE QUESNOY between F.3.c.9.1 and F.3.c.2.3 under Lt. Jarvis.
		Battery forward Hd. Qrs under Capt. E. J. Saunders were taken up at E.5.d.1.5.
		The following casualties occurred at LE QUESNOY on the night of the 11th.
		Sergt Steel Killed. Pte Allsopp } Wounded
		Pte Waring " Coombs
		    Jones Died of Wounds. " Evans
		          " Baxter
		          " Williams
		positions shown above.	

	12 Fri.	Battery with guns at positions shown above.	

War Diary for April 1918 of 3rd T.M.By

Place	Date	Hour	Summary of events and information	Remarks
BETHUNE	1918 13	Sat	Battery with guns at positions as on the 11th inst	
	14	Sun	ditto	
GORRE	15	Mon	Battery relieved 165th T.M.By in the FESTUBERT SECTOR. Advanced Hd Qrs were established at GORRE CHATEAU	
	16	Tues	1 Officer + 18 O.R. in the line with 4 guns	
	17	Wed.	ditto	
	18	Thurs.	Guns in the front line took part in repelling attack by the enemy. A total of 290 rounds were fired during the day with good effect. One gun was destroyed by shell fire. The following Congratulatory Order was received by Capt. Saunders from the Brigadier General. "Please convey to all concerned, and to Lt Williams and his detachment especially my appreciation of the good work done by the Trench Mortars yesterday. To have every confidence from yesterday's experience that any call on the Trench Mortars will be fully	

War Diary for April 1918 of 3rd I.M.B.Y.

Place	Date	Hour	Summary of Events and Information	Remarks
	18 Thurs (continued)		responded to and that they could be efficiently used to the best advantage of the Infantry." sd. H.S. Morant, Brig Genl. Comd'g 3rd Inf. Brigade

The following messages were also received.

"The Commander in Chief requests the Army Commander to convey to Major General E.P. Strickland and to all ranks of the 1st Division his congratulations on the successful operations carried out this morning."

from G.O.C First Army "Well done, 1st Division."

from the Army Commander.

"The Army Commander has watched with much interest and anxiety the course of the fighting to-day, and the splendid defense put up by the Division against a very heavy attack. The units engaged are much to be congratulated."

from Major General Strickland, Commanding 1st Division.
"I wish to express to all ranks my unbounded admiration and pride at the way they fought. When a battle has once commenced it is principally on the action of the Junior Commanders and the rank and | |

GORRE

War Diary for April 1918 of 3rd T.M.BY.

Summary of Events and Information

Place	Date	Hour	
	18 Thurs (continued)		felt that success or failure depends, and the nerve and endurance under all exceptionally heavy bombardment, and fine fighting spirit displayed when in contact with the Scottish Infantry were chiefly responsible for our success. All units of the First Division, and the Artillery fighting with us, may well be proud of the result of the days fighting. For their good work on this day, Cpl Evans & L/Cpl Edmundson & Pte Nash & Simpson were recommended for the D.C.M, & L/Cpl Hull & Pte Hone for the M.M. For continuous good work Pte W. Jones was also recommended for the M.M. Our casualties on this day were one killed and two wounded.
	19 Fri.		Usual harassing fire was done by guns on this day, but nothing of importance to report.
	20 Sat.		On this date the Battery co-operated with 1st S.W.B. in an attack on ROUTE A KEEP, and the special idea, prepared by the Battery Commander, was as follows

GORRE

War Diary for April 1918 of 3rd. T.M. B.Y.

Summary of Events and Information.

Place	Date	Hour		Remarks
	20 Sat. (continued)		" 2 Mortars & teams under the command of Lt. E.A. Savors will take up positions about X.29.a.5.5. in the JUNING FORK SWITCH, and at Zero will open a concentrated bombardment on ROUTE A KEEP. Fire will be maintained for 3 minutes at the rate of 15 rounds per minute per Mortar. At zero plus 3 the Mortars will "lie Motraw". A total of 80 rounds were fired, and the attack by the S.W.B's was carried out successfully.	
GORRE	21. Sun.		Battery were relieved in the line by the 166 K.G.M. Battery, and moved to LA BOURSE.	
LA-BOURSE	22 Mon.		Battery engaged in cleaning & overhauling Guns, Rifles & Equipment.	
	23 Tues.		Battery moved to MAZINGARBE.	
SAILLY LA BOURSE	24. Wed.		Battery relieved 32nd. T.M. BY in HOLLENZOLLERN SECTOR. 2 Officers & 25 men with 6 guns in the Line. B'y Hd. Qrs moved to SAILLY-LA-BOURSE.	

Army Form C. 2118.

WAR DIARY of 3rd T.M.BY.
or
INTELLIGENCE SUMMARY. for April 1918.
(Erase heading not required).

Instructions regarding War Diaries and Intelligence Summaries are contained in F. S. Regs., Part II. and the Staff Manual respectively. Title pages will be prepared in manuscript.

Place	Date	Hour	Summary of Events and Information	Remarks and references to Appendices
SAILLY-LA-BOURSE	1918. 25.	Thurs.	2 Officers + 25 men with guns in the Line. 235 rounds were fired on this day. Capt. Saunders visited the guns.	
	26	Fri.	do. 140 rounds fired this day.	
	27	Sat.	do * guns again fired on various targets. Capt. Saunders visited the guns. 2/Lt. Mann, 2nd Welsh joined Battery	
	28	Sun.	do. 2/Lt. K.J. Williams, 2nd Welsh rejoined his Battalion & relinquished Acting Rank of Lieutenant. Lt. E.B. Jarvis 1st S.W.B. assumes 2nd in Command of Battery.	
	29	Mon.	do. Capt. Saunders visited the Line.	
	30	Tues.	do. 2/Lt. W. Davies 1st S.W.B. joined Battery as Section Officer.	

J. Saunders
.... CAPTAIN,
003089 3RD TRENCH MORTAR BATTY

Army Form C. 2118.

WAR DIARY
or
INTELLIGENCE SUMMARY
(Erase heading not required.)

3RD TRENCH MORTAR BATTERY.

No. .... Date 1/6/18

Instructions regarding War Diaries and Intelligence Summaries are contained in F. S. Regs., Part II. and the Staff Manual respectively. Title Pages will be prepared in manuscript.

Place	Date	Hour	Summary of Events and Information	Remarks and references to Appendices
HOHENZOLLERN SECTOR	May 1 WED		Battery in the Line 3 officers & 25 men with 6 guns at posts in the HOHENZOLLERN SECTOR (CAPT. SAUNDERS) visited the guns	W Davis 2/Lt.
	2 THURS		ditto Lt. E.A. Jarvis admitted to Hospital 2/Lt. W Davis & 2/Lt. O.R. Marrected to I Corps School for 7 days Course on L.T.M.	W Davis 2/Lt.
	3 FRI		ditto: All guns were action during the day 146 rounds were fired Capt Saunders visited the Line	W Davis 2/Lt.
	4 SAT		ditto: Capt. Saunders and three other ranks gassed at LA BOURSE	W Davis 2/Lt.
	5 SUN		ditto Usual activity	W Davis 2/Lt.
	6 MON		ditto 2/Lt. W.W. Lambert reported for duty with the Battery 2/Lt. W. Read R.A. engaged in Gun Drill	W Davis 2/Lt.

The following Decorations were Published in Corps Routine Orders
No. 164105. No. E. Simpson Bdr to M.M. No. 1018 Cpl A. Evans M.M.
56825 L/Cpl Edmondson M.M. 1727 Pte W. Wiley M.M. 39087 Pte Hoare M.M.
for gallantry at GORRE on the of 18th April/18.

2449 Wt. W14957/M90 750,000 1/16 J.B.C. & A. Forms/C.2118/12.

Army Form C. 2118.

WAR DIARY
or
INTELLIGENCE SUMMARY

(Erase heading not required.)

Instructions regarding War Diaries and Intelligence Summaries are contained in F. S. Regs., Part II. and the Staff Manual respectively. Title Pages will be prepared in manuscript.

Place	Date	Hour	Summary of Events and Information	Remarks and references to Appendices
LA BOURSE	MAY 7 TUES		2 officers + 25 men with guns in the Line & 190 rounds were fired on the usual targets. Men at Rear H.Q. engaged in gun drill & drill in S.A.A. & Fatigue party was also provided for carrying ammunition to the gun emplacements.	W Davies 2/Lt
	8 WED		2 additional gun teams with guns under Capt. Saunders & 2/Lt. Lambert went up to the front line.	W Davies 2/Lt
	9 THUR		8 guns with teams with 4 officers & 32 men in the line. Remainder of Battery at H.Q. engaged in gun drill & S.B.R. Drill & Carrying party was also engaged in taking up ammunition to the gun positions.	W Davies 2/Lt
	10 FRI		do.	W Davies 2/Lt
NOEUX-LES-MINES	11 SAT		8 guns with full teams in the line and about 170 rounds were fired on the usual targets. 2/Lt. E.A. Jarvis rejoined Battery from hospital. Battery were relieved in the line by the 2nd P.M.B. and moved to NOEUX-LES-MINES. (Battery engaged in thorough cleaning of guns, equipment, rifles, & clothing.)	W Davies 2/Lt
	12 SUN			
	13 MON			
	14 TUES		Arms Drill. Steady Drill. Musketry & Gun drill 2/Lt. W.H. Lambert 1st G Loshr Regt rejoined his Battalion on return of Lt. E.A. Jarvis from Hospital.	W Davies 2/Lt
	15 WED		Lecture "Action in case of alarm". Practice in moving to assembly position in case of alarm.	W Davies 2/Lt
	16 THUR		Physical Training & Bayonet fighting. Part of Battery engaged in demonstration before G.O.C. in Chief firing Farmour of Battery on Gun Drill & Emplacements.	W Davies 2/Lt

WAR DIARY or INTELLIGENCE SUMMARY

Army Form C. 2118.

(Erase heading not required.)

Place	Date	Hour	Summary of Events and Information	Remarks and references to Appendices
NOEUX-LES-MINES / LA BOURSE / CAMBRIN SECTOR	May 1918 17 FRI		Battery engaged in Physical Training, Bayonet fighting & Dummy firing. 2/Lt H.G. Clark visited 1st T.M.B. in the line with a view to taking over. Capt Saunders visited Canadian Corps and saw Demonstration of models of 6" shelters in open warfare.	with anx 9/34
	18 SAT		Musketry & Box Respirator Drill. Gun Drill & Dummy firing. Capt Saunders & 2/Lt Mann visited Post in the front line to be taken over from 1st T.M.B.	with anx 9/34
	19 SUN		Church Parade in the morning. Brigade Sports afternoon & evening in which the Battery were very successful and first in Brigade.	with anx
	20 MON		Battery relieved 1st T.M.B. in the line. 8 Guns, all Officers and teams at the various Posts. 9 O.R. sent to "B" Echelon. A carrying party taking ammunition to the line were gassed.	G/Saunders Capt
	21 TUES.		Two guns were active, principally ranging. All accommodation and emplacements were improved and repaired.	G/Saunders Capt
	22 WED:		80 rounds fired on various targets and E.A.	G/Saunders Capt
	23 THUR:		ditto	G/Saunders Capt
	24 FRI:		40 rounds fired this day on usual targets, principally AUBURN TRENCH and roads at A.29 B.6.3. - Assistance was also given to 516th Field Coy R.E. in constructing tunnel and dug-outs between A.15.c.St.21 and A.15.c.92.30.	G/Saunders Capt

Army Form C. 2118.

WAR DIARY
or
INTELLIGENCE SUMMARY

(Erase heading not required.)

Instructions regarding War Diaries and Intelligence Summaries are contained in F. S. Regs., Part II. and the Staff Manual respectively. Title Pages will be prepared in manuscript.

Place	Date	Hour	Summary of Events and Information	Remarks and references to Appendices
CAMBRIN SECTOR	May 25	SAT:	45 rounds fired on the usual targets. Two new emplacements and ammunition recesses constructed at A.21.D.1/4.65.	E/Saunders Capt.
	26	SUN:	60 rounds fired on all usual targets, principally AUBURN TRENCH.	E/Saunders Capt.
	27	MON:	143 rounds fired this day, including 61 at E.A. At 11.40 a.m. whilst engaging E.A. a premature burst occurred, causing the instantaneous death of No. 11314 - Corpl. D. Pugh and No. 16535 Pte. J. Turner, both 2nd Welch Regt, attached to this Battery.	E/Saunders Capt.
	28	TUES:	49 rounds fired this day, including 29 at E.A, one of which was turned back. No 15747 Pte. E.J. Davies, 2nd Welch Regt. attached to this Battery, wounded in the left eye and evacuated to Hospital.	E/Saunders Capt.
	29	WED:	Various targets, including E.A. were engaged, and a total of 64 rounds fired. A new emplacement was completed at A.15.C.8.3.	E/Saunders Capt.
	30	THURS:	The usual targets were engaged and 87 rounds fired. This includes 12 rounds fired at E.A, one of which was distinctly observed to rock through the explosion of one of the shells fired at it.	E/Saunders Capt.
	31	FRI:	60 rounds fired this day, principally on AUBURN TRENCH and FRANKS KEEP.	E/Saunders Capt.

Army Form C. 2118.

WAR DIARY of 3rd I.C. Battery for June 1918.

INTELLIGENCE SUMMARY.
(Erase heading not required.)

Instructions regarding War Diaries and Intelligence Summaries are contained in F.S. Regs., Part II. and the Staff Manual respectively. Title pages will be prepared in manuscript.

Place	Date	Hour	Summary of Events and Information	Remarks and references to Appendices
CAMBRIN SECTOR	June 1918 1.	SAT.	Battery in the line with 8 guns at posts in the CAMBRIN SECTOR. 75 Rounds fired on various targets. Two emplacements altered and improved.	M/Canfield
	2	SUN.	The following targets were engaged:— Enemy front line (40 rounds) AUBURN TRENCH (10 rounds) Hostile T.M's (35 rounds). Ranging was carried out in preparation for Raid by 1st Q'sters. Captain Saunders attended Court of Enquiry at NOEUX-LES-MINES with reference to premature which occurred on 27/5/18.	M/Canfield
	3	MON.	85 rounds were fired on enemy front and support lines & hostile T.M's with apparent good results. Preparation was again made in readiness for raid on the night of the 4th inst. 300 rounds were carried from HARLEY STREET to the 4 guns taking part in the raid.	M/Canfield
	4	TUES.	During the day men were engaged in cleaning and preparing ammunition for the guns assisting in the Raid. At night the Battery co-operated with the 9st Q'sters in a raid on the enemy's front and support lines. 6 guns were in action, and a total of 462 rounds were fired. The following Congratulatory Order from the 1st Divisional Commander was received by the Units taking part in	M/Canfield

WAR DIARY of 3rd J.ch Battery

INTELLIGENCE SUMMARY for June 1918

Army Form C. 2118.

Place	Date 1918. JUNE	Hour	Summary of Events and Information	Remarks and references to Appendices
	4 TUES (continued)		The raid. "Please convey to all ranks taking part in raid last night the Divisional Commanders great appreciation of the preliminary arrangements made and of the success of the raid generally. All arms concerned are deserving of high praise." During the raid a premature occurred which resulted in the death of No. 25594 L/Cpl. A. Hull and No. 13798 Pte. G. Goulding, both of the 1st Lin. Borderers attached this Unit.	My Cauft Lt
	5 WED.		Battery were relieved in the line by 2nd T.M.B. & moved to billets at NOEUX-LES-MINES.	My Cauft Lt
	6 THUR.		Battery engaged in cleaning & overhauling guns, ammunition & equipment. Captain Saunders attended Conference of C.B.'s at Bois Nr. Drs. Lt. Banks and 2nd Lt Mann accompanied the Brigadier & party of 6 Officers to training area at BOIS D'OKHAIN where a few tactical exercises were explained by the Brigadier.	My Cauft Lt
	7 FRI.		The following programme was carried out:- Musketry, Physical training and Gun Drill in gas masks. Battery also practised in moving to Assembly positions	My Cauft Lt

NOEUX-LES-MINES.

WAR DIARY of 3rd T.M. Battery
INTELLIGENCE SUMMARY for June 1918.

Army Form C. 2118.

Place	Date 1918 June	Hour	Summary of Events and Information	Remarks and references to Appendices
NOEUX-LES-MINES	7. FRI. (Continued)		2/Lt. H.G. Clarke assumed 2nd in Command of Battery vice Lt. E.A. Davies who relinquished the appointment at his own request. 2/Lt. W. Davies, 1st S.W.B rejoined the Battalion vide B.R.O. 4089.	Hyland Lt
	8. SAT.		The training carried out this day included Gun drill and Dummy firing, also Musketry - Rapid loading and Rapid firing.	Hyland Lt
	9. SUN.		A distribution of Medal Ribbons was held by the CORPS COMMANDER at the Patronage NOEUX-LES-MINES at which the following recipients of the Battery were decorated. No 14706 Sgt. W. Hodges. No 39087 Pte J. Howe " 1018 " A. Evans. " 1727 " D. Clark. " 56823 Cpl. B. Edmundson. Remainder of distribution. 1 Officer and 10 O.R. attended the distribution. Remainder of Battery attended Church Parade.	Hyland Lt
	10. MON.		Battery attended Baths at 7 a.m. Remainder of morning spent in Gun drill, Dummy firing & Musketry.	Hyland Lt

WAR DIARY of 3rd L.M. Battery for June 1918.

INTELLIGENCE SUMMARY.

Army Form C. 2118.

Place	Date 1918.	Hour	Summary of Events and Information	Remarks and references to Appendices
NOEUX- LES- MINES	JUNE 11 TUES.		Battery engaged in training as follows :- Physical training, Gun Drill in Gas Masks (M.S.), Musketry, Guard Mounting, Lecture by C.O. "Use of Stokes as A.A. Weapon."	Wyhanfield
	12. WED.		The following training was carried out :- Physical training, Gun Drill, Musketry & Box Respirator Inspection. Men also engaged in overhauling Mules, equipment, clothing &c. preparatory to going in the line.	Wyhanfield
HOHENZOLLERN SECTOR	13. THUR.		Battery relieved 1st L.M.B. in the HOHENZOLLERN SECTOR. Owing to sickness (P.U.O.) being prevalent in the Battery 32 O.R. were this day admitted to Hospital. This necessitated 5 gun teams of the 1st L.M.B. (under Lt. Clapton) remaining in the line – 8 theo Battery providing 3 teams only its complete 8 guns.	Wyhanfield
	14 FRI.		Guns were engaged to-day chiefly in registering. Gun teams were also engaged in improving and repairing accommodation, recesses, latrines &c.	Wyhanfield
	15 SAT.		95 rounds were fired during the day on various targets.	

WAR DIARY of 3rd. L.M. Battery for June 1918.

Army Form C. 2118.

INTELLIGENCE SUMMARY.
(Erase heading not required.)

Place: HOHENZOLLERN SECTOR

Date 1918 JUNE	Hour	Summary of Events and Information	Remarks and references to Appendices
15 SAT (continued)		Two new emplacements were commenced at QUARRY TUNNEL and QUARRY ALLEY and work on KENSINGTON WALK and LEWIS ALLEY Emplacements was continued.	H/Flank ft
16 SUN.		Various targets (including RAILWAY CRATER TRAIN ALLEY and FOSSE TRENCH) were engaged and a total of 120 rounds were fired. Work on existing emplacements was continued.	H/Flank 26
17 MON.		106 rounds were fired on this day, the following being the chief targets:- TRAIN ALLEY (57 rounds) FOSSE TRENCH (13 rounds) AUDIT TRENCH (16 rounds). Men continued to work on emplacements & accommodation. L/Bdr. Farhi and L/Bdr. Masterton (1st & 3rd T.M.B attached 3rd T.M.B) were this day admitted to Hospital sick.	H/Flank2 tr
18 TUES.		Various targets were engaged, a total of 97 rounds being fired. Work continued on emplacements and accommodation. Assistance given to Infantry carrying party in taking 200 rounds Stokes gun Ammunition.	H/Flank ts
19 WED.		124 rounds fired on usual trench targets. Two new emplacements commenced on orders from G.O.C. Brigade Ammunition brought up from CAMBRIN to local gun pits.	H/Flank ts 5

WAR DIARY of 3rd T.M. Battery for June 1918.

INTELLIGENCE SUMMARY.

(Erase heading not required.)

Army Form C. 2118.

Place	Date	Hour	Summary of Events and Information	Remarks and references to Appendices
HOHENZOLLERN SECTOR	1918 JUNE 20 THUR.		116 Rounds on usual trench targets. Desultory H.E. and T.M. fire from enemy during raid by anzacs on our left, shells falling near Battery H.Q. New Emplacement commenced at CANNON STREET and CENTRAL KEEP. Usual routine continued.	HyClarkR
	21. FRI.		Fired on usual trench targets. 300 rounds brought up from VERMELLES to night gun pits. One of our Balloons near NOEUX-LES-MINES brought down by an enemy 'plane.	HyClarkR
	22. SAT.		Work on new emplacement hindered by inclement weather. Battery H.Q. shelled intermittently for 3 hours (6.30 a.m. to 9.30 a.m) by 4.2's and occasional 5.9's. CANNON STREET emplacement (in construction) seriously damaged by a direct hit during day. This shelling - no Casualties. 115 rounds fired during day. L/B. Clarke returns from Hospital.	HyClarkR
	23. SUN.		Various targets were Engaged. 130 rounds being fired. Work on five new emplacements continued. CANNON STREET emplacement finished. Insufficient men of this Battery being discharged from Hospital, the Unit was able to man the 8 Mortars for the time, and consequently the men loaned from the	HyClarkR

Army Form C. 2118.

WAR DIARY of 3rd T.M. Battery for June 1918.

INTELLIGENCE SUMMARY.

(Erase heading not required.)

Place	Date	Hour	Summary of Events and Information	Remarks and references to Appendices
	1918 JUNE			
	23 SUN (continued)		1st and 2nd. T.M.B's were returned to their Units.	
	24 MON.		The following targets were engaged:- TRAIN ALLEY to FOSSE TRENCH, LITTLE WILLIE TRENCH, CROSS TRENCH and enemy T.M's - 110 rounds being fired. Work continued on new emplacements. Captain Saunders attended interviews to H. Corps Ammunition Officer at Bde H.Q. with reference to premature which occurred on the 4/6/18.	Appendix 6.
	25. TUES.		140 rounds fired including 30 rounds harassing fire on TRAIN ALLEY to FOSSE TRENCH + 30 rounds on enemy O.P (A.28.d.60.10) Class emplacement + messes at CANNON STREET and LEWIS ALLEY completed and work continued on remaining 3 new emplacements. Captain Saunders attended Conference of T.B.O's at H.Q. 1st Glouster Regt.	Appendix 6.
	26. WED.		Usual trench targets engaged + registration carried out. 98 rounds being fired.	Appendix 6.
	27. THURS.		143 rounds fired on enemy front + Support lines + Hostile T.M's. Demonstration of firing was carried out by one of our guns in the presence of S.2 of T.B.O's of the American Army.	Appendix 6.
	28. FRI.		124 rounds fired following the days on selected targets in the Enemy's Lines. Work continued on new emplacements + assistance was given to carrying parties in conveying Ammunition to Gun Pits.	Appendix 6.

HOHENZOLLERN SECTOR

WAR DIARY of 3rd T.M. Battery for June 1918.

INTELLIGENCE SUMMARY.

(Erase heading not required.)

Army Form C. 2118.

Place	Date 1918.	Hour	Summary of Events and Information	Remarks and references to Appendices
HOHENZOLLERN SECTOR	JUNE 29. SAT.		Several targets were engaged & fired. All new Emplacements completed and ready for occupation. Lt. C.A. Farris, 1/4th S.W. Borderers attached this Unit, rejoined his Battalion, by Order of G.O.C. Brigade.	Appendix A.
	30. SUN.		125 rounds fired, chiefly on Enemy front and support lines and hostile T.M's. 600 rounds conveyed from CAMBRIN & VERMELLES to Local Dumps, and Emp: of boxes returned.	Appendix A.

E. Saunders
CAPTAIN.
COMD'G 3RD TRENCH MORTAR BATY

Army Form C. 2118.

WAR DIARY of 3rd T.M. Battery

INTELLIGENCE SUMMARY. for July 1918.

(Erase heading not required.)

Instructions regarding War Diaries and Intelligence Summaries are contained in F. S. Regs., Part II. and the Staff Manual respectively. Title pages will be prepared in manuscript.

Place	Date	Hour	Summary of Events and Information	Remarks and references to Appendices
	July 1.	MON.	Battery in the line at HOHENZOLLERN SECTOR with 8 guns. 120 rounds fired in short trench target. Men engaged in cleaning & overhauling ammunition &c preparatory to relief.	Appendix attached
	2.	TUES.	Battery relieved in the line by 2nd T.M.B and moved to billets at NOEUX-LES-MINES.	Appendix attached
	3.	WED.	Battery engaged in cleaning & overhauling guns equipment clothing &c. 2/Lt Mann & 6 O.R. proceeded to I. Corps School for Stokes for Mortar Course.	Appendix attached
	4.	THUR.	The majority of the Battery were inoculated this day & consequently no training was carried out. In accordance with 1st Division No. G 155/1 the surplus men of this unit were to-day returned to their Battalions.	Appendix attached
	5.	FRI.	No training was carried out on account of inoculation. Capt. Saunders proceeded to I. Corps School for Course of A.A. firing. Practice was carried out in loading two limbers each & Jordans and Battery Stores with a view of possible allotment of transport to the Battery.	Appendix attached
	6.	SAT.	The training for this day was as follows:- Box Respiration drill. Gun drill, Musketry & Physical Training.	Appendix attached
	7.	SUN.	Church Parades.	Appendix attached

NOEUX-LES-MINES

Army Form C. 2118.

WAR DIARY of 3rd S.A. Battery

INTELLIGENCE SUMMARY. for July 1916.

(Erase heading not required.)

Place	Date	Hour	Summary of Events and Information	Remarks and references to Appendices
CAMBRIN SECTOR · AFS · MINES	JULY 8	MON.	Battery engaged in Bayonet fighting, Gun Drill, Gun Laying by Compass. Concealed emplacements etc. Six further demonstrations of Loading Limbers were carried out in the presence of the G.O.C. Division.	
	9.	TUES.	Training:- Gun Drill in Gas Masks. Dummy firing overhead. Rep. fearing of Corpus Shoot 26. W.J. Plants attended a 6" S.T.M. Demonstration at LA COMTE.	
	10	WED	Training programme was as follows:- Heavy Drill. Dummy firing (part time in) Gun Laying, Gun Drill. Sets. Lieut. W.J. Clarke was sent to inspect the Brigade Tactical Scheme (without troops) under the direction of the Divisional Commander. Lt. Plants attended a C.O's Conference held at B'de H. Qrs. Capt. Saunders reported the Units from I. Corps. A.F. Course.	
	11.	THUR.	Battery relieved 190. T.M.B. in the CAMBRIN Sector. 6 Mortars were manned and 2 retained at by H.Qrs. for use in case of emergency. It is the intention of the O.C. Battery. 2/Lt. S. Barnes, 1/c. 2/Lt. S. Jolmo. joined this unit for duty:- also Lieut. Crowseby, 1/L. Gloster reported to the Battery for 1 month's course of instruction.	
	12.	FRI.	During this day 55 rounds were spent chiefly Registration. When employed in cleaning & overhauling ammunition.	

D. D. & L., London, E.C.
(A8041) Wt. W1771/M-31 750,000 5/17 Sch. 52 Forms/C2118/14

Army Form C. 2118.

WAR DIARY of 3rd T.M. Battery
INTELLIGENCE SUMMARY. for July 1918.

(Erase heading not required.)

Place	Date	Hour	Summary of Events and Information	Remarks and references to Appendices
CAMBRIN SECTOR	July 13	SAT.	During the day 80 rounds fired on observed hostile T.M.; also 350 rounds in co-operation with artillery in AUBURN TRENCH	Appx 1
	14	SUN.	The targets engaged this day were FRANKS KEEP, CHATEAU ALLEY & DOSN ALLEY, 90 rounds being fired. Assistance was given to carrying party in carrying 358 rounds from HARLEY ST. Dump to Cave gun pits.	Appx 1
	15	MON	80 rounds fired on enemy front & support lines & nine trench targets.	Appx 1
	16	TUES.	200 rounds fired on the following targets :- AUBURN TRENCH CHATEAU ALLEY & FRANKS KEEP, & supplied hostile Pairs in A.22.c & A.21.D gun Emplacements. Ammunition carrying in clearing Ammunition Emplacements &c. Ammunition was conveyed from HARLEY STREET DUMP to gun pits.	Appx 1
	17	WED.	nine trench targets engaged. 160 rounds being fired.	Appx 1
	18	THUR.	Harassing fire was carried out on enemy front & support lines, Hostile T.M.'s in addition to other trench targets, a total of 260 rounds being fired.	Appx 1
	19	FRI.	153 rounds fired on selected targets in the enemy lines.	Appx 1

WAR DIARY of 3rd T.O.B. Battery for July 1918.

INTELLIGENCE SUMMARY.

Army Form C. 2118.

Place	Date	Hour	Summary of Events and Information	Remarks and references to Appendices
CHAMPIEN SECTOR	July 20	SAT	The chief targets engaged were FRANKS KEEP, Enemy FRONT & SUPPORT LINES & CHATEAU. They _____ 112 rounds being fired. During registration by one of our guns an accident occurred causing the death of the N.C.O. & gun C/No.14,106. H/Sgt. O. Hodges M.M. 1/6. J.O.B. atte the Battery) & also the destruction of the gun. The Rev. Father J. Fiené 3rd Bde C.D. joined this Unit. 2/Lt. Mann & 6 O.R. returned from 1 Corps school L.M. Gun.	
	21.	SUN.	344 rounds fired this day, including 200 rounds in conjunction with fixed fly S.O.S.	
	22.	MON.	During this day we carried out a AUBURN TRENCH, FRANKS KKEEP & hostile T.M. pt. 4.22.c.30.35, 84 rounds being fired.	
	23.	TUES.	Various targets were engaged a total of 95 rounds being fired. T.O.B. Gask intended Inquiry of Enquiry into T.Boe H. No. 51 pit. after the reference to the accident which occurred on the 20 inst. After the above the Cause were of the opinion this accident was connected from the traversing of the York of the gun becoming disconnected from the traversing screw in short of discharge, this allowing the breeze to fall forward & causing the shell in contact with the front of the emplacement to explode in the gun pit. I unable to trace found that no blame to attaching to anyone.	

WAR DIARY of 3rd I.O.B. Battery for July 1918.

INTELLIGENCE SUMMARY.

(Erase heading not required.)

Army Form C. 2118.

CHABRIN SECTOR.

Place	Date	Hour	Summary of Events and Information	Remarks and references to Appendices
	JULY			
	24.	WED.	Several targets were engaged chiefly HOBORN TRENCH, CHATEAU ALLEY trench M.G's. - 145 rounds fired. Enemy hostile shelling this morning the gun emplacement at BRAINSWIY in addition to numerous rodus of ammunition was destroyed.	1st Lieut 1st Lieut
	25.	THUR.	65 rounds were fired on usual trench targets.	1st Lieut
	26.	FRI.	Mortars active on usual trench targets - 80 rounds being fired	1st Lieut
	27.	SAT.	60 rounds fired on HOBORN TRENCH, CHATEAU ALLEY & FRANKS KEEP. R.F.'s in opposing gun Pits at BRAINSWY. Assistance given	1st Lieut
	28.	SUN.	90 rounds fired on various targets.	1st Lieut
	29.	MON.	Harassing fire carried out on various targets, 90 rounds being fired	1st Lieut
	30.	TUES.	100 rounds fired on numerous trench targets.	1st Lieut
	31.	WED.	Battery relieved in the line by 2nd T.M.B. & moved to Billets at NOEOX. LES-MINES.	1st Lieut

G.J. Saunders
CAPTAIN,
COM'ng 3RD TRENCH MORTAR BATTY

Army Form C. 2118.

WAR DIARY
INTELLIGENCE SUMMARY.

for August, 1918.

3rd Trench Mortar Battery

(Erase heading not required.)

Instructions regarding War Diaries and Intelligence Summaries are contained in F. S. Regs., Part II. and the Staff Manual respectively. Title pages will be prepared in manuscript.

Place	Date 1918	Hour	Summary of Events and Information	Remarks and references to Appendices
	Aug. 1. Thurs		Battery engaged in cleaning guns, equipment, clothing, etc.	Adm. 1
	2 Fri.		One hour gun drill was carried out, but owing to inclement weather the remainder of the morning was devoted to lectures on various subjects in billets. 10 N.C.O.s are seen attended a lecture on the co-operation of Aircraft with other arms.	Adm. 2
	3 Sat		Morning devoted to gun drill and practise in moving to positions of Assembly. (Defence Scheme — Brigade in reserve) Captain Saunders attended a Tactical Exercise (without troops) under Director of Brigade Commander.	Adm. 3
	4 Sun		Battery present at combined Church Parade & Green Howards Divisional Horse Show in the afternoon.	Adm. 4
	5 Mon		The morning on the day was as follows:— Steady drill, Gun drill, and Lewis Gun firing. Capt Saunders proceeded to Officers Rest home, Paris Plage.	Adm. 5
	6 Tues		Battery training in Gun drill, Machinery, P.T. and B.F. and 1 Lieut W. Davies attended a Brigade Summary hurry (without troops) under direction of Tactical Exercise — Brigade Commander.	Adm. 6

NOEUX - LES - MINES

WAR DIARY for AUGUST, 1918.

INTELLIGENCE SUMMARY.

(Erase heading not required.)

Army Form C. 2118.

Place	Date	Hour	Summary of Events and Information	Remarks and references to Appendices
NOEUX-LES-MINES	AUG 7 1918	WED	Battery engaged in Gun Drill, practice in Mapping and Arm Drill. The afternoon was spent on GAVIN RANGE when different parts were carried out. Lt. N. DAVIES acted as Arty.	
	8	THUR	Practical exercise. Battery having as follows:- Gun Drill, Sammy Gunnery, PL and B.F. (N.C.O.'s - map reading and compass). Box respirator drill. Musketry 4. Gun Drill.	
	9	FRI	Employing by compass and construction of emplacements.	
HOHENZOLLERN SECTOR	10	SAT	Battery relieved 1st. T.M.B. in HOHENZOLLERN SECTOR - 3 officers and 3 Lieutenants & guns being wounded, and men immediately engaged in cleaning & overhauling ammunition.	
	11	SUN	Registration was carried out and the following targets engaged ie. N. DAVIES proceeded to G.H.Q. L.T.M. School for course.	
	12	MON	Harassing fire carried out on FOSSE TRENCH(GALLANT and GAMBLE ALLEYS 20 rounds being fired.	
	13	TUES	(Word illegible) targets were engaged and a hostile working party was dispersed near RAILWAY CRATER, 215 rounds fired.	

Army Form C. 2118.

WAR DIARY for AUGUST 1916.
or
INTELLIGENCE SUMMARY.

(Erase heading not required.)

Instructions regarding War Diaries and Intelligence Summaries are contained in F. S. Regs., Part II. and the Staff Manual respectively. Title pages will be prepared in manuscript.

Place	Date 1916	Hour	Summary of Events and Information	Remarks and references to Appendices
HOHENZOLLERN REDOUBT	AUG 14	WED	Over 200 rounds were fired on wounded head targets during the day. Capt. Saunders returned from Officers Rest Home.	
	15	THUR	Harassing fire carried out on enemy trenches and hostile T.M. Retaliation given to harassing party in covering party in Convoy at SAVILE ROW. 197 rounds fired. 160 ammunition recess constructed for shells to gun pits.	
	16	FRI	355 rounds fired during the day and harassing fire with Besa gun. Was carried out on trenches as far as AUBIT TRENCH.	
	17	SAT	Usual activity on head targets, 225 rounds being fired. Work commenced on new accommodation at KENSINGTON WALK.	
	18	SUN	125 rounds fired on targets in enemy lines.	
	19	MON	Various head targets were engaged, a total of 120 rounds being fired. New accommodation at KENSINGTON WALK completed.	
	20	TUES	105 rounds fired on wounded head targets. The following Casualties occurred to N.C.O's and men of the unit.	

No 56825 Cpl. N. EDMUNDSON, M.M. killed in action
1018 L/Sgt. A. EVANS, M.M. wounded
18424 Pte. W. LANE "

WAR DIARY OR INTELLIGENCE SUMMARY.

Army Form C. 2118.

August, 1918.

Place	Date	Hour	Summary of Events and Information	Remarks and references to Appendices
HOHENZOLLERN SECTOR	Aug 21 WED		Battery/Wagon lines taken over by 47 T.M.B. and moved by route march and bus to SACHIN.	
	22 THUR		Battery engaged in general cleaning of guns, rifles, equipment & clothing, &c. Surplus proceeded to U.K. on leave.	
	23 FRI		The following training was carried out: Inspections, Steady Drill, P.T. and B.F. Gun Drill and Musketry.	
	24 SAT		Batteries having Steady Drill, Gundrayne by Subsec Guards, advancing to unprepared Emplacements, Rapidly forming into Action &c. Afternoon - football. Church Parade.	
	25 SUN			
	26 MON		Owing to inclement weather, the morning was devoted to lectures & kit inspections in Billets.	
	27 TUES		The training on the day was - Steady Drill, Box respirator Drill and Gundrayning. Lt. N. DAVIES reported to Battery from G.H.Q. L.T.M. Course.	

SACHIN

WAR DIARY
or
INTELLIGENCE SUMMARY.

(Erase heading not required.)

Army Form C. 2118.

August, 1918.

Place	Date	Hour	Summary of Events and Information	Remarks and references to Appendices
ACHIET	August 1918 28	WED	Battery having in General Musketry, P.T. and Gunnery training.	
	29	THUR	The following day was as follows:- Musketry, Gas drill & gun drill and Gunnery training. C.O. Clark attested & had advance fire carried out by 1st Brigade.	
	30	FRI	This day training was as follows:- Gun drill, P.T., Practice rapidly in coming into action and Gunnery training.	
	31	SAT	Battery preparing to move to new area.	

W.J. Park Lieut for
O.C. 3rd E. By. C.F.A. 15Y

Army Form C. 2118.

Copy of WAR DIARY or INTELLIGENCE SUMMARY. 3rd TRENCH MORTAR BATTERY.
For Sept. 1918

(Erase heading not required.)

Instructions regarding War Diaries and Intelligence Summaries are contained in F. S. Regs., Part II. and the Staff Manual respectively. Title pages will be prepared in manuscript.

Place	Date	Hour	Summary of Events and Information	Remarks and references to Appendices
	1918 Sept			
	1st	SUN	Battery Entrained at 1 A.m. for ARRAS, arriving at 9 A.m. Battery moved by route march to place of assembly on the E. side of WANCOURT.	GSM
	2	MON	Battery awaiting orders at place of assembly.	GSM
	3	TUES	Ditto	GSM
	4	WED	In accordance with orders of Bde. H.Q. Battery moved to B. Echelon Lambert Lines	GSM
	5	THURS	Battery engaged all day in salvage work in vicinity of 'B' Echelon, Bangart Lines	GSM
	6	FRI	Battery moved by route march to Billets at ARRAS	GSM
	7	SAT	Battery at ARRAS awaiting orders. 1st Lt G.B. MANN proceeded to U.K. on leave.	GSM
	8	SUN	Battery left ARRAS at 7.15 A.M. & marched to NOYELLE-VION. arriving at 11.30 A.M. Capt. SAUNDERS returned from leave and resumed command of Battery.	GSM

D. D. & L., London, E.C.
(A800g) Wt. W277/M2 31 750,000 5/17 Sch. 53 Forms/C2118/14

Army Form C. 2113.

Copy of WAR DIARY of Sept: 1918

INTELLIGENCE SUMMARY.

(Erase heading not required.)

Instructions regarding War Diaries and Intelligence Summaries are contained in F. S. Regs., Part II. and the Staff Manual respectively. Title pages will be prepared in manuscript.

Place	Date 1918	Hour	Summary of Events and Information	Remarks and references to Appendices
	SEPT 9 MON		Battery resting at NOYELLE-VION	G XII
	10 TUES		Moved from billets at 3am and entrained at AUBIGNY station for VILLERS-BRETONNEUX arriving at billets here at 6.30 pm	G XII
	11 WED		Battery resting and waiting orders at VILLERS-BRETONNEUX	G XII
	12 THUR		Battery embussed at 6am for CAULAINCOURT arriving there at about 12 noon	G XII
	13 FRI		Battery moved at 5.30 AM by route march to VERNAND. At 7 pm with 16 more 2 guns and ammunition to take positions from Bde H.Q. (R.3.d.) to assume offensive position in vicinity of SUNKEN ROAD in support of 1st Gloucs.	G XII
	14 SAT		100 rounds per gun ammunition were placed at disposal of 1st Sw.B. Group as offensive patrols to assist in advance of our infantry took up offensive positions to assist	G XII
	15 SUN		At 9am (dark) Battery made a visit Sw B) sent in order to assist advance on MASSENY belonging to the Directors of Kimberly. The guns were not required.	G XII
	16 MON		Guns remained with the 1st Sw.B. Group of O.C. 1st Gloucs and O.C. 1st Sw.B. till about 5 p.m. when the whole Brigade relieved returned to the line	G XII

D. D. & I., London, E.C.
(A8004) Wt. W2771/M2 31 750,000 5/17 Sch. 53 Forms/C2118/14

Army Form C. 2118.

Copy of WAR DIARY for SEPT, 1918

Instructions regarding War Diaries and Intelligence
Summaries are contained in F. S. Regs., Part II.
and the Staff Manual respectively. Title pages
will be prepared in manuscript.

INTELLIGENCE SUMMARY.
(Erase heading not required.)

Place	Date 1918	Hour	Summary of Events and Information	Remarks and references to Appendices
CAULAINCOURT	SEPT 17	TUES	1 Officer & 23 O.R. employed as ??? Dump, CAULAINCOURT. Bakery H.Q. remained at VERMAND.	CRM
	18	WED	ditto	CRM
VERMAND	19	THUR	ditto	CRM
	20	FRI	Bn ? late recognizing ???? front line. 2/Lt DAVIES 2/Lt CLARKE proceeded to OC ? ??? Battery under ? Bde H.Q. E. CLARKE proceeded to OC of Same	CRM
	21	SAT	The 23 O.R. employed at Dump CAULAINCOURT rejoined Battery at VERMAND in afternoon (no orders)	CRM
	22	SUN	Battery awaiting orders to proceed to front line	CRM
	23	MON	Moved with 4 guns to front line	CRM
E 7	24	TUES	Guns arrived 3.a.m. Bn in ? between FRESNOY. 2 ??? Rifles to 2nd Bde H.Q. and 2 Rifles @ Glatery Be ??? with K6 ??? Rifles R. Bde opened ??? with K6 15 ???? of the infantry and K6 opened ??? at zero Fired ??? artillery barrage on FRESNOY. In the afternoon ??? the Battery advanced to FRESNOY TRENCH to bombard positions through hills by Enemy.	CRM

Army Form C. 2118.

Copy of **WAR DIARY** for Sept. 1918
or
INTELLIGENCE SUMMARY.
(Erase heading not required.)

Instructions regarding War Diaries and Intelligence Summaries are contained in F. S. Regs., Part II. and the Staff Manual respectively. Title pages will be prepared in manuscript.

Place	Date	Hour	Summary of Events and Information	Remarks and references to Appendices
	Sept 1918			
	25 WED		Guns took up defensive positions with the 71st on being the long Arras day. 2nd E. NANN reported by 1st home leave	9/XM
	26 THUR		One manned in defensive positions. 131 gun when battery was relieved by 71st T.M.B.	9/XM
	27 FRI		Battery station at VERMAND morning. Devoted to general clean up - repairing clothes etc.	9/XM
	28 SAT		Battery relieved 2 Lt T.M.B. in line, 2 guns 11th, 2 Gloster's and 2 with 11 S.W.B.	9/XII
	29 SUN		3 guns in defensive positions, 1 gun moved forward to "D" Coy 11 SWB in front line.	9/XII
	30 MON		1 gun went forward with S.W.B. in attack on THERIGNY and TALANA HILL. Remaining 3 guns in defensive positions one	9/XII

Army Form C. 2118.

WAR DIARY for October 1918
or
INTELLIGENCE SUMMARY.
(Erase heading not required.)

3rd Trench Mortar Battery

Place	Date	Hour	Summary of Events and Information	Remarks and references to Appendices
	Oct.1.	Tues.	Guns were withdrawn from Line and moved back to Batty. H.Q. (M.11.C.2.4.)	
	2	Wed.	Battery resting and awaiting orders	
	3	Thurs.	Battery moved to MAGNY-LA-FOSSE.	
	4	Fri.	On the evening of this date, Batty moved with Bde in support of 46th Divn and took up positions near SEQUEHART.	
	5	Sat.	Battery were relieved by 16th T.M.B. and moved to M.11.C.2.4.	
	6	Sun.	Resting	
	7	Mon.	Guns overhauled and cleaned and clothing & equipment looked to. 2nd/Lt. Clarke rejoined unit from leave	
	8	Tues.	Battery "Standing To" from 6a.m. to 6p.m in anticipation of move forward to engage in active operations.	
	9	Wed.	"Stand Down" received. Day devoted to training.	
	10	Thurs.	Following training carried out — P.T. Arms Drill, Bay't. & Gun drill.	
	11	Fri.	Owing to bad weather no training was carried out. Men attended Divl. Baths.	
	12	Sat.	Battery training	
	13	Sun.	Church parade	
	14	Mon.	Battery drill — consisting mainly of speed in coming into action.	
	15	Tues.	Battery training.	
	16	Wed.	Battery moved with Bde to area between BOHAIN and BRANCOURT where they bivouacked for the night	

(Cont.)

Army Form C. 2118.

WAR DIARY for October 1918
or
INTELLIGENCE SUMMARY.   3rd T.M.B.

(Erase heading not required.)

Instructions regarding War Diaries and Intelligence Summaries are contained in F. S. Regs., Part II. and the Staff Manual respectively. Title pages will be prepared in manuscript.

Place	Date	Hour	Summary of Events and Information	Remarks and references to Appendices
	17	Thurs.	Battery moved at 8am. to position of assembly S. of VAUX-AUDIGNY	
	18	Fri.	At 02:00 hours 4 guns moved to further position of assembly, S. of MOLAIN and at 10:30 hours the 4 guns went forward (2 with the 2nd Welch and 2 with the 1st W.B.) in the advance on the WASSIGNY – RIBEAUVILLE road	
	19	Sat.	At 05:30 the 4 guns continued with the infantry in the advance on REJET DE BEAULIEU which objective was eventually gained at 11:30. The guns were not called upon to fire during this advance	
	20	Sun.	Guns in position on the line – 2 with Rt. Battn. & 2 with Left Battn. The two guns with Left Battn. carried out harrassing fire on hostile M.G's.	
	21	Mon.	Guns disposed as on the 20th.	
	22	Tues.	Do.	
	23	Wed.	4 guns of the 1st I.M.B. were attached to this unit to assist infantry in attack on the high ground running from the elbow of the SAMBRE CANAL (S.7.b.3.7.) to the road R.35.c.8.7. The task of mortars as directed by 3de H.Q was as follows:— (a) To leave 2 guns in position on right Battn front (1st Glos) to fire on eastern bank of canal (b) Remaining 6 guns to fire on selected spots on the front of the Left Battn. (2nd Welch). Two of these guns were to move forward under the instructions of O.C. 2nd Welch. The 2 guns (a) carried out their allotted task, but only 2 guns on the Left Battn front were allowed to fire by the O.C. 2nd Welch. (cont⁴)	

D. D. & L., London, E.C.
(A804) WL W1771/M2:31 750,000 5/17 **Sch 52** Forms/C2118/14

Army Form C. 2118.

WAR DIARY
or
INTELLIGENCE SUMMARY.

(Erase heading not required.)

for October 1918   3rd I.M.B.

Instructions regarding War Diaries and Intelligence Summaries are contained in F. S. Regs., Part II. and the Staff Manual respectively. Title pages will be prepared in manuscript.

Place	Date	Hour	Summary of Events and Information	Remarks and references to Appendices
	23	Wed. (Cont)	2 guns went forward with the attacking infantry, but were not called upon to fire. The following casualties were sustained - 1 Officer (Lt. G.B. Mann, 2nd Beds. Wounded) + O.R.	
	24	Thurs.	During the day guns were in position in the line, but were withdrawn in the evening on Bde relief. Battery moved to billets at VAUX-AUDIGNY.	
	25	Fri.	Morning devoted to cleaning and overhauling guns, clothing, equipt etc. Capt. W.J. Bradley, M.C., 1st Glos Regt returned from England to this unit, after a tour of 6 mths light duty, and re-assumed command vice Capt. G.H. Clarke. Usual battery training was carried out.	
	26	Sat.		
	27	Sun.	Church parades	
	28	Mon.	Battery training. 2nd Lt. C. Davis, 2nd Welch reported for duty with this unit vice 2nd Lt. G.B. Mann, 2nd Welch, wounded in action 23/10/18	
	29	Tues.	Usual training	
	30	Wed.	Morning spent in cleaning overhauling guns, prior to evening relief of 2nd Bde. Relief completed by 21.30 hrs. 4 guns in line 2 with left Battn, 2 with centre Battn and 1 with right Battn.	
	31	Thurs.	Work of supplying necessary ammunition to guns carried out, and two forward dumps replenished. Gun positions of Rt Battn gun destroyed by Shell fire. The afternoon Alternative positions chosen and ranging carried out. Left and centre guns supplied each with 20 boxes of ammn	

Army Form C. 2118.

WAR DIARY for November 1918.
or
INTELLIGENCE SUMMARY.

3rd Trench Mortar Battery

(Erase heading not required.)

Instructions regarding War Diaries and Intelligence Summaries are contained in F. S. Regs., Part II. and the Staff Manual respectively. Title pages will be prepared in manuscript.

Place	Date	Hour	Summary of Events and Information	Remarks and references to Appendices
	Nov 1918			
	1	Fri	Battery in the line at CANAL BANK. Guns being with Left Battalion, 2 with centre battalion and 1 with right battalion. Guns teams were engaged in cleaning, firing and carrying ammunition.	
	2	SAT	Further ammunition was carried to gun emplacements and preparations for firing. Ranging was carried out.	
	3	SUN	Preparations were made for assisting the Infantry on the following attack. Further emplacements were prepared and ranging on the BRIDGEHEAD was carried out.	
	4	MON	Two guns under Lt. G. Davies were attached to C Coy 2nd Welch Regt at Lieu after Zero temporarily, the others participated by enemy. Machine Gunners at The BRIDGEHEAD. Guns were activated for 30 minutes (300 rounds being fired) and 17 enemy dead were afterwards found. One gun under Lt. H.G. Clarke attacked with the Infantry (8 Co.) 14th Brigade) in the attack on CAPINGHEM, but were not called upon to fire. On the evening the battery with the remainder of brigade were withdrawn from the line and moved to billets at VAUX ANDIGNY.	
	5	TUES	Battery left VAUX ANDIGNY at mid-day and moved by route march to BOHAIN.	
	6	WED	Moves by route march to FRESNOY-LE-GRAND, arriving at billets at 11.30 hours.	
	7	THUR	Baggage handed in cleaning and overhauling guns equipment and clothing and kit inspection.	
	8	FRI	Battery engaged for three hours in training.	
	9	SAT	The following training was carried out:- Guns Drill Physical Drill Bayonet Fighting with Regimental Drill.	

Army Form C. 2118.

WAR DIARY
of
INTELLIGENCE SUMMARY.

(Erase heading not required.)

Instructions regarding War Diaries and Intelligence Summaries are contained in F. S. Regs., Part II. and the Staff Manual respectively. Title pages will be prepared in manuscript.

Place	Date	Hour	Summary of Events and Information	Remarks and references to Appendices
	Nov 10	SUN	Battery attended Church Parade	
	11	MON	Morning spent on Fatigues	
	12	TUES	Battery engaged in Battery during the morning and attended Foot- washing Parade in the afternoon	
	13	WED	Battery moved by Bus to BAZUEL	
	14	THUR	Battery engaged in Fatigues during the morning	
	15	FRI	Battery moved by route march to MARBAIX	
	16	SAT	ditto to SARS POTERIES	
	17	SUN	Battery resting at SARS POTERIES. Attended Church Service in the morning	
	18	MON	Battery moved by route march to BEAUMONT.	
	19	TUES	ditto to WALCOURT	
	20	WED	Morning devoted to general cleaning up, and inspection in full marching order	
	21	THUR	Morning spent in turnout, and afternoon Football Match.	
	22	FRI	Battery engaged in general cleaning up and short route march.	
	23	SAT	Battery moved to FLORENNES.	
	24	SUN	Church Parade	
	25	MON	Battery engaged in cleaning harness, equipment and clothing	
	26	TUES	Morning spent in turnout, including 5 mile route march	
	27	WED	do	

Army Form C. 2118.

WAR DIARY
INTELLIGENCE SUMMARY.
(Erase heading not required.)

Place	Date	Hour	Summary of Events and Information	Remarks and references to Appendices
	Nov.			
	28	THUR	Battery engaged for short period in Training and cleaning up.	
	29	FRI.	Route March, Ceremonial Drill and cleaning reserve ammunition.	
	30	SAT.	Cleaning guns, equipment & checking stores. Kit Inspection.	

W. Alexander Capt
O.C. 3

Copy of War Diary of 3rd B. I. Ch. Batty. for Dec. 1918.

Army Form C. 2118.

WAR DIARY or INTELLIGENCE SUMMARY.

(Erase heading not required.)

Instructions regarding War Diaries and Intelligence Summaries are contained in F. S. Regs., Part II. and the Staff Manual respectively. Title pages will be prepared in manuscript.

Place	Date	Hour	Summary of Events and Information	Remarks and references to Appendices
	DEC. 1918			
	1.	SUN.	Battery participating in March to the Rhine. Left FLORENNES at about 10.30 hours and moved to FLAVION.	
	2.	MON.	Battery marched to WEIKEN.	
	3.	TUES.	do MIRANDA CHATEAU near CELLES.	
	4.	WED.	Battery resting. do	
	5.	THUR.	do morning devoted to cleaning billets, equipment, clothing &c.	
	6.	FRI.	do morning spent in training including 5 mile route march.	
	7.	SAT.	do General cleaning up of equipment & Battery stores.	
	8.	SUN.	do Church Parades.	
	9.	MON.	Battery moved by route march to CHEVETOGNE	
	10.	TUES	do do HEURE	
	11.	WED.	do do HOTTON.	
	12.	THUR.	Battery resting at HOTTON. Men engaged in cleaning & overhauling equipment & clothing.	
	13.	FRI.	do do	
	14.	SAT.	Moved by route march to LES ROCHES.	
	15.	SUN.	do do GRANDMENIL.	

Army Form C. 2118.

Copy of WAR DIARY of 3rd L.I.H. Batty for Dec - 1918.

or

INTELLIGENCE SUMMARY.

(Erase heading not required.)

Place	Date	Hour	Summary of Events and Information	Remarks and references to Appendices
	1918 DEC			
	16. MON.		Moved by route march to JOUBIEVAL.	
	17 TUES.		do do BEHO.	
	18. WED.		Battery moved with remainder of Brigade & crossed the German Frontier at about 10.00 hours Battery reached NEUBRUCK about 12.30 + were billeted there.	
	19. THUR.		Moved by route march to LOSHEIM.	
	20. FRI.		Battery resting at LOSHEIM. Morning devoted to cleaning Clothes + Equipment.	
	21. SAT.		Battery moved by route march to HAMMERHUTTE.	
	22. SUN		do do MULHEIM.	
	23. MON		do do MUNSTEREIFEL.	
	24. TUES.		do do LUDENDORF.	
	25. WED.		Christmas day. Battery at LUDENDORF. Holiday.	
	26. THUR.		Battery engaged in cleaning guns, equipment, ammunition + clothing.	
	27. FRI.		Devisional Holiday. Battery dinner in the evening.	

Copy of WAR DIARY of 3rd L.T.M.B/y. Army Form C. 2118.
or
INTELLIGENCE SUMMARY. for Dec 1916.
(Erase heading not required.)

Place	Date 1916	Hour	Summary of Events and Information	Remarks and references to Appendices
	DEC. 28. SAT.		Morning spent in general cleaning up.	
	29. SUN.		Battery resting. Kit inspection in the morning.	
	30. MON.		Battery left BODENDORF & moved by route march to billets at SCHWEINHEIM.	
	31. TUES.		Men engaged in thoroughly cleaning & oiling guns & ammunition.	

W Whalley Capt".
Comm dg. 3rd L.T.M.B/y.

Army Form C. 2118.

WAR DIARY
or
INTELLIGENCE SUMMARY. 3rd French Mortar Battery.

(Erase heading not required.)

January 1919.

Instructions regarding War Diaries and Intelligence Summaries are contained in F. S. Regs., Part II. and the Staff Manual respectively. Title pages will be prepared in manuscript.

Place	Date	Hour	Summary of Events and Information	Remarks and references to Appendices
Schwanheim	1st to 31st Jany.		Nothing worthy of record to note throughout the month. Each day has seen the usual routine of military and educational training. Guns and ammunition have been cleaned and overhauled twice weekly. Occasional football matches in the afternoon. Lieut Davies proceeded on leave to England on 29th. " Clarke " " " " " 12th. 2 left for demobilization on 12th. Average Battery strength present. 2 and 22 OR.	

W/S Bradley Capt B
OC 3 T.M.B.

WO 95/1282
3 INF BDE
MGC
Feb 16 - Feb 18

1ST DIVISION
3RD BRIGADE

3RD MACHINE GUN COMPANY

~~FEB - DEC 1916~~
~~(APL MISSING)~~

1916 FEB — ~~1918 FEB~~ Sept 1916

3rd Brigade.
1st Division.

3rd MACHINE GUN COMPANY:: FEBRUARY 1916.

D.A.G.
3rd Echelon

Herewith War Diary of 3rd Bn
M.G. Coy from 14th Feb to 29th Feb

A.G. Lyttelton Capt
O.C. 3rd M.G. Coy.

4.3.16

26.Inf

3 Bde M Gun Coy

WAR DIARY or INTELLIGENCE SUMMARY

Army Form C. 2118.

3rd Bn. M.G.C.

Place	Date	Hour	Summary of Events and Information	Remarks and references to Appendices
Les Brebis	14/2/16		The Coy marched from LOZINGHEM to LILLERS & entrained at 4.0 pm for NOEUX-LES-MINES. Marched from there to LES BREBIS & relieved the 140th Coy in the LOOS sector in the evening. 6 guns in front line, 6 guns in second line, & 2 guns in LOOS as part of the defences.	
"	15/2/16		C.O. went round the line in the morning. There were no emplacement of any value as far as cover was concerned. Siting on the whole good. The Germans having exploded a mine in HARRISONS CRATER the previous morning & attempted to occupy crater, arrangements were made to bring cross fire on [crossed out] from Lige during night.	
"	16/2/16		Quiet day. C.O. visited line in afternoon & recommended positions for Lewis guns on to 2 emplacements on LOOS CRASSIER. The two guns there having no cover at all at 4am	
"	17/2/16		The Germans exploded a mine at Hart's crater Nos 1 & 5 guns opened fire on German line in rear of Crater. No 5 gun was slightly damaged by a shell. Reserve gun Sections Nos 1 & 4 Sections relieved front line	

Army Form C. 2118.

WAR DIARY
or
INTELLIGENCE SUMMARY 3rd Bn M.G.C.

(Erase heading not required.)

Place	Date	Hour	Summary of Events and Information	Remarks and references to Appendices
Nr Poelis	10/7/16		No 1 Gun Section the Second line	
			Rainy day. Wished to start work on permanent emplacement, but Brigadier unable to spare any R.E. or infantry carrying parties. Trenches in very bad & muddy.	
	19/7/16		C.O. visited left of 2nd Bn to inspect permanent emplacement under construction. Went & part of second line. No 7 gun in enclosure had barrel casing badly perforated by stray bullets at evening Stand To. 16:01 Pte SHANAHAN S/watch at 2nd 3rd Sec wounded. 7 O.C. 1st Sec ordered attack on HARTS & HARRISON'S CRATERS. Nos 3 & 5 guns co-operated in attack by firing on ground between HART's Crater & German line. Attack started 9.30 p.m. Casualties. 1 O.R. wounded.	
	20/7/16		HARRISON Crater consolidated by S.W.B. but attack on HART'S failed owing to enemy M.G. fire. All guns that went bear according laid on Crater lists to prevent establishment of German post. Nos 3 & 5 guns instructed to keep constant look out for any sign of movement by enemy between Craters & front line.	

2449 Wt. W14957/M90 750,000 1/16 J.B.C. & A. Forms/C.2118/12.

WAR DIARY or INTELLIGENCE SUMMARY

Army Form C. 2118.

3rd B'ty M.G.C.?

Place	Date	Hour	Summary of Events and Information	Remarks and references to Appendices
"	20/7/16	(?)	All guns & dead Germans relieved in evening.	
"	21/7/16		2/Lt Nelson relieved by 2/Lt McLean in afternoon. Altered position of No 1 gun & began new emplacement owing to consistent trouble with craters. No assistance could be got from R.E. owing to infantry carrying parties. Fire at intervals on HART'S crater during night. Reinforcements 1 O.R.	
"	22/7/16		No. 5 gun engaged enemy working party on HART's crater during night. No 1 also fired on crater. E.O. visited line in afternoon. Reinforcements 1 O.R.	
"	23/7/16		Quiet Day. German working party E. of HART'S crater, & in s/s gun emp.t of gun position engaged during night by No 5 gun. Work continued on No 1 emplacement. Reinforcements 1 O.R.	
"	24/7/16		Same targets engaged nightly by No 5. E.O. visited line in afternoon. Continued work on No 1 emplacement & began new emplacements for Nos 2 & 5 guns. This gun was shelled	

WAR DIARY

INTELLIGENCE SUMMARY   3rd Bn M.G.C.

Army Form C. 2118.

Place	Date	Hour	Summary of Events and Information	Remarks and references to Appendices
In the Field	25/9/16		O.C. & M.G.C.y reconnoitred line with C.O. in the morning. In evening 1/5 Mining C.y explored & mined under HART'S crater at 7.0 p.m. The I/Glam occupied western lip of crater formed by the explosion & dug themselves in under cover of heavy bombardment of German front line by 1st Div. Artillery. The M.g. C.y co-operated by firing on the back of HART'S crater with nos 3 & 5 guns from their emplacements. Splinter proof overhead cover was placed over these as soon as it was dark. 2 gun was damaged by hostile shell fire. No 4 gun was moved to No.3 Bay position & laid on crater & a Lewis gun taken to top of LOOS CRASSIER placed in position near No 5 gun. No 5 gun moved up to fire of crater. When artillery fire slackened the M.g. opened fire & continued at intervals throughout night. Germans made no advance on the open against crater. Work on No 2 emplacement continued. Reinforcements 2 O.R.	
	26/9/16		German artillery fire been heavy. O.C. from line guns ordered to get B" Lewis guns to co-operate in firing on damaged wire & parapets	
	27/9/16		Quiet day. At 6.0 p.m mine was exploded by us in front of CHALK PIT & lip of crater consolidated. No 5 gun ordered to fire on usual Coy relieved at dusk by No 2 C.y. Forget.	

WAR DIARY
or
INTELLIGENCE SUMMARY

3rd B⁽ⁿ⁾ M.G.C.⁽ᵒ²⁾

Army Form C. 2118.

Place	Date	Hour	Summary of Events and Information	Remarks and references to Appendices
In the Field	28/2/16		Relief not complete till midnight. Bn. spent in cleaning up & checking stores. C.O. attended conference at Div. H.Q. at 3. p.m.	
"	29/2/16		Began training of extra men attached for duty, most of whom are very ignorant. Remainder employed in cleaning roads & billets.	

3rd Brigade.

1st Division.

3rd MACHINE GUN COMPANY ::: MARCH 1916.

3 Bde M Gun Coy

~~Vol I & II~~

I . II

II . III

"A" Form.
Army Form C. 2121.

MESSAGES AND SIGNALS.

Prefix	Code	m.	Words	Charge	This message is on a/c of	Rec'd. at	m
Office of Origin and Service Instructions.			Sent At m. To By		Service. (Signature of "Franking Officer.")	Date From By	

TO D.A.G. 3RD Echelon

Sender's Number.	Day of Month	In reply to Number		AAA
	9/4/16.			

Herewith Original War Diaries for
Feb 15 – 29th
March 1st – 31st 1916.

From N°3 Company
Place Machine Gun Corps.
Time

The above may be forwarded as now corrected. (Z)

Censor. Signature of Addressor or person authorised to telegraph in his name.

* This line should be erased if not required.

WAR DIARY 3rd Bn M.G. Co

Army Form C. 2118.

Instructions regarding War Diaries and Intelligence Summaries are contained in F.S. Regs., Part II. and the Staff Manual respectively. Title Pages will be prepared in manuscript.

INTELLIGENCE SUMMARY
(Erase heading not required.)

Place	Date	Hour	Summary of Events and Information	Remarks and references to Appendices
My Hd Qrs	1/3/16		Training of men attached from battn for duty, & men of whom known nothing. Remainder of Company employed in cleaning billets & obtaining a gun room. One officer per section reconnoitred the Reserve Line & the MAROC Defences. Company washed.	
"	2/3/16		Training continued. All guns were tested on range, & off attached men fired a few rounds. O.C. arranged details of relief with O.C. 1st & 13th M.G. Co's.	
"	3/3/16		C.O. reconnoitred line in Right Section. Heavy snowfall. Again training in mechanism continued.	
"	4/3/16		Co. relieved 1st Bn B'y Co's in No 4 section on Right Section. Reserve line. Two extra guns on extreme right of Reserve line manned by mixed detachment & known as MAROC Detachment. Relief complete by 11.0 p.m.	

WAR DIARY or INTELLIGENCE SUMMARY

Army Form C. 2118.

3 ∕ 3 ∕ M.G. Coy

Instructions regarding War Diaries and Intelligence Summaries are contained in F. S. Regs., Part II. and the Staff Manual respectively. Title Pages will be prepared in manuscript.

(Erase heading not required.)

Place	Date	Hour	Summary of Events and Information	Remarks and references to Appendices
Y Sector	5/3/16		C.O visited line in morning. Bearings & area of fire of all guns checked & with help of 2 officers and 4th Division work on No. 6 & permanent emplacements continued by R.E. Timber emplacement for No. 7 completed by No. 2 Section. Mr HEWETT relieved 2/Lt BARRETT in Loos & Annex	
"	6/3/16		C.O. visited line in afternoon & chose a place for night firing on CROSNE ALLEY. Sandy, the proposed target being the road past PUITS 16. Work done in front line in Reserve in front of No 6 gun cleared. Trench cleared at No 4, 5, & 7 gun Reserve line. R.E. made good progress with emplacement for No 5 gun on Crassier M > at S. 3. One trench between Nos & TREIZE ALLEY cleared	
"	7/3/16		C.O. visited No 2 section's guns on left of line in morning & also Nos 5, 6, 7, 8 & 9 in reserve line. Work done. R.E. continued work on Nos 1, 2 & 3 in forward line. Trench to No 2 Reserve cleared & trench boards laid. Trench from TREIZE ALLEY to Reserve Hd qrs. cleared & trench boards laid. In evening half 6 Squad. (No 1) gun returned by reserve half section under 2/Lt G. Davis all Langton (No 2) & McCann (No 4)	

WAR DIARY or INTELLIGENCE SUMMARY

Army Form C. 2118.

3 — 11.9 C.S.

Place	Date	Hour	Summary of Events and Information	Remarks and references to Appendices
Field	8/16		C.O. visited No 1 section at night in front line with O.C. Lowland Field Co. to discuss siting of construction of permanent emplacements. Night firing emplacement on CHONNE Bvmt nearly completed. No 5 Reserve Emplacement commenced by R.E.	
	9/16		4 Officers & 15 men attended Innovation of German Flammen Werfer at NOEUX-les-MINES. Object of which was to show all ranks limitation of weapon. Report received from O.C. No 2 Section that sounds of mining near No 7 gun emplacement to be heard. This was communicated to O.C. 173 Co R.E. CATONNE Bomb Emplacement & No 5 Reserve Emplacement complete. Trench boards laid at Nos 2 & 3 Reserve Gun positions. Open emplacement in support line prepared for No 7 gun in case of accidents. No 2 Reserve Gun fired 100 rounds in short bursts on road S.E. of PUITS 16. Range 1800 x	

WAR DIARY or INTELLIGENCE SUMMARY

Army Form C. 2118.

Place	Date	Hour	Summary of Events and Information	Remarks and references to Appendices
Pits	10/3/16		C.O. visited No 2 Section on left of line & inspected new open sap & open trench in front of No 2 Gun. Arranged for working party to deepen trench leading to No 5 Reserve Emplacement. Began instruction of resting half sections in bombing & use of Mills grenades. Corrugated iron placed on roof of No 3 Emplacement, trench boards laid in Sap G, & new Nos 3 & 4 Reserve Emplacements. No 2 Reserve Gun fired till midnight on same target as previous night.	
	11/3/16		Bombing instruction continued. Night firing on same target. Continued work on roof of No 1 Emplacement, & cleaned & sand bagged walls of No 5. Nr Cronch accidentally wounded.	
	12/3/16		C.O. & L/Lyttard visited left section. Nos 5 & 6 Reserve Nos 2 Reserve Trench to No 5 Reserve Improved for 30 yds. Continued work on Nos 5, 7, & 6 & 7 Reserve Emplacements. Repairing O.P. completed. Column Slag Heaps. Began trench to Right Sap.	

WAR DIARY
INTELLIGENCE SUMMARY 3rd M.G.C.

Army Form C. 2118.

Place	Date	Hour	Summary of Events and Information	Remarks and references to Appendices
Field	12/3/16		Considerable night firing on German working parties none fired to 16 by Nos 1, 2 & 3 guns during night. Arrangements made to get more accurate fire on to their parties in future. No 2 Reserve fired on same target as before. Considerable shelling of South Eresin with rain-searching shells during day. Eg 3 mm gun of No 4 gun buried during our	
"	13/3/16		C.O. visited No 4 Section on left. No 4 gun not yet recovered owing to hostile shelling interfering with working party. 2 out of the 3 mm buried got out. Mr Molony fired. During previous night Nos 1, 2, & 3 guns fired on Pints 16 & neighbourhood & No 7 Reserve Gun on same target. No enemy working party heard after 8.30 p.m. Completed another open emplacement on Calonne trench trench no 6 N9 5 Reserve & began trench No 6 Reserve. In evening visited whole line with ringing half section. Casualties 1 man killed	
"	14/3/16		C.O. visited line & arranged fresh night firing pr units 2/Lt Langton to have ..... on to Point 11 & CORON Trenches Officer & com- trenches	

WAR DIARY or INTELLIGENCE SUMMARY — 3rd / 119 Coy

Army Form C. 2118.

Place	Date	Hour	Summary of Events and Information	Remarks and references to Appendices
H.Q.	15/3/16		Leading out of stores. During previous night No 3 gun engaged enemy working party. No 2 Reserve fired from CAIONNE during VERY lights. Post 16. the infantry in front line sending up VERY lights whenever any heavy transport on the road. No 9 Reserve fired at intervals on cross roads N10 e 44. No 4 gun was firing on + normal in No 5 alternative Emplacement.	
	16/3/16		CO visited No 1 Section on night of his + arranged for working party to finish loopholes on in No 1 emplacement, + also for another party to complete construction to No 6 Reserve. Visited No 1 again in evening to inspect emplacement in front his from Adjunct (Canna) and some night firing from Calonne Dump. Firing was received during afternoon that 3 mines were to be blown upon Southern arm of South Crater at 6.0 a.m. on 16th, arranged for Nos 2 + 3 + 4 Reserve guns to cooperate in event of enemy attempting any movement. Mines exploded successfully at 6.0 a.m. No movement by Germany.	

2449 Wt. W14957/M90 750,000 1/16 J.B.C. & A. Forms/C.2118/12.

Army Form C. 2118.

WAR DIARY
or
INTELLIGENCE SUMMARY   3rd M.G. Co.
(Erase heading not required.)

Instructions regarding War Diaries and Intelligence Summaries are contained in F. S. Regs., Part II. and the Staff Manual respectively. Title Pages will be prepared in manuscript.

Place	Date	Hour	Summary of Events and Information	Remarks and references to Appendices
Fits	16/3/16		In evening Company was relieved by 2nd M.G. Co. On relief whole Co. moved to billets in GRENAY with the object of being nearer Reserve line emplacements in event of an attack.	
Fins	17/3/16		Morning spent cleaning up & checking stores. Co. provided working party of 2 officers & 50 men for 153rd Co. & also continued 5 open emplacements in Reserve line between CALONNE ALLEY & TREIZE ALLEY	
Field	18/3/16		C.O. attended conference in morning on new Lewis Gun defence scheme in Divisional Area. Capt Rackey has taken round reserve line to be revising and to look hands over & this. Instructional training of new men begun.	
Field	19/3/16		Capt A.C. Lyttelton proceeded on 10 days leave to England. Capt Rackey – acting C.O. had round Kensington & reserve line with S.O.1 9th Div. to see the proposed sites for new M.G. Emplacements. Conference at C.R.E. H.Q. at 3 p.m. to arrange details of co-operation for work. Training continued under section officers	
Field	20/3/16		7.30 p.m. in convoy for R.E. personnel exploded a small mine between Northern & Southern arms of Double Crassier at 7.46 p.m. Working party of 100 men & 2 officers sent out at	

Army Form C. 2118.

WAR DIARY
or
INTELLIGENCE SUMMARY 3rd M.G. Coy
(Erase heading not required.)

Instructions regarding War Diaries and Intelligence Summaries are contained in F.S. Regs., Part II. and the Staff Manual respectively. Title Pages will be prepared in manuscript.

Place	Date	Hour	Summary of Events and Information	Remarks and references to Appendices
Field	21/3/16	9.0 a.m.	C.O. visited new G.O.C. 1st Div. & Brigade Comdr. and O.C. 1st DWR Bat. finally selecting sites for M.G. Emplacements. Section Officers reconnoitring known positions in Bulls Road. Morning spent by Sections in preparing for Reliefs. C.O. met C.O. 15th M.G. Coy & arranged relief.	
Field	22/3/16		Reliefs were allotted to the Coys. From 9.0 a.m. to 11.30 a.m. Interview with C.O. Wiltshire N⁰1 M.G. Coy in the LOOS Redbt. Reliefs 6.0 p.m. Relief complete 10.30 p.m. Reserve gunners & officers moved back to billets in LES BREBIS.	
Field	23/3/16		C.O. went up the line at 7.30 a.m. Work was commenced at once on Reserve Emplacements R.4, R.5, R.6, R.8 & R.9.	
Field	24/3/16		C.O. went up the line at 3.30 a.m. in moderate weather. But R.E. has turned up framework for R.4 & R.6. In the afternoon N⁰ 8 Emplacement in the COPSE was hit by a small shell & wrecked. The gun was damaged but no casualties to men.	
Field	25/3/16		Gun mounters stood to from 4.a.m to 6.30.a.m as Germans were expected to blow a mine just N. of COPSE. This did not take place. C.O. went up in afternoon. Work progressing satisfactorily in all the house emplacements especially at R.6. Where almost entire roof is filled with bullet & bombproof baulks. Own visited trenches supplemented by possibility & schedule ...	[?]Bomb ditches & 3/14 Platoon ...

Army Form C. 2118

WAR DIARY
or
INTELLIGENCE SUMMARY 3rd M.S. C"

(Erase heading not required.)

Instructions regarding War Diaries and Intelligence Summaries are contained in F. S. Regs., Part II. and the Staff Manual respectively. Title Pages will be prepared in manuscript.

Place	Date	Hour	Summary of Events and Information	Remarks and references to Appendices
In the Field	26/3/16		C.O. went up to 2/Lt Gildons in the afternoon. Work done mainly consisted in digging Traverses to or round new emplacements. Rubble carefully cleared away from entrance to Emplacements. Also numbering of guns confirmed. had line MG etc Support his MG etc. Reserve line MG etc. Received from Royal W. Regt. 2 guns from M.M.G.S arrived late at night. Returns (C.W.S.B./16) of establishments over & recently MG & MG. M.M.G. officer relieves 2/Lt McGann.	
	27/3/16		C.O. & 2/Lt Gildons went down in morning with Capt Black I.O. 1st Div, & Saw all reserve emplacements. Idea of taking COPSE into Vickers Guns given up. Material salvaged from Vickers Emplacement & brought restored. Both Vickers guns in COPSE to be replaced by Lewis with Deep Dug outs. 2/Lt Gildons leave postponed till hour of 2 2/Lt Nichr (Lean from 9/3/16) received.	
	28/3/16		2/Lt Kaye returned from leaving sign orders & took over from 2 2/Lt Cook. 3 = Lt McLean went up again. Stake on his Guns from M.M.G Officers ante relief was not approved by Div. C.O. will hand Vickers Guns to nearest schools on position to be re 9 Eastern Vickers guns. There will be 4 9 these were sent from COPSE and intervene Since M.M.G.S. have taken over 2 9 guns. 2/Lt Nichr should not except - handicap bounded 18/3/16.	
	29/3/16		C.O. went up to Line with 2/Lt Gildons in the afternoon. MG R8 R6 R8 completed. MG my satisfactory Numerous Staff reports a Rx 7 strengthen with Rubble & sandbags. Sandbags are very scarce as are also steel girders.	
	30/3/16		Officers leave hopes up is to a house in GRENAY to avoid necessity of moving up every 12 days. 2/Lt Gildons proceeds on leave to England from 3/4 to 9/4 April.	

WAR DIARY
or
INTELLIGENCE SUMMARY

(Erase heading not required.)

Army Form C. 2118

3 - M.G.C "?"

Place	Date	Hour	Summary of Events and Information	Remarks and references to Appendices
In the Field	31/3/16		C.O went round with Brigadier in the morning & selected further positions for M.G.s in support line. Precious position confirmed & one additional site selected. On way up to 2nd reliefs wounded Enemy bombards the copse between the CRATERS & especially HART'S CRATER with 5.9 shells all the morning. Considerable material damage. Our Strombos & Bererial casualties 6th Infantry. No M.G damaged. Capt A.C Lyttelton returned from leave in the evening.	
	1/4/16			

3rd MACHINE GUN COMPANY

1st to 28th APRIL 1916 MISSING

3rd Brigade.

1st Division.

3rd <u>MACHINE GUN COMPANY</u> :::   29th APRIL - <u>30th MAY 1916</u>.

WAR DIARY
or
INTELLIGENCE SUMMARY

Army Form C. 2118.

3 Bde M G Coy
Vol 475

Place	Date	Hour	Summary of Events and Information	Remarks and references to Appendices
La Brebis	29/4/16		Gas attack at about 5 a.m. The wind brought some of the gas through LOOS & MAROC, as far as Le PREUX, but not in enough strength to make wearing of gas helmet necessary. All teams in post had to wear them on two reprimands to support — very favourably on the lots. Absolute MG & MG silenced a hostile MG which had been located one wishes a Diagram working party of sappers to be throwing their wire continued work on S1 & S2 on several R E placements.	
"	30/4/16		Capt. Raikes & B' Major visited all M.G. emplacements in front line to check positions & arcs of fire for 1st Div. Positions of Lewis guns somewhat irregular & we is helping with 1st Div. instructional 11 p.m. S.O.S. right B. Lt. Bde Gun Cpl. to Small boating raid by Germans which reached our trench & Copelina Lewis gun. Party however were cut up on return party & guns manned. Enemy wire opposite N front was 2/Lt Love & party Helped 2/Lt He Levere & Gibaud with rescue team. Trench to R7 partly flood. Continued movement of Vickers trench at CORDIALE AVENUE.	
"	1/5/16		Quiet day, weather very hot. The team of MG down to have knocked out 1st party of Germans making off with its Lewis gun. Began repairing of dividing (Chiefly) trench to R5 (Maroc) Combined evacuation of MIDDLE ALLEY emplacement CORDIALE AVENUE Compartis - foot of trench.	

Army Form C. 2118.

WAR DIARY
or
INTELLIGENCE SUMMARY
(Erase heading not required.)

Instructions regarding War Diaries and Intelligence Summaries are contained in F. S. Regs., Part II. and the Staff Manual respectively. Title Pages will be prepared in manuscript.

Place	Date	Hour	Summary of Events and Information	Remarks and references to Appendices
Le Tr. obus	1/5/16		Capt. Rourke visited line & Lieut. Stimpson & Snipers. N of LOOS CRASSIER. At 2 am there was a short N.9 + Snipers. N of LOOS CRASSIER. At 2 am there was a short bombardment of the front + comm trenches in the 14 B¹s sector followed by an alarm of gas, which was false. Continued work on both Queen & emplacements & on the Lens R⁴ samp. 3 dug outs at HQ finished 10 yds N of Alphonse, third trench to R⁴ (Maroc), enlarged + deepened. NORE ALLEY P.b. Sanitary conditions in Loos becoming rather bad, all stone men were employed in clearing up	
	2/5/16		Staff bay & McCann returned 1/Lt Cook + Joyce + H formerly Adams Ashton continued work on HQ dug out + Lens Road, also cleans up new in Loos. 1⁵ B⁵ exploded a mine under British Crown at Knee made a small raid afterwards (screening our prisoners to be prisoners in one shows 26⁶ Reg⁴. to be still holding crater hour of the lie.	
	3/5/16		Enclosure shelling by Germans above. 3.45 a.m. Gas gone to cellars moved into support, had emplacements at E1. E2. Work continued on LENS R⁴ + trench to RO(Maroc) Junker and 19 men carried to Middle Alley. Infantry carrying party Lt Hewett proceeded to leave to England	

Army Form C. 2118.

WAR DIARY
or
INTELLIGENCE SUMMARY

(Erase heading not required.)

Instructions regarding War Diaries and Intelligence Summaries are contained in F. S. Regs., Part II. and the Staff Manual respectively. Title Pages will be prepared in manuscript.

Place	Date	Hour	Summary of Events and Information	Remarks and references to Appendices
LES BREBIS	5/5/16		Nos. 2 & 3 in front line carried out some night firing on Roads running S.W. from Enemy line of DOUBLE CRASSIER. Quiet day except for enemy shelling of HAYMARKET. Work was continued on all emplacements and dug-outs in front. Remainder of Ride carried on Tristan Alley. Emplacement & emplacement roofs & finishes except to the opening of Kloosters. Capt Rankin visited line in evening.	
	6.5.16.		2/Lt Cooke & 2/Lt Joyce relieved 2/Lt McCann & 2/Lt Gilland respectively. Considerable activity in part of enemy Snipers & bombers & Machine guns at night. Our German aeroplane flew over loot at 4.30 a.m. 9 hostile Shelling began immediately afterwards. P.G. was hit by a trench mortar bomb and emplacement slightly damaged. Work continued mostly on dug-outs.	
	7.5.16		Front line guns engaged enemy working parties during twilight and also fired at sniper's flashes all along line. Communication trenches and reserve line were heavily shelled during today. Work continued on Tristan Alley, etc. 2/Lt McCann went up to ----- in afternoon. 2/Lt on Inside Avenue, RS/Major gall Roos dug-outs. 2/Lt Rankin & 2/Lt Gilland went to reconnoitre Kristo Alley & Capt Section. C.O. developed influenza and 2/Lt Bennett returned from leave.	
	8.5.16		C.O. to Hospital. Capt Rankin arranged relief not O.C. 2/16 in afternoon. Work continued on Dug-outs in loos. 2/Lt Gilland took up working party to NEUVELLY in afternoon to complete unsortes on supports to NEUVE ALLEY.	

2449 Wt. W14957/Mgo 750,000 1/16 J.B.C. & A. Forms/C.2118/12.

WAR DIARY or INTELLIGENCE SUMMARY

Army Form C. 2118.

Place	Date	Hour	Summary of Events and Information	Remarks and references to Appendices
L.F.S. BREFUS	9/5/16		2/1st Bn nth went up to Loos in afternoon to supervise relief of Loos DEFENCES. Horses M.G. took Crosses in shells into S.G's during morning. Relief by 2 WL Coy. & M.G. Sector & we relieved the 4 Coys of 2nd LF in Loos Defences. Relief not complete till 2.20 a.m. Coy marches & Enemy inactive.	
	10/5/16		Morning spent cleaning up billets & otherwise, jumble etc. In afternoon inspected & arranged for improvement of framework in North Alley. Cmpt. Bonning allotted work & made canvas up Kllan Cup forward.	
	11/5/16		2/Lt Glenn took party up & more of work in North Alley. Framework completed through to entire about mid day. Heavy shells started up for EC left & started up N. breve ferres of Platoon H.Q. quadre. 1F's BREFUS Car Sunday till about 8 p.m. Then Loos been hit too a turned by 4.2's specially dumped. 2/Lt Cook firing), 2/Bennett & Joyce in return Rifles. Quarter- masters QMS Slight damages. Our casualties 2/ABennett took up party burns to RB at night. 2/Lt Killern proceeded (cook).	
	12/5/16		Aftn. parts to GRENAY. C.O. and several others live to MAROC looker our O.G./87 Co. to morrow. Very slack day. Atmosphere now going in to Scurrey. Heard Cpl & Hill had gone to twenty three horses tin within. 2/Lt Joyce took a party to complete River ARP by night.	
	13/—		C.O. went up to CORDIAKE AVENUE w/Capt Major to meet. Railway Churches next control (Left) meet by — Rumble Quilter into yarn.	

WAR DIARY or INTELLIGENCE SUMMARY

Army Form C. 2118.

(Erase heading not required.)

Instructions regarding War Diaries and Intelligence Summaries are contained in F. S. Regs., Part II. and the Staff Manual respectively. Title Pages will be prepared in manuscript.

Place	Date	Hour	Summary of Events and Information	Remarks and references to Appendices
H.Q. B. Sec.	14.5.16		2/1st Barnett took Church Parade in the morning. 2/1st look took parade in private. Lieut D. Burns Hulme & Rev. reported. Coy returned 1st Coy to March coster. Shooting at 6.30 p.m. 2/1st Jones & Greaves to trenches. 2/1st Barnett moved up to relieve them. Employment at R.15, S.O.S. message rec'd at 9.30. Guns in action. Had a small land N. of lost Crater &c. Lt. Hewitt returned from leave.	
	15th		Colonel round the line. Lt. Staff Capton to H.Q. making alterations & made by staff. All arrangements for relief of No. 4 guns in hope by H/5 R.G. were left by rail to Mont [Abbey] Practically complete. Rendezvous to Cordiale Avenue Carried out. 2/1st look succeeded in Leave.	
	16th		All preparations for Relief. Look proceeded on guns in CORDIALE AVENUE. M.G.3 was heavily shelled during afternoon. Rail was carried to Cordiale Avenue.	
	17		Mr. M. Carr left from Dedfor and took over R.8 & R.9. New trench informer own front line guns.	
	18		Co. went on leave to England. 2/Lt. Cornish reports for duty and was posted to No. 2 Section. Gunner Weir Carries up to Cordiale Avenue. 2/Lt. Barnett returned Y'prge	

WAR DIARY or INTELLIGENCE SUMMARY

Army Form C. 2118.

(Erase heading not required.)

Instructions regarding War Diaries and Intelligence Summaries are contained in F. S. Regs., Part II. and the Staff Manual respectively. Title Pages will be prepared in manuscript.

Place	Date	Hour	Summary of Events and Information	Remarks and references to Appendices
Hebuterne	19		2/Lt Conrad alured 2/Lt Helsord and 20 men of 1/5 hrs returned to unit. 1 cope men of 1/5 hrs returned to unit	
	20		Germans raided our frontline near M.G/3 - 3 of Double Coys. and succeeded in capturing one of our M.G./3 returning with M-G/3	
	21st		C.O. went round the line to ascertain the cause. Two yolk day overlap - unable to find any the accurate views - Found 4 todies of Gunners. Claimed to have been killed by M.G.	
	22nd		2/Lt Barnett relieved 2/Lt Pope... Party from Infantry Camas left Hebuterne to Sh + Orchard Avenue. 2/Lt McCann returned permanent	
	23rd		CO. went to Brigade Office to give reason for loss of M.G.3. 2/Lt Geloader went round the trenches and examined proposed moves on dugouts	

2/Lt McCann Peters of Comd

2449 Wt. W14957/M90 750,000 1/16 J.B.C. & A. Forms/C.2118/12.

Army Form C. 2118.

WAR DIARY
or
INTELLIGENCE SUMMARY
(Erase heading not required.)

Place	Date	Hour	Summary of Events and Information	Remarks and references to Appendices
	24th		CO went round the line with Supplements in West Alley, Keep St & in Edgware Rd. Keep St. Party carried cement to Cord Rue Avenue. 54 completed.	
	25th		Arranged with 2nd Corp 2nd in Command about relief. Lt Gelderd visited HQrs. - Interview with GOC. 'D' were 109 B Aug/3	
	26th		Relieved by 2nd Corp. Moved to Billets in BULLY GRENAY. GRENAY having become very inhabitable owing to shell fire	
	27th		Morning spent in cleaning up guns. No Reel-lieut for a recruit march. Cole to Slaws to came at 5pm. & out came B Supplements at 6pm. She was funded by 7pm	
	28th		Still standing to & manning B emplacement	
	29th		Still standing to & manning B Supplements. 4th Gelderd attended to proceed on a Court Martial	
	30th		No change as B Supplements still filled. 4th Gelderd returned	

2449 Wt. W14957/M90 750,000 1/16 J.B.C. & A. Forms/C.2118/12.

3rd Brigade.

1st Division.

3rd MACHINE GUN COMPANY :::: JUNE 1916.

Army Form C. 2118.

WAR DIARY
or
INTELLIGENCE SUMMARY
(Erase heading not required.)

Instructions regarding War Diaries and Intelligence Summaries are contained in F. S. Regs., Part II. and the Staff Manual respectively. Title Pages will be prepared in manuscript.

Place	Date	Hour	Summary of Events and Information	Remarks and references to Appendices
Bully May Pit	31		Guns withdrawn from "B" emplacements. Capt W Mallet returned from leave.	
	1		Spent cleaning up guns etc. Mules were marched to Les Brebis for bath.	
	2.9		C.O. went round CALONNE Sector with O.C. No 1 Coy, on - C. Corps and arranged relief. The guns moved back to main "B" emplacements	
	3rd		The Company relieved No 1 Coy in CALONNE Sector. Five guns in front line (No Emplacements) 6 Guns support line - (5 emplacements) Lt Geddards & Named blue Reserve Line - Spool emplacements. Lt Goddards & Named blue. 3rd C.O. & Advent Officers visited round the line in the morning	
	4.		New M.G Scheme brought out by division necessitating withdrawal of 4 Vickers Guns from front line	
	5		C.O. went round to study new scheme - discussed same with Brigade & the officers. A quiet day except for heavy shelling & heavy mortaring of our front & support line area Railway	
	6		C.O. went round with C.J. O.C 3rd Brigade - Germans very quiet as result of strong retaliation by our T. Ms. started work on S4, S6.	
	7		J. Jewell went round the line & inspected work - 1 Officer (Mr Savage) & 9 O.R. reinforcements arrived from Base. J. McCann relieved Lt Bagnell	

2449 Wt. W14957/M90 750,000 1/16 J.B.C. & A. Forms/C.2118/12.

WAR DIARY
or
INTELLIGENCE SUMMARY

(Erase heading not required.)

Army Form C. 2118.

Place	Date	Hour	Summary of Events and Information	Remarks and references to Appendices
Bully	8th		C.O. round with G.O.C. Divn. Alterations approved & work on all our positions the Statue - of - Savage Leave fr devilar Kealnemp	
	9th		Co + L. Hewlett round trenches in afternoon to arrange work St heaps finished. Capt. W.T. Raines appointed C.O. Lt. W.G. Hewell " " 2nd in Command	
	10th		Major W took working fort. E.R.3 with morning Lt. Corniot ambulance work in afternoon. Work took the Sappers during the same a Thurs. C.O. & Hewett went round in afternoon to receive & inspt/all emplacements in right sector.	
	11			
	13		B went round with Rev Hugh & arranged memory blufts in tumel man (Lt Junett) to take pogs in afternoon. Rev Hugh's company Heavy rain had stopped all work & excavators at R.3 had subsides - 2/Lt Corniot returned Lt Getaad & Lt McCann returned to Lt Joyce	

Army Form C. 2118.

WAR DIARY
or
INTELLIGENCE SUMMARY

(Erase heading not required.)

Instructions regarding War Diaries and Intelligence Summaries are contained in F. S. Regs., Part II. and the Staff Manual respectively. Title Pages will be prepared in manuscript.

Place	Date	Hour	Summary of Events and Information	Remarks and references to Appendices
Bucy	12		C.O. went round line, work begun on C-3 behind flag trap; gun & tear Newhall's new line. C.O. & Sgt. Mead completed tunnelling continued	
	13		R1 & R1. Major J. R E. Ktrick – S4 complete hurricane Newell went round & inspected C3, S7, S6; work progressing satisfactorily. Y-Savage rejoined – S4 shinghiened	
	14		C.O went round with G.O.C.'s surge and Major Pursey & L.F. I inspected Reserve emplacements before line of tunnelling & to Further Jap at R3, obliged to give up idea of tunnelling & to Continue by –	
	15		Y-Savage attacked Lt Cornwall for instruction. M.S.7 moves Ones position made by R E & becomes no. 8 C.O. & Newell round line see reserve emplacements & M.S.8	
	16		C.O. to Support line, S7 also to same work S6 complete R.E. slow work on R1 – C/3 continued & was of great value Behind it	
	17		2nd Savage (afterfire to instruction. In 5, 8 (new position) flew up by shell fire – Of aircraft regulation) Lt Newell went round line	

2449 Wt. W14957/M90 750,000 1/16 J.B.C. & A. Forms/C.2118/12.

WAR DIARY
or
INTELLIGENCE SUMMARY

(Erase heading not required.)

Army Form C. 2118.

Place	Date	Hour	Summary of Events and Information	Remarks and references to Appendices
	18		C.O. went round reserve line of MAROC section with G.S.O.I. T. Div. Check loopholes & fields of fire - All new loopholes retained at 1 foot to clear parapet. Left Church Parade team TM actions on airstrip line near Railway - Fleet of 16 hostile aeroplanes flew over lines, 1 brought down	
	19		C.O. with V.C. Geldard around left-sector checked learning for Range Cards. Enemy T.Ms very active near S3 Sq. Open emplacements wires to MGs, Sq, initial Construction complete. Leaflet of this & S6 ranges of right Khan Graa. Range Cards made from map in afternoon. Lt Barrett relieved Lt Cornish Lt McCann relieved Lt Joyce - Lt Savage left for Gymnasium Course	
	20		C.O. round line in morning will map hill as Eng C. Dugouts started at S1, S6 R3, - S2 pt complete - Lt Hewett & Lt Gellers flew in afternoon.	

Place	Date	Hour	Summary of Events and Information	Remarks and references to Appendices
BULLY	21st		C.O and Lt. Hewett went round trenches and made careful notes of all work done during period of leave; so as to hand over plan of work to 151st Brigade	
	22		C.O to HQ 1st Divisional HQ with morning - Lt Hewett E civil. C.3 & C4 C.O arranged with No1 Coy to cover to Noeux-les-Mines for a Symmetric Course.	
	23		C.O. and Lt. Hewett round divisional area and sited 4 guns on the high ground and withdrew fire on overhead and indirect fire on back areas of the German positions. The Coy were relieved by No 1 Coy & returned to BULLY. Parties went out under C.O. & Lt Hewett to work on proposed position. Bearings were taken	
	24		C.O. Major Lindsay M.C. and Lieut. Field and sited four more emplacements for overhead fire in more and on the high ground near NORTH STREET. Working parties under Lt. McCann and Carnie made these during night.	

WAR DIARY or INTELLIGENCE SUMMARY

Army Form C. 2118.

Place	Date	Hour	Summary of Events and Information	Remarks and references to Appendices
BULLY	26		C.O Spent whole day in works up out-bearing, angles, and ranges, for use in connection with Divisional scheme issued 22nd. Guns moved up and occupied emplacements under Lt Barrett and 2t Cornish. During the night guns fired on base lines of Noewong & Each Gun firing about 100 rounds. There was no retaliation. The C.O and Lt Steward went up to various guns during the night.	
	26		Guns fired by day as follows: Each Gun fired at stated times 6 times during the day. They fired 280 rounds per line thus making about 2000 rounds per gun in all. Target various billets behind the German lines. By Night: at 11p - 11.20, 11.40, 12, 12.10, 12.45 am 12.55, 1.30 2, 2.20. Guns opened on various billets and areas. Very little retaliation was experienced. Special item: Shots fired rapid on to various billets between 1.20 - 1.3 am 1.27 to 1.30 am 1.35 - 1.38 am	

WAR DIARY or INTELLIGENCE SUMMARY

Army Form C. 2118.

Place	Date	Hour	Summary of Events and Information	Remarks and references to Appendices
27th			Guns fired by day as follows - Gun A on billets 6 lines Total 1800 rounds. Gun B fired the same amount, tri-traverses and vertically searched. Gun C " " " " " " Gun D " " " " " " Gun E fired seven lines on enemy billets Gun F " " " " " " Gun G " " " " " " Guns F & G fired on neighbouring towns & billets. By night: All guns fired at - 10; 10.15p, 10.35, 11.5p, 11.20p, 11.50p, 12.10 am, 12.20-12.40, 1 a, 2 am. All guns were searching roads. In connection with an operation all guns fired rapid on the following lines 1.20 - 1.23 am, 1.27 - 1.30 am, 1.35 - 1.38. Targets: Billets, Roads near Billets, and Cutaways to Ammunition trench	

Army Form C. 2118.

WAR DIARY
or
INTELLIGENCE SUMMARY
(Erase heading not required.)

Instructions regarding War Diaries and Intelligence Summaries are contained in F. S. Regs., Part II. and the Staff Manual respectively. Title Pages will be prepared in manuscript.

Place	Date	Hour	Summary of Events and Information	Remarks and references to Appendices

T8			Guns fired by day as follows
			Gun A on 3a 2b (initials)
			    B — 10 3b (initials)
			    C — 3b (")
			    D — 12 (")
			    — 12 — 9 (")
			    F — 5b (")
			    G — 5b (")
			    — 11 — 9
			        } About strewn by day 0170
			          about 70 rounds a gun
			
			By night- Guns deneches Roads
			A gun Target-1 }
			B — 5 }
			C — 9 } About 70 rounds
			D — 12 } a little per gun.
			E — 11
			F — 19
			G — 20
			Guns retaliation by the enemy	

WAR DIARY
or
INTELLIGENCE SUMMARY

Army Form C. 2118.

Place	Date	Hour	Summary of Events and Information	Remarks and references to Appendices
	28.	By day	Bullet Target	32
		4a – 5a	B & D gun fires	26 a & b
		5a – 6a	A B C D	29 a x 30
		6a – 7a	B x D	
		Argren	A	29
		" "	C	30
		6p – 7p	A B C D	27 x 28
		7p – 8p	A & D	31
		10.30a – 1.30p	m E, F G	
		4p – 5p	F & G gun	33
		"	M gun	30
		7p – 8p	E F G H	31
		By night		E gun target 11 roads
		A gun target No 4 bullets	F " " 19	
		" "	G " roads 20	
		C " " 1	H " " 19	
		Combined sight has been when possible. None elsewhere.		

3rd Bde.
1st Div.

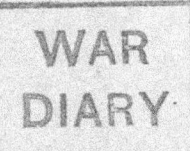

3rd MACHINE GUN COMPANY

JULY 1916.

Army Form C. 2118.

WAR DIARY
or
INTELLIGENCE SUMMARY
(Erase heading not required.)

No 3 Coy Machine Gun Corps.

Vol 6

Place	Date	Hour	Summary of Events and Information	Remarks and references to Appendices
Gezaincourt	2/7	—	Divisional activities ceased at midnight — owing to some late warning of withdrawing guns. 2/Lt Hewett to Hospital: travel fever. Coy remains late ready/throw at Stonehill.	
	3/7	—	Up of 120th Coy came up and went round line — Re-crews at Gezaincourt. John Stone arr being relieved by 120 Coy tomorrow.	
	4/7	—	120 arrived about 11 am and Coy moved off by sections. No 1 Section has orders for relief with late and came on a independent-ly. He was Blew. G.S. wagon for other stores went ahead. Wister ain to BRUAY. Arriving 5 pm no additional transport trains exhausting.	
	5/7	—	Warned early of probable move again. Refilled at 8 am and got orders at 11.30 pm No 3 Sect 1am No 4 6am. No 2 Zero CHOQUES STATION 6am.	
	6/7	—	Brig ace moved in 5 trains at 3 hour intervals starting 10 am. Coy H Q arrived CHOQUES STATION army are not leaving Head allocation in zero till 9 am. Delaying bgy VIENE COURT H.Q. arrived at Doullens at 5pm. and marched to No 3 Sect 1am No 4 6am. No 2 bivouacked for the night on the road.	

WAR DIARY
or
INTELLIGENCE SUMMARY

Army Form C. 2118.

Place	Date	Hour	Summary of Events and Information	Remarks and references to Appendices
Ismailia	2/7		Divisional artillery bombard at midnight - some Turkish villages set on fire - enemy light lifts and swept field over. Cry marched into outskirts of Ismailia.	
	3/7		Rep. of 1st Corps came up and went round lines - Pairins cheer. Turks shown as being about 6,000. Cry Commander	
	4/7		R.O arrived about 11 am and Cry moved off by sections. No 1 section had transport for whole cry. Little advance before 1 Q.S. wagon for detail 9 times a second party, which in pursuit, to TORUAY. Arrived early at hotels more again. Ovalde - Refill & etc from and got own horses throwing Zero CHOQUES STATION Camp.	
	5/7		Routes were in 3 hours of horses. Cry HQ. arrived CHOQUES STATION upon Francis. Arrived Ville a lieu in Zero test gun Belward at - Drillage a tep and has advanced by VIENA COURT for Commodor at 11:30 pm 1st. Dat 1 one may 1 am no 3 marched on the troops -	

WAR DIARY or INTELLIGENCE SUMMARY

Army Form C. 2118.

Place	Date	Hour	Summary of Events and Information	Remarks and references to Appendices
PIQUIGNY	7/7		No 2 Sect. joined us at 1 pm. Coy Moved off at 5.45 hours. No 2 Sect (Stytton) in the preparing. 2/Lt Bakeley developed mumps this aernoon had he dropped at 7 AM on line of march. Got to RAINNEVILLE at 7 am & billeted in very good barns.	
Rainneville	8/7		C.O. & ₤₤ Coy at RAINNEVILLE at 7 pm. Coy moved at 9.30 p to FRANVILLERS getting into billets at 3 AM.	
FRANVILLERS	9/7		Slept all day but no orders to move. HQ in afternoon	
"	10/7		Moved off at 5.45 pm for ALBERT — getting in 10 pm	
ALBERT	11/7		C.O. with Lt BARRETT & Lt Cornier reconnoitred the "line" of division	
	12/7		Lt Jewett rejoined; C.O. & Lt Jewett to RAINVILLE ? Behind "B" Court. 2/Lt Savage gave over this O.P.	

2449 Wt. W14957/M90 750,000 1/16 J.B.C. & A. Forms/C.2118/12.

WAR DIARY
or
INTELLIGENCE SUMMARY

(Erase heading not required.)

Army Form C. 2118.

Instructions regarding War Diaries and Intelligence Summaries are contained in F.S. Regs., Part II. and the Staff Manual respectively. Title Pages will be prepared in manuscript.

Place	Date	Hour	Summary of Events and Information	Remarks and references to Appendices
?	7/7		Recd. Self went to see Bn. Coy moved off at 4.45. Horses & Det. left with no. 1 Bakery developed mumps. Coys horses stopped at 7AM on line of march Buttooshe. Had an Grm Barrage Raismsville.	
Raismsville	8/7		C.O. & [crossed out] ALBERT to see the country – got back at 9.30 & Bn at Ramsville at 7pm. Bn moved at 3 AM. Transport & stores but Battn— at your own on Bivouac Staff all day but in clear weather HQ in afternoon.	
Ramsville	9/7		Moved off at 5.45 fm to ALBERT – Getting in touch with	
"	10/7		nothing J. Bassett & formia recommaces Sn Tm	
LARRT	11/7		J Lomon	
	12/7		J Smith offms & Co & J Ashurt to Flamencouret me Belched to E'COURT at Pelago. gave own our the Q.F.	

2449 Wt. W14957/M90 750,000 1/16 J.B.C. & A. Forms/C.2118/12.

Army Form C. 2118.

WAR DIARY
or
INTELLIGENCE SUMMARY
(Erase heading not required.)

Instructions regarding War Diaries and Intelligence Summaries are contained in F. S. Regs., Part II. and the Staff Manual respectively. Title Pages will be prepared in manuscript.

Place	Date	Hour	Summary of Events and Information	Remarks and references to Appendices
ALBERT	13/7		Closed by all as; more P.T. by Lt. Savage. Heavy bombardment at night on right. Preps along on advance on German second system.	
	14/7		Col. & Fellows tree at No. 1 Coy with a view to ratify – stood by all day. Lt. Hewett to a Court Martial. Lt. Rewett to a conference at Bde H.Q. Orders from rec'd re copy got up to O.C. 2. 9.30. Number to 2 & 4 sections in CONTALMAISON. The Villa & LOWER WOOD (Front Line) 2 guns of No. 3 m. sup post. Remaining 5 in reserve with Bn H.Q. Relief completed at 5 am.	
Jula	15/7		C.O. & Lt. Hewett to MAMETZ WOOD 178th HQ. Brigade arr. Bombing all aft on German 2nd System N.W. of BAZENTIN LE PETIT WOOD – Successful attack and No. 1 section sent up to assist in control station.	

Place	Date	Hour	Summary of Events and Information	Remarks and references to Appendices
MESSINES	6/7		[illegible handwriting - largely illegible due to faded pencil]	
	7/7			

WAR DIARY
or
INTELLIGENCE SUMMARY

Army Form C. 2118.

Place	Date	Hour	Summary of Events and Information	Remarks and references to Appendices
Fees	15/7		Otters held up at 2.30 pm after again of 250 yds. Anoth attack organised at 5.30. also held up but Nº1 Sect got 2 gun targets in open & knocked about 80 Germans. Bn & MG Ho to Bn CONTALMAISON	
CONTALMAISON	16/7		Given a general use of plan for night attack Bn. to attack 2nd System between POZIERES & PB-LE-SP	
		(1.00): Zero 12 mdn 16/17. MB arrett & MB Sect detailed to work after left flank facing POZIERES & keep down any reflast fire or confuse attack. 2/Lt SAVAGE (No1) & MB moved up from ALBERT, MAnnett bit followed by heavy (Shrapnel) BLACK-WATCH alley up positions at BLACK-WATCH alley after bombardment. Bombardment attack at 2 am 16/17 - Everywhere successful - 2 guns from CONTALMAISON VILLA moved up under Lt McLaren to CONTALMAISON. Men owing 2 guns of Nº4 + 2 guns of Nº1 Sec under 2/Lt Martin PUICH.	
	17/7			

WAR DIARY or INTELLIGENCE SUMMARY

Army Form C. 2118.

Place	Date	Hour	Summary of Events and Information	Remarks and references to Appendices
	7/7		0.7 a.m. Held up at 2.30 p.m. after 2 guns got up. Rifle attack organized at 5.30. N° 1 Sect got 2 good targets on our front about 80. German and Bos. 2 M.G. H.Q. to be at CONTALMAISON	
CONTALMAISON	16/7		Guns in general area B. 8 for support attack B2. to attack outly system. Relieved POZIÈRES & B-S-S. (MOD.) Zero 12 mdr 16/17. M3 ment + M3 Sect Lt. BARRETT + M3 Sect. We ought to start off without being spotted to get down any reinforst guns. MG's on our right left about 11 gge moved up from ALBERT & Lt. SAVAGE (m.) followed by Heavy Schrapnel + Rifle not up position we BLACK - WATCH Alley. Bombardment about launches.	
	17/7		At 1 am on a 16/17 - Every were successful - 2 guns Last M.G. bombard then enemy 2 gun N° 4 + 2 guns from CONTALMAISON with moved by centre of MALTESE CROSS. It up to stite M. then enemy 2 gun N° 4 + 2 guns N° 2 with to Copse + Rifle at CONTALMAISON with M.G. to MAMETZ WOOD	

WAR DIARY or INTELLIGENCE SUMMARY

Army Form C. 2118.

Place	Date	Hour	Summary of Events and Information	Remarks and references to Appendices
CONTALMAISON			Man: One of McCanns guns out of action and replaced by gun from Villa. Casualties: 1 Off. 4 O.R. wounded; 1 O.R. Killed (gas) a.m. Harassing by shells during day — an attack anticipated by demolition left at to L/Cpl Powells gun Knocked out — 1 OR Killed 3 wounded — Gas Shells — Enemy Barrage heard. Coy just relieved by Rants in evening — moves from a MARTINPUICH Shelters. Very quiet night; all OR1 slipped.	
O.B. 1	18/		No operations during day; Germ artillery fairly active on our front line: specially on Right when Germans were witnessed counter attack. B-le — at night — Bn relieved by 2 Bn. Coy moved Back to OB1. adjoining Relief complete by 10.30 p.m.	
	19/		Day spent in resting. Cleaning up guns etc: damaged guns repaired. Row stopped Tuesday, February 18th — Back to BEDRUIT on Bruges Recruits this BECOURT in evening. Nothing doing all day — relieved by Lancs in evening. AUSTRACK to ALBERT	58
MAKSE REDOUBT	24/			
ALBERT	(9)		Spent day cleaning and resting. Conference at B.Q. HQ in afternoon. W. C.S. Ships attached for hour fr. aug. from 1/5 W.B.	
	22		Day spent resting — moves into support in SAUSAGE VALLY	
		01730	in Support	
	23		Owing to operations being unsuccessful we moved back at 12 Noon & a quiet Evening and relief given in the line	

WAR DIARY or INTELLIGENCE SUMMARY

Army Form C. 2118.

Place	Date	Hour	Summary of Events and Information	Remarks and references to Appendices
Contalmaison	24		Relief completed 5.30 am. 1 Sect. in tr. Linie, 2 Sect in CONTALMAISON 1 Sect reserve. Quiet day – attack by Bns in MUNSTER ALLEY in the evening. Talks over from 4 – 5 pm.	
	25		A quiet day. Saw for a Strong counter attack on our left. No 4 Sect relieved No 3 in front line. Attack by Welsh on front 4.1 at night.	
	26		Walsh & Anzacs continued bomb attack on MUNSTER ALLEY all day. No Sect. got decent small targets. Relieved by 68 Cy in the evening and went to MILLENCOURT into Bivouacs	
	27		all Troops of division on grounds 48 hrs rest – Conference at Bde Hd qts.	
	28		No hrs on day	
	29			
	30		Training under Section arrangements.	
	31		CHURCH parade under C.O. Evening 1 x 4 Sect night operation – got suspects. Taking census in rest – Taking census continued. Drafts in afternoon	

Army Form C. 2118.

WAR DIARY
or
INTELLIGENCE SUMMARY
(Erase heading not required.)

Instructions regarding War Diaries and Intelligence Summaries are contained in F. S. Regs., Part II. and the Staff Manual respectively. Title Pages will be prepared in manuscript.

Place	Date	Hour	Summary of Events and Information	Remarks and references to Appendices
Lesars	24		Relief completed 5.10 am. 1 Coy in trenches, 3 Coys in CONTALMAISON. "Z" reserve against enemy attack 2 Bn/s in MINSTER ALLEY in the evening Falls away 4 pm - 5 pm	
	25		A quiet day. Saw for a time connets attack on our left No 4 Coy self find No 3 in front line. Attack 5 "effies" on prism. 4.1 artillery bombardment old set on MINSTER	
	26		Visited & bushes lor(unerd) point. No fact Bgr. Durnal small Targets ALLEY all day. Relieved 18 Cov in the evening and took to MILLENCOURT into Bivouacs	
	27		All Troops of division found as to rest - Conference at Bge HdR rest of	
	28		Nothing on day	
	29			
	30		Trained and made scheme of movements	
	31		Church Parad to Divisional General evening 1 am set night operation tr company exercises resp	

3rd Brigade.
1st Division.

—————

3rd BRIGADE

MACHINE GUN COMPANY

AUGUST 1 9 1 6

Army Form C. 2118.

WAR DIARY
or
INTELLIGENCE SUMMARY 3rd M.G. Coy. Vol 7
(Erase heading not required.)

Instructions regarding War Diaries and Intelligence Summaries are contained in F.S. Regs., Part II. and the Staff Manual respectively. Title Pages will be prepared in manuscript.

Place	Date	Hour	Summary of Events and Information	Remarks and references to Appendices
MILLENCOURT	AUG 1915 1st		Parade in morning consisting mostly of drill for the afternoon's inspection. Afternoon G.O.C. III Corps inspects the Brigade on the big Parade ground.	
	2nd		Training continued with section arrangements.	
	3rd		Weather getting too hot for much midday work. Parades in the morning of all 11 a.m. No 2 & 3 sections did night operations in HENENCOURT WOOD	
	4th		Company has batter allotted 6th — 11 a.m. — 1 p.m. Div! Sports in the afternoon.	
	5th		Training continued — Section in the attack in open warfare.	
	6th		Brigade Church Parade 11 a.m. in the Parade ground. Very hot weather continuing parades were done in morning up till 11 a.m. and again in evening after 6.0 p.m. A certain amount of sickness in the company mainly diarrhoea & the condition of men walks cant which was noticed the weekly inspection.	
	7th			
	8th		Company out to the morning on a scheme between SENLIS & MILLENCOURT	
	9th		Training continued.	

2449 Wt. W14957/M90 750,000 1/16 J.B.C. & A. Forms/C.2118/12.

Army Form C. 2118.

WAR DIARY
or
INTELLIGENCE SUMMARY 3rd M.G. Coy
(Erase heading not required.)

Place	Date	Hour	Summary of Events and Information	Remarks and references to Appendices
MILLENCOURT	Aug 10		Training in the morning. 3rd Bde Horse Show in the afternoon.	
	11th		Training by sections in the morning. Evening Officers & N.C.O.'s in their own + Indicator recognition of targets.	
	12th		Whole Company out all night on a night scheme. 3 sections on outpost + one section attacking.	
	13th		Some training in the morning. Reorganisation of sections ready for going up into the line.	
	14th		Orders arrived re moving up ↑ it Sick. Sgt Spul in cleaning up Gunners etc & in packing up. Lt S.H. Gelaced to Hospital Sick	
BECOURT	15th		Coy. moved off from MILLENCOURT 9.30 a.m by transport road + Kit over MAXSE REDOUBT near BECOURT from 110th M.G. Coy about 11.20 a.m. Coy. is vacuum 1st + 2nd Coys in the line. 2/Lt W.J. McCann to hospital Sick.	
	16th		Very wet day, men are living in little dug outs & shelters.	
	17th		C.O & Lt Hewitt went up to reconnoitre the line between HIGHWOOD & BAZENTIN -/15- PETIT with a view to relieving the 15th Coy. Did Physical training in Coy afternoon for 1 hour.	

Army Form C. 2118.

WAR DIARY
or
INTELLIGENCE SUMMARY 3rd Coy M.G.C.

(Erase heading not required.)

Place	Date	Hour	Summary of Events and Information	Remarks and references to Appendices
BECOURT	18.		Lt W.G. HEWETT appointed C.O. 6th M.G. Coy. left 1st Company during the morning. This left the Company with only 5 Officers including 1st Staff attached.	
	19.		No orders re relief arrived during morning. Capt. Stanley by is here. Lt K.V. Barrett to Hospital Sick. 2/Lt Joyce went up to the line in the evening to arrange details about taking over this from 100th Brigade. Relieved out about 10 p.m. with orders to entrain at relieve at 6 a.m. next morning. Four Officers joined the Company from M.G. Heavy Course at 6 p.m. 2/Lt R.B. BAKER 3rd S. Staffs " T. MORGAN 5th R. Scotts " J. FRASER 6th Seaforths " W.L. CAMPBELL 5th Essex Regt.	
HIGHWOOD BAZENTIN -LE-PETIT	20.		C.O. went up at 2 a.m. to arrange about guides &c. Company moved off at 3.30 a.m. & arrived at new 2nd Coy H.Q. at 5.45 a.m. Relief completed by 10.30 a.m. No 2 Sect: with 2/Lt Avent to left — 2 guns in 3 sect under 1/Lt Fraser — No 1 Sect under 2/Lt Morgan — 2 guns in 3 sect on Right. No 4 Sect in Reserve. Very heavy shelling all day. Our 9 hrs/ sect. guns knocked out by Enemy shell 1.30 p.m. Casualties 1 O.R. killed. 1 O.R. wounded.	

Army Form C. 2118.

WAR DIARY
or
INTELLIGENCE SUMMARY   2nd R.M.S. Bn
(Erase heading not required.)

Instructions regarding War Diaries and Intelligence Summaries are contained in F. S. Regs., Part II. and the Staff Manual respectively. Title Pages will be prepared in manuscript.

Place	Date	Hour	Summary of Events and Information	Remarks and references to Appendices
HIGH WOOD TO BAZENTIN -LE - PETIT	Aug 21st		C.O. went round left section of line in early morning. Trenches in very bad state from shell fire. Continuous shelling. Communication trenches practicable. Tally up rations and water about 5 a.m. when it is comparatively quiet. Very heavy shelling again during afternoon. Casualties 2 O.R's (wounded).	
	22nd		C.O. visited Right Section. Trenches here also badly damaged. No. 4 E artillery tis could be traced to the Windmill. No. 2 sun & No. 1 sect. This was blown up in early morning by T.R.S. Heavy shelly during afternoon. 6n gun. & No. 2 sect knocked out by direct hit from H.E. Casualties 1 O.R. wounded. No. 4 Sect relieved No. 3 Sect. 2/Lt Campbell & Baker relieved 2/Lt Arnold & Fraser.	
	23rd		On visiting support line where 3 guns of No. 2 sect were, trench was found to have been completely blown in by heavy shell, the driving trigger. No troops had been left except two three guns. These guns were accordingly withdrawn at 1.30pm to O.C. 7 Coy about Bazentin-le-Petit Wood. Casualties 2 O.R.'s Wounded. On gun & No. 4 sect & No. 4 sect G.S.O. ford taught against Germans in the Village.	
	24th		No. 1 BATTERY reinforcing from Hospital. Unsuccessful. On gun of No. 4 sect supporting the 2nd R.M.F. in INTERMEDIATE line at 5-45 p.m. Unsuccessful. And night 2700 musnel & infantilis Considerable losses on enemy. Casualties NI 3 guns of No 2 sect Nr Cornish sent up to support 2nd R.M.F. in case of Counter-attack. Germans but up heavy barrage with gas shells between MAMETZ & BAZENTIN LE PETIT woods.	

WAR DIARY
or
INTELLIGENCE SUMMARY 3rd Coy M.G.C.

Army Form C. 2118.

(Erase heading not required.)

Place	Date	Hour	Summary of Events and Information	Remarks and references to Appendices
HIGH-WOOD TO BAZENTIN -LE- PETIT	Aug 24th		C.O & Lt Barrett went up to Regt Head near HIGH WOOD when one gun under 2/Lt AVENT was sent up. From the Regt an excellent view was obtained of all the ground behind HIGH WOOD & the SWITCH LINE on the RIGHT. Also a good view looking N.E towards FLERS. Position itself good but 200 yds at beginning of Sep obstinately held this.	
	25th		A comparatively quiet day except to relieve Lt No 2 Sect (2 guns/relieved 2 guns) to 4 under 2/Lt Fraser	(3/Lt Conboy)
			C.O & Lt Barrett went up in afternoon to HQ S.W.B. when wrote Gun attack on INTERMEDIATE LINE at night to arrange M.G. support. S.W.B. raided unsuccessful in afternoon & captured 7 prisoners. Attack at night unsuccessful 9/Lt Baker relieved 1/Lt Avent in the Reg. Nos 3 sect held No 4.	
	26th		S.W.B. attacked again at 6.30 pm and gained about 200 yds of a trench. Enemy machine Gun Lt Currah got on target (6 min bursts) before the attack 5 (south) & another 9 (north) during enemy retiring after attack. In the morning another target was offered by a counter-attack about dawn. About 100 casualties are believed to have been inflicted. Gun in the Gap & 2 Lewis machine Gun target but 6 runners were killed by the gun team. 4 units of C.O of 48th Coy from front of the line in the afternoon & arrangements made for relief	

Army Form C. 2118.

WAR DIARY or INTELLIGENCE SUMMARY

(Erase heading not required.)

L. Stickler Capt

Place	Date	Hour	Summary of Events and Information	Remarks and references to Appendices
BECOURT	Aug 27		Company less 2 guns proceeded to RIGHT Nlewis G 46th M.G Coy at 6.30 a.m. With exception of guns in Rear lines 2/L7 BAKER relief was completed by 11 a.m. The guns in tête-de-pont were delayed by guns covering this way, guns in relieved all 13.0 p.m. Remaining 2 guns were taken out of trenches without relief at 8.0 p.m & got back to MAXSE REDOUBT about midnight. Very heavy rain all day also considerably & the difficulties & relief of which tête-de-pont & left hand had been considerable. Sixteen seven tape-wire trenches had been blown in. Lt F.G. GURNEY 1/1/96 West Yorks Regt. joined the Coy before relief to assume duties of 2 i/c Company. vice Lt W.E. Hewitt	
	28.		Day spent cleaning up as far as possible. This involved a considerable recasting. 7 guns were inevitably sent down taken over guns & ammo from one another in line.	
	29.		Lists of various deficiencies obtained & all shew checked. Physical drill under Lt Baker during a free interval. Pay drawn & afternoon Batt'n allotted to Coy 3.30 to 5.30 p.m. Pay parade postponed owing to weather.	
	30.		The weather very little better. 2 cases occurred of our falling in of very severe	
	31st		Battery for parade stables 9.30 – 10.0 a.m Paraded to Company at 12 noon	

3rd Brigade.

1st Division.

3rd MACHINE GUN COMPANY ::: SEPTEMBER 1916.

WAR DIARY or INTELLIGENCE SUMMARY

Army Form C. 2118
3rd Coy M.G.C. Vol 8

Place	Date	Hour	Summary of Events and Information	Remarks and references to Appendices
ALBERT (MAYSE REDOUBT)	1916 Sep 1st		Weather improved. Learned in the morning Coy would be moving up its line next day. Rest of day spent in re-organising sections etc. for this and drying & cleaning ammunition belts.	
MAMETZ WOOD	Sep 2nd		Coy moved up by sections to support in MAMETZ WOOD starting at 2 p.m. O.C. & Lt GURNEY went up in the morning to take over.	
"	Sep 3rd		Attack by 1st Bde on HIGH WOOD at 12 noon. Not successful. C.O. & Lt GURNEY went up at 6 p.m. to BAZENTIN-LE-GRAND to arrange about M/c up with O.C. 1st Coy. Lt's BARRETT and JOYCE proceeded to CARNIERS for advanced M.G. course. Orders to relieve 1st Coy during the night 4th/5th. It was decided that early morning was best down to relieving guns.	
"	Sep 4th		Coy started up to relieve 1st Coy at 5.30 a.m. Relief complete 10 a.m. Six guns in the line. 3 guns had set up w/ Lt BAKER in HIGHWOOD. 3 guns No 2 sect " Lt AVENT in SEAFORTH & WORCESTER TRENCHES (RIGHT) Remainder of Coy in BAZENTIN-LE-GRAND	
"	Sep 5th		Coy & Lt Guns went to line. Slight attention in gun positions during tr[en]ch shelling in Seaforth trench. Six gun moved up into Sect. C. Casualties. 1. O.R. KILLED (Pte KEATING) Lt Campbell relieved Lt AVENT [gun] Lt Morgan rld Lt Baker 3. O.R.'s wounded	
BAZENTIN-LE-GRAND (HIGH WOOD)	Sep 6th		Day spent in making arrangements to support attack on HIGHWOOD to be carried out on Sep 8th as in selecting places for advanced fire to m.c. reach _____ behind Cpl Iselina	
"	Sep 7th		all shell fire.	

WAR DIARY or INTELLIGENCE SUMMARY

Army Form C. 2118.

3rd Coy M.G.C.

Place	Date	Hour	Summary of Events and Information	Remarks and references to Appendices
BAZENTIN -LE-GRAND (HIGH WOOD)	1916 Sep 7th		1st Relief with 3 guns No 3 section relieving Lt Campbell & 8 guns No 2 section. Casualties 1.O.R. killed (L.Cpl Cormack No 3 section) and 3.O.R. wounded. 3.O.R. wounded	[signature] E. T. Walker Major
	Sep 8th		Lt Baker relieves Lt Morgan in High Wood. Bombardment began at 12 noon. Attack at 6.10 p.m. Three guns No 3 section in cage on Right of High Wood fires N & Eastward. Objective from zero onwards. Three guns in High Wood firing to wards High Wood during bombardment. 2 guns of No 1 section under Lt Cornish at the disposal of 1st Gloucesters to consolidate. 4 guns fired barrage fire from 12 noon to Zero deliberate & rapid till 7 p.m. from Windmill and remaining 4 did same from BAZENTIN-LE-GRAND. Attack successful at first but died up to extreme left and had to come back tonight. 3rd west fire maintained all night. 120,000 rounds fired by all guns during the 24 hours. Casualties 4 wounded. ORs. Lt Cornish wounded. Attack repeated. Bombardment began 3 p.m. attack at 4.45 p.m. 2nd B.ion took over to line on Right of High Wood relieving No 3 guns of No 3 section (Partly got 25 mm No 2 sect that is tying & m.g.'s as 7 on Sep 8th. Attack on Right successful - failed on left - i.e on High Wood. Indirect fire maintained during the night. Casualties Nil.	
	Sep 10th		2nd B.ion took over remainder of High Wood during input and early morning 9/10th. Coy moved back transport in MAMETZ Wood about 8.30 a.m. 5 p.m. moved back to LOZENGE WOOD - have 3 Lyz in 3 well huts. Officers had one tent	

WAR DIARY or INTELLIGENCE SUMMARY

Army Form C. 2118.

3 W Coy M.G.C

Place	Date	Hour	Summary of Events and Information	Remarks and references to Appendices
HENENCOURT	1916 Sep 11th		Coy moved from LOZENGE WOOD to HENENCOURT WOOD starting at 3 p.m. and getting in about 7 p.m. The 3 officers were crowded but only for one night.	
FRANVILLERS	Sep 12th		Coy moved to FRANVILLERS starting at 6.30 a.m and getting in about 10 a.m. Practically same billets as Coy occupied in July on trench down. All rather more room and no section was crowded. Officers had as last 3 rooms. Day spent settling in & cleaning up. Cpl Jones and Pte WOODWARD (2nd) awarded MILITARY MEDAL.	MILITARY MEDAL.
	Sep 13		A day allotted to rating & cleaning up. Lists of Deficiencies etc. A conference at Bn HQ. at 6 p.m. to discuss programme & example of training. Half Coy & 12 Guns rose for half an hour afternoon.	
	Sep 14		Company training area Bresnanis in throwing. Short parades were done in throwing - arms drill, P.T. and saluting. An exhibition was given in throwing by Lt A/T. 4th Div "Follies". Running hay Coy to Baila.	
	Sep 15th		Coy had an inspection. Drill etc. Lewis section arrangements began. Inspection Stewardson. COUREELETTE - MARTINPUICH & FAERS captured. "TANK"	
HENENCOURT	Sep 16th		Big advance up the line. Coy left FRANVILLERS at 6 a.m and marched back to HENENCOURT WOOD. Accommodation had altered but later we were put in another camp and had excellent accommodation.	

WAR DIARY or INTELLIGENCE SUMMARY

Army Form C. 2118

3rd Coy M.G.C.

Place	Date	Hour	Summary of Events and Information	Remarks and references to Appendices
HENENCOURT	1916 Sep 17		Church parade with P.W.R. in the morning. Our Lewis parade in afternoon. Arrangements were being made for new training areas when orders came in afternoon that we should move up (which they never did).	
BLACK WOOD (ALBERT)	Sep 18		Left HENENCOURT 4.30 p.m. and moved to BLACK WOOD (S.E. of ALBERT). A very bad march in very heavy rain & tracks in places being flooded. Everything very congested. Did not get in till 7.30 p.m. Men living in shelters in very wet ground. Officers in tents.	
MAMETZ WOOD	Sep 19		Left BLACK WOOD 1.30 p.m. and moved up to MAMETZ WOOD. Another bad march through mud. Coy bivouacked in MAMETZ WOOD. Rain very heavy. Seven men went sick into observation.	
	Sep 20		Weather improved a little. Lt Gurney went up to Bn HQ to find out situation and orders. A successful attack by 15th Bde at night.	
	Sep 21		Waited in MAMETZ WOOD for orders. 6.0 p.m. Bde gave orders up of the line. Lt Morgan with No. 1 Section and Lt Baker with 2 g Sec & Coy went up & came under orders of 15th Coy.	
	Sep 22		Orders to relieve 15th Coy on 23rd. Lt Gurney went up to Reserve Lr - Green to arrange relief with O.C. 15th M.G. Coy and attack over rules & water arrangements etc.	

2449 Wt. W14957/M90 750,000 1/16 J.B.C. & A. Forms/C.2118/12.

WAR DIARY
or
INTELLIGENCE SUMMARY 2/3 M.S.C

Army Form C. 2118

(Erase heading not required.)

Instructions regarding War Diaries and Intelligence Summaries are contained in F.S. Regs., Part II. and the Staff Manual respectively. Title Pages will be prepared in manuscript.

Place	Date	Hour	Summary of Events and Information	Remarks and references to Appendices
BAZENTIN-LE-GRAND (HIGH WOOD)	1916 Sep 23rd		C.O. & Lt Guiney went to BAZENTIN-LE-GRAND to arrange details of relief. Remainder brought up remainder of Coy at 5-30 p.m. Relief completed by 12 midnight. Runaway 2 guns & 4 sets in new front ON DROP ALLEY. 4 guns & no 2 section under Lt Avent in DROP ALLEY and COUGH DROP. 1 gun & no 3 section in new front line Runaway 3 in STARFISH under Lt Fraser. All 16 guns in the line. Casualties 3 O.R's wounded	
	Sep 24th		Lt Guiney & Lt Skipp undertaking intensive bombing attack by 2nd R.M.P at night. Unsuccessful. Casualties 1 O.R killed 2 O.R's wounded	* 1 since Died of wounds
	Sep 25th		C.O. & Lt Guiney up to HIGH WOOD to assist in terming. Offensive moved at 12-30 p.m Germans bombing attack in early morning repulsed. No 14 section guns in action. Offensive renewed at 12-30 p.m. BLACK WATCH took 3eps in FLERS LINE and XIV CORPS took MORVAL and LESBOEUFS. B&c relieved at night by 2nd B.N. except M.G. Coy. O.C No 2 Coy came up to arrange relief for morning of Sep 26th. Casualties 2/Lt A.B. Baker wounded by bomb. O.R's 1 missing 16 wounded	
ALBERT	Sep 26th		Coy relieved in morning by 2nd Coy M.G.C. Relief completed by 10.30 a.m. Battalion marched back independently to billets in ALBERT very good billets. GEUDECOURT, COMBLES and THIEPVAL Captured. 2/Lt A.B Baker died of wounds at No 1 Midland Casualty Clearing Station.	
	Sep 27		Day spent in cleaning guns & equipment etc. Clean clothes issued. Brigade Order read known RMillencourt 6.285	[signature] Major

3rd Brigade.

1st Division.

3rd MACHINE GUN COMPANY ::: OCTOBER 1916.

WAR DIARY or INTELLIGENCE SUMMARY

No. 3 Machine Gun Company
3RD MACHINE GUN COY

Army Form C.2118

(Erase heading not required.)

Place	Date	Hour	Summary of Events and Information	Remarks and references to Appendices
ALBERT	1916 28 Sept		Company moved into billets at MILLENCOURT leaving at 3 p.m. Move completed by 5.30 p.m.	
MILLENCOURT	29		Company moved into huts in HENENCOURT WOOD leaving on 2 p.m.	
HENENCOURT WOOD	30		Day spent in cleaning up	
"	Oct 1		Church Parade with 12th South Wales Borderers	
	2		Training commenced. Parades made certain arrangements.	
	3		Company marched to ALBERT - AMIENS road and entrained near BRESLE: which proceeded via AMIENS - ABBEVILLE to FREVENVILLE arriving there at about 8.30 p.m. Marched from this place to HOCQUELUS. Company billeted in out-buildings of Chateau	
HOCQUELUS	4		Day spent in cleaning up and making billets, there was good and men were quite comfortable. Major RAIKES sick and reported to bed. Lt BURNEY attended conference with [illeg] Divisional General at Bde HQ (FEUQUIERES) whereupon system of training was discussed in the afternoon all officers present at conference to discuss system of Company training.	
	5		Training commenced with certain arrangement. Lt L.V. PEACOCK 1/6 Suffolk Rgt. Reported for duty and was attached to No.1 section for instruction.	
	6		Training continued.	
	7			
	8		Owing to bad weather Church Parade was cancelled. A short Route March was carried out by the Company. Pay Parade in afternoon. Lt AYENT proceeded on leave	[illeg]

Army Form C. 2118

WAR DIARY or INTELLIGENCE SUMMARY

(Erase heading not required.)

3rd MACHINE GUN Coy.

Place	Date	Hour	Summary of Events and Information	Remarks and references to Appendices
HOCQUELUS	Oct 9		Training continued. Major RAIKES - went into hospital at LE TREPORT. Lt PEACOCK posted to Instruction.	
	10		Lt CORNISH struck off Company strength -	
	11		Company carried out firing on range in volley sand of HOCQUELUS. Guns fired well - mts.	
	12		Training continued. Lt BARRETT attached 2nd in command of unit Coy. left early in camp. In afternoon lecture by Capt. Bayliss Range in Battalion H. at AIGNEVILLE.	
	13		Training in field work. (Sectional Tactical schemes)	
	14		Training continued. Centre inspected by Lt Colonel CRAIGBROWN commanding 3rd bank house at 2.30 pm Church parade with 16 South Wales Borderers at AIGNEVILLE. Pay Parade in afternoon.	
	15			
	16		Company carried out firing on organised tactical gun, Rifle and Revolver.	
	17		L/FINSLR went to salvol mtg. demonstration at Canvas. Lt SHIPLEY went into hospital sick - Lt N.E. HUMPHREYS, 4/9 Suffolk Regt reported to Company and posted to No 17. Lecture for instruction.	
	18		Training in field work. Lt JOYCE went on leave -	
	19		Training continued.	
	20		Bde Route March. Route Company joined column at HOCQUELUS. Route HOCQUELUS - FEUVIRCES - FEUQUIERES - HOCQUELUS. Bn Commanded arrival. Arrived Hocqueles expected 2 no in line of march.	
	21		Training continued	
	22		Church Parade with 1st S. Wels. Borderers. Pay Parade in afternoon.	
	23		Firing on Range -	

Army Form C. 2118.

WAR DIARY
or
INTELLIGENCE SUMMARY   3rd M.G. Company

(Erase heading not required.)

Instructions regarding War Diaries and Intelligence Summaries are contained in F. S. Regs., Part II. and the Staff Manual respectively. Title Pages will be prepared in manuscript.

Place	Date 1916	Hour	Summary of Events and Information	Remarks and references to Appendices
HOCQUEUS	Oct. 27		LIEUT. A.B. FINDLAY took command of the Company as from the 26th inst.	
"	28		Weather fine. The Company were inspected by the G.O.C. Division.	
"	29		Wet and cold. Kit and equipment inspection by section Officers. Church parade and pay parade, heavy transport went on ahead to BAZIEUX.	
"	30		Fine. Route march and inspection by O.C. Company. Infantry drill. Remainder of transport went on to BAZIEUX.	
"	31		Company entrained and travelled via AMIENS to BAZIEUX arriving at our camp at 7 p.m.	

Alex. B. Findlay Lt.
O.C. 3rd M.G. Coy.

3rd Brigade.

1st Division.

3rd MACHINE GUN COMPANY ::: NOVEMBER 1916.

WAR DIARY or INTELLIGENCE SUMMARY

Army Form C. 2118

Vol 10
3rd MACHINE GUN Coy.

Place	Date	Hour	Summary of Events and Information	Remarks and references to Appendices
BAZIEUX	1916 Nov. 1		Cleaning up. Recomm. Training	
	2		Training as per programme of work. Wet.	
	3		Training as per programme of work.	
	4		Training as per programme. Wet. Major W.T. Raikes struck off Company Strength.	
	5		Church Parade 9 a.m. The Company moved to Millencourt - moving at 2.15 p.m. Arrived at Millencourt at 4.15 p.m. Took up Quarters in No. 1 Camp. 2 Lt. J. Fraser returned to duty from No. 4 Camp at Cavilion.	
MILLENCOURT	6		Training. 2 Lt. W.S. Doyle returned from leave to U.K. One coy of machine admitted to hospital.	
	7		The Company was ordered for weather. Training as usual. 3 cases of measles.	
	8		Firing on range. One case of measles.	
	9		Training	
	10		Rests leaves	
	11		Training. Tactical Scheme. machine gun in attack.	
	12		Firing.	
	13		Training on range. Gun Revolvers.	
	14		Training. Tactical Scheme. guns in Defence	
	15		Training	
	16		Training. Rartahack. 2 more cases of measles.	
	17		Training	
	18		Training by Revolver	
	19		Training	

W. Nugent
for O.C. 3 M.G.Coy.

Army Form C. 2118.

WAR DIARY
or
INTELLIGENCE SUMMARY.   3RD MACHINE GUN Cy.

(Erase heading not required.)

Place	Date	Hour	Summary of Events and Information	Remarks and references to Appendices
MILLENCOURT	1916 Nov. 20		Training. Tactical Scheme.	
	21		Training. Retrenchment.	
	22		Training. Lt F.G Gurney returned for leave.	
	23		Training. Horse race for officers in afternoon.	
	24		Training. Tactical Scheme - no firm attack no defence. Spoken w/Framen	
	25		Training. Retrenchment.	
	26		Training. Very bad weather.	
	27		Kit inspection. Bad weather.	
	28		Training. Sections re-arranged. Pay Parade.	
	29		Coy on extended days of weather. Orders received to move up line	
			Company marched to MAMETZ where shelter was provided. Left MILLENCOURT at 8am	
MAMETZ WOOD	30		Co. and Lt. GURNEY to PEACOCK arrived. Relief of Company marched. EARLGS	
			On Flers Relief completed at 11pm. Four guns of No 2 section	
			No. 1 & Peacock and Humphreys on bn right. Two guns of No 1 rect. & Lt	
			Cameron + Pont Bis and two guns of No 1 sect with Lt Morgan	
			line.	

Whiting 8 G
Lt OC 3rd...

3rd Brigade.

1st Division.

3rd MACHINE GUN COMPANY ::: DECEMBER 1916.

Army Form C. 2118.

WAR DIARY
or
INTELLIGENCE SUMMARY
(Erase heading not required.)

3rd Machine Gun Coy

Place	Date 1916	Hour	Summary of Events and Information	Remarks and references to Appendices
FLERS	Dec. 1		C.O and Lieut Furray at Coy H.Q. FLERS. Lieut Peacock-Humphrey in right reserve position with 1st section No 2. Flatfell in front line with one team.	
BAZENTIN LE PETIT		3	Coy. H.Q. moved to old R. BAZENTIN-LE-PETIT. Lt Morgan in Centre Reserve line with half section. Front line gun withdrawn. Gun in right reserve position. relieved by No 2 Company.	
		4	Lt Avent with half section took up position in Post C.	
		5	Lt Eason with half section relieved Lt Morgan in reserve line	
		6	C.O and Lt Peacock went round line.	
		7	Front line position again occupied - by Lt Crompton with one gun team	
		8	Lieut Joyce relieved Lt Eason in reserve position	
		10	C.O and Lt Peacock round line.	
		12	Lieut Peacock Mansfield relieved Lt Morgan and Crompton	
		13	C.O and Lt Furray round the line - visited all positions except Q. Lt Humphrey to hospital sick	
		14	Lt Furray visited C.D. and E positions and 1st Bde. HQ.	
		15	C.O went on leave	
		16	Lieuts Fraser and Avent relieved Lieuts Peacock Mansfield	
		17	Lt Furray round line.	
		18	Company (less section in line) moved back to camp at MAMETZ WOOD WEST.	
		19	Lt Crompton relieved Lt Avent. Conference at Bde HQ. regarding camps &	
MAMETZ		20	A.Compton sent 50 fr. for men Christmas now Xmas dinners. Ordn Joyce to MAMETZ to obtain half new ar chicken & for dinners. wait until Capt Gray out in to line. Ordig NCOs civilian cleaners	

Army Form C. 2118

WAR DIARY
or
INTELLIGENCE SUMMARY.
(Erase heading not required.)

3rd M. G. Coy.

Instructions regarding War Diaries and Intelligence Summaries are contained in F. S. Regs., Part II. and the Staff Manual respectively. Title pages will be prepared in manuscript.

Place	Date 1916	Hour	Summary of Events and Information	Remarks and references to Appendices
MAMETZ	Dec 21		Lieut Furey on Peacock round line.	
	22		Lieut Grafsia wounded in hand at No. 3 position. Lieut Campbell took over command of No. 1 and 2 parties.	
	23		Lieut Peacock round line.	
	24		Lieut Morgan relieved Lt Joyce. Lieut Brown on leave.	
	25		Lieut Furey and Peacock round line	
	27		Bus Peacock visited Batt. H.Q. went round H.Q. office of 149 Coy, observed relief	
	28		21 HVKYPRE joined the Company	
	29		C.O. of 149 M.G. Coy arranged relief. Emm & Spurr held a Con & recce taken. Sec A divide. All Sections and guns in the line relieved.	
BÉCOURT	30		Company moved into Nissen huts at BECOURT. having camp at 10 a.m.	
	31		Morning spent in cleaning equipment and guns. Kit inspection. Voluntary Church Service at 10 a.m.	

Murphy
Lieut

A5834 Wt. W4973/M687 750,000 8/16 D. D. & L. Ltd. Forms/C.2118/13.

Army Form C. 2118.

WAR DIARY
or
INTELLIGENCE SUMMARY
(Erase heading not required.)

3RD MACHINE GUN COY

Place	Date	Hour	Summary of Events and Information	Remarks and references to Appendices
MORVILLERS	1916 24 Sept		Proposed firing on range etc. cancelled owing to wet weather. Training carried on in billets. L't AVENT returned from leave. L't SHIPLEY returned from hospital.	
	25		Preparing for move in accordance with warning order received last night — dull weather — no further outdoor training — in the afternoon instructions received re- 1st Sth Andrean forces going on AIGNEVILLE with G Gurney to H.Q.C. 11th Division generated. Badges to follow NCO's and men of the Company. 19313 Sgt. W. FITZGERALD, 19339 A/t W. HAGGERTY 19378 Sgt G. H. BLACK 18907 - G. WOODWARD 19349 Cpl A. JONES 1750 — W. BELL	
	26		All of men received the military medal. Orders received late last on. This there was tattoo of Brigade today for these days.	
	27		Hot weather again heated attack training. Cleaned up during morning and rare done order work was carried out. 57 Inf. Coy afforded to take over command of Coy — but Lieut. A. B. FINDLAY was not Coy to assume command until Auckinah had his Brigade instructions. Divisional Route march carried out in morning — received from Divn	

2449 Wt. W14957/M90 750,000 1/16 J.B.C. & A. Forms/C.2118/12.

1st Division
3rd M. G. COMPANY
3rd Infantry Brigade
From 1st January. To 30th June 1917

WAR DIARY.

3rd. M.G. Company.

3rd. INFANTRY BRIGADE.

1st. DIVISION.

JANUARY. 1917.

Army Form C. 2118.

WAR DIARY
or
INTELLIGENCE SUMMARY
(Erase heading not required.)

3RD MACHINE GUN COY

Place	Date	Hour	Summary of Events and Information	Remarks and references to Appendices
BECOURT	1917 Jan 1	1	Morning spent in cleaning guns, equipment &c. M.O.C. 3rd Bde went round huts in evening and wished all officers and men good luck in the new year.	
		2	Cleaning carried on - technical ammunition and spare parts. Arrived on Mafeham at ALBERT. Improvements to camp and transport lines.	
		3	Captain C.O. returned from leave. Company also on working parties - improving ALBERT - BECOURT road.	
		4	Training. B. GURNEY attended lecture on S.G.Ct Montals or 4th Bde HQ in the afternoon. Company interested by C.O.	
		5	New Ids also New Year dinner.	
		6	Training.	
		7	Working Parties. (ALBERT - BECOURT road).	
		8	Training. Camp improved much also a transport lines. D PINCOCK on leave to England. Lt FRASER returned fro leave.	
		9	Working Parties. Elementary training for new carifts.	
		10	"	
		11	"	
		12	Baths. working parties.	
		13	Working parties. (ALBERT - BECOURT road). Lieut MORGAN and 4. O.R. July and 4. O.R. July Lieut JOYCE & Lt Learm at CARRIERS ho for working parties.	
		14	Church parade at 10.20.	
		15	Working Parties. (Transport lines and Jr-major). Lecture on Defense of quarters at ALBERT. 3 - O.R. on leave to England.	
		16	Working Parties (ALBERT - BECOURT road). Lieut. WILLATT Joined Company, 2Lt.	
		17	CAMPBELL returned from leave. Working Parties.	Signed Lieut.
		18	Training.	

Army Form C. 2118.

3rd M. G. Coy

WAR DIARY
or
INTELLIGENCE SUMMARY.

(Erase heading not required.)

Instructions regarding War Diaries and Intelligence Summaries are contained in F. S. Regs., Part II. and the Staff Manual respectively. Title pages will be prepared in manuscript.

Place	Date (1917)	Hour	Summary of Events and Information	Remarks and references to Appendices
BÉCOURT	Jan 19		Working Parties (ALBERT-BÉCOURT ROAD) Training, making fire work.	
	20			
	21		Church Parade at 11. with 2nd Welsh Regt.	
	22		Working Parties (ALBERT-BÉCOURT ROAD) Lectures on offensive war afar at ALBERT. Lt ALBERT on leave warning	
VADENCOURT	23		Company marched via ALBERT, LAVIEVILLE, HÉNENCOURT, WARLOY to billets at VADENCOURT.	
	24		Cleaning guns - and Billets - the latter were very dirty - Pay Parade. Pte PEACOCK returned from leave.	
	25		Routemarch	
	26.		C.O's conference with R.Q. when Training was discussed. Captain J. Willatt arrived command of the Company. Brigadier inspected Company at work in the morning.	
	27		Training continued. Lieut Peace admitted to hospital sick.	
	28		C.O. inspected the Company. Church Parade at 12 o'clock.	
	29		Training in open warfare - No 1 section near 2d Canifield and 1st Gloucestershire	
			No 2 - " " Sant Jersey - 1st Royston	
			No 3 " " 1st Dyckes - 2nd Rifle Brigade	
			No 3 section continued with training	
	30		Pay Parade in afternoon. Training in open warfare - 2 lectures No 2 at Breakwater on MGN Operations Lt Peacock was 1st Gloucestershire Lewis gunners 2nd Welsh Lt Hughes - 3rd Parkinson	
	31		No 1 section carried on Training - All lectures at an MGN operation Reported holdings - All lectures at an MGN operation Training carried on in Training - on tactical ideas C.O. at Bde H.Q. 9.20. for conference regarding disposed Coys. Commanding in afternoon. Came Townsend A786D M.S. in afternoon.	W.Willatt Lieut

WAR DIARY.

3rd. M. G. Company.

3rd. INFANTRY BRIGADE.

1st. DIVISION.

FEBRUARY. 1917.

Army Form C. 2118

WAR DIARY or INTELLIGENCE SUMMARY
(Erase heading not required.)

3rd MACHINE GUN COY

Vol 3

Place	Date 10/17	Hour	Summary of Events and Information	Remarks and references to Appendices
VADENCOURT MORCOURT	30.1.	1	Brigades Tactical School. All guns went into Brigades Tactical School at Divisional School.	
		2	Company moved to billets at MORCOURT being VADENCOURT at 9am. Route via WARLOY, BAIZIEUX, RIBEMONT, MERICOURT, SAILLY-LE-SEC, SAILLY-LAURETTE, CERISY. Road bad in places.	
		3	Guns tested in morning. News received that D.V. BEGAN admitted to hospital sick from CERISY M/G Camp.	
		4	CO left as O. for his time when he will away retail and remain until Coy release tomorrow. Heavy fall in cleaning all limbers and bring them. New anti-aircraft measures carried out in the afternoon.	
BARLEUX	5		Company left MORCOURT at 8.15 a.m. and marched to Telegraph Camp via CHUIGNES, marched from B.O.C. Division. No billets had been arranged so Company had arrived in order of march. Orders received to move off about 6 o'clock and the Three sections marched via BOMPIERRE to HERBECOURT where Brigade HQ was. One section in support this and two sections Reserve line.	Coy H.Q. at TELEGRAPH CAMP
		6	Temporary established on Tr. de Cavey.	
		7	Infantry relieved Brench. Quiet day.	
		8	Quiet. Sgt. J. BLAIR joined Centre on Q.H. Seqt.	Lieut-Voyce returned from leave.
		9	Reg. HQ moved from TELEGRAPH CAMP to new position about 500 yards to CAPPY. CO revd. Recom this evd. G.S.O. 2 to pre-position from 2nd M.G.Coy in Right Supports, Instructions where Cele Tape took over their position.	
		10	Gun established to have 3 guns Left Support Line, 3 guns Right Support line, 2 guns in Roucourt Reserve on Railway line, one old Junction with Mole or Real line, Relief of Section carried out.	
		11	Rain. One cames out throughout night and relieved German front system.	
		12	No guns. Harsh fire carried on on night. Rain. One returned from leave. Very Quiet day. One O'Sutton his gun fired no Sgt. A.M. HOLMES the av high.	
		13	Relief of Section carried out. Guns did no fire from 7:30 p.m. to 8 p.m. owing to Artillery firing very much.	
		14	Quiet day. No reports on night.	
		15	Pte Rook & No 2 arebs wounded in Support line. Relieved. The Comrad.	
		16	Heavy shrapnel Support line into Div't Station at 5.20 am. New families made - Sgt. BEAVERSOE.	
		17	Relief of section carried out. Than commenced - today very sickly. New Aeroplanes made a raid. Wo inflicted on our artifices from Rear HQ. Heavier fire.	

A 5834 Wt. W4973/M687 750,000 8/16 D. D. & L. Ltd. Forms/C.2118/13

Army Form C. 2118.

3rd M.G. Coy

WAR DIARY
or
INTELLIGENCE SUMMARY

(Erase heading not required.)

Place	Date	Hour	Summary of Events and Information	Remarks and references to Appendices
FARLEUX	18		Employed now for special purpose. Work on emplacements	
	19		Work entirely carried on by artillery. Wire entanglements. Kept these open at night by small fire trenches. No very bad casualties owing to wet.	
	20		Test gas alarm carried out. Carrier H.Q. moved to MEUDON Avenue. No interest for carried out. Very light weather.	Yes
	21		Order for relief received in usage terms of one day earlier. Removed details.	Yes
	22		Coyn relieved by 2nd M.G. Coy. Relief commenced at 11.30 p.m.	
CAVIGNES	23		Relief of guns carried by 6 a.m. - Remainder of machines made the relief a very long and difficult one. Company moved back to CAVIGNES and tent per billets moved to by 2nd Coy. In large threads tents quite attacked village. C.O. went to 42nd Division to arrange details as to being being attached to them for special purpose.	Yes
	24		Morning spent in cleaning guns, equipment and machinery of machine by machine to.	
	25		C.O. again at 42nd Division. G.O.C. Brigade inspected Company billets. Copies list of officers attached.	Yes
	26		Morning spent in cleaning equipment and in Bell Drill	
	27		Bullets material & Company by 3.G.C. instruments checked by the Contractor White - especially the transport.	
	28		Morning spent in cleaning bushes by section. There were not enough clean out ??? Grove Drill, bistron Drill and gun Drill. Afternoon - inspection of spare parts & probable cleaning of equipment etc.	
			Arrangements made for 2nd F. M.G.C to go in the trenches.	

WAR DIARY.

3rd. M. G. Company.

3rd. INFANTRY BRIGADE.

1st. DIVISION.

MARCH. 1917.

Army Form C. 2118.

WAR DIARY
or
INTELLIGENCE SUMMARY
(Erase heading not required.)

37 M.G. Coy.
Vol 14

Place	Date	Hour	Summary of Events and Information	Remarks and references to Appendices
CHUIGNES	1 Aug 17	—	Full months rest including first to guns into trenches; from chateau to un heated Coy Hars. 8.9. at 6 pm. Chivers in relief. No 1 M.G. Coy in in right section. No 4 section in right support line. No 2 section left support line 1, No 2 Reserve line; No 3 rest; Gunners new at ammunition.	
	2/Aug	—	Rest & musketry. 2 hrs. Trenches in very bad condition, full of mud & slimy mud; irrigation trenches wet & slippery. No gunners wounded (shell fire) in support line. Gunners find caverns wet at mg 11.	
	3	—	Misty day; front & support line - trench materials used steadily. Took over - returnable? Quarry & Tortune Wavieux Rd. No Rifles billet (shell fire) ma Cinghen. Ground gun by Artillery, menefully kept down by mg fire night. Extra living wire) made.	
	4	—	Another wurs day. Calm. Wind masters & artillery again active. Enemy explains the my line new new lines; standed they emufied un to mg's but offered the hit. Situation front a enemy sunders. Trenches again caused in. Gates in emery line found in E 7/27 Knyser deployed from current.	
	5	—	Guiet delay; 7 on m g.s. evacuated; they fire in emery lines & roads; n. and caused in to Bus n.m. Left. A. g. Fraser signed from Hospital. Served relief carried out. Ammunition supplies to complete.	
	6	—	Own mg S.S. after fires on roads; attempts to mens trenches is emery lies of artillery want back to Bus n.m. Left	
	7	—	Quiet day. Work commenced slappty? emery stations sheet never still a new back anderim wire Others were. Intense pr caused out at night. Improvement of kiden & emplacements commenced. T.O.R reinforcements arrived from base.	
	8	—	Quiet day.	
	9	—	Coy H.Q's shelled. Served gas hay alert.	

Army Form C. 2118.

WAR DIARY
or
INTELLIGENCE SUMMARY

J.M.Q.L.

(Erase heading not required.)

Instructions regarding War Diaries and Intelligence Summaries are contained in F. S. Regs., Part II. and the Staff Manual respectively. Title Pages will be prepared in manuscript.

Place	Date	Hour	Summary of Events and Information	Remarks and references to Appendices
Brooklyn	10/9/17	—	Received relay equipment. Received from by night	
	11/9/17	—	Received four cement mixers and eight	
	12/9/17	—	at L.P.D. rate. With new trainees, my Capt. A 703 further trainees	Ref App I
		from 2.30 a.m. to All groups trained.	
	13/9/17	—	All guns attacked from base U.K. Quiet day.	Received pent and night
	14/9/17	—	Quiet day.	
	15/9/17	—	Received relay	
	16/9/17	—	Very quiet day. 3rd Bttn. carried out two raids at night to ascertain whether	
			enemy was still holding his trenches. Returned he carried out by 6 p.m. a new	
			man after Enemy attempted E. raid. Returned + Wilson returned	
			from Trenches. Jude to have evacuated his front line trenches w. result that	
			our patrols took at attack pty great	
			results. Battn. in Whiteh. Sunne. The Sunne canal onfour successive	
	17/9/17	—	nights advance established. Relay 93 & 9 to 4 2nd S Co.	
	18/9/17	—	Commenced training. Last 2 Sundays. Coys arrived back + settled at Chaynes.	
			Relay supplies at 2.am	
			Day spent in general cleaning up.	
	19/9/17	—	Company as training working parties of 25 men to R.E. at FROISSY.	
	20		Found Cyclist + officer t share officers	Rev. Peacock
	21		Reveillely at noon. C.O. inspected Coys in the afternoon.	W.P. marks
	22		Found Coy. - Par Parade	
	23		Training continued	

Army Form C. 2118.

WAR DIARY
or
INTELLIGENCE SUMMARY

3RD M G Coy

(Erase heading not required.)

Instructions regarding War Diaries and Intelligence Summaries are contained in F.S. Regs., Part II. and the Staff Manual respectively. Title Pages will be prepared in manuscript.

Place	Date	Hour	Summary of Events and Information	Remarks and references to Appendices
QUIGNES	Mar 24		Training continued.	
	25		Church Parade – for Coy at 9.30 a.m. transfer at 3.30 p.m.	
	26		Company on working parties – as ordered on batt. Orders. Inspected two camps at CHUIGNOLLES – on ground unsuitable as was intimated after reconn.	
	27		Two sections on tactical training – one with 2½ Welch Bgd. as will 1st Plat. One section firing – one fourth section carried on general training.	
	28		Be section training with 1st Battn. S. Lan. Fusiliers. Two section general training. Range on firing. Pay parade. Company carried on the morning.	
	29		3 section training with 1st Bank Shrops. Foresters, 2 & Welsh Rgt. & 2nd Royal Munsters. Sunders, respectively. No 2 section on Range. Brigade wateries billets –	
	30		Trench training with 2nd Rajput Munster Fusiliers. No 3 section on range ofter Section general training. 2/Lt L G Grant to Hospital for influenza.	
	31		Training continued.	

Murphy
Major
O.C.

Copy No 7. War Diary Appendix I SECRET.

Operation Order by LIEUT L. P. DA COSTA
Commanding 3rd M.G. Company

On night of the 15TH/16TH inst.

Section 1	At present at	will be relieved by	On relief move to	Relieve
IV	Right support line (guns 1-4)	I	Reserve line	III
II	Left support line (guns 5-8)	III	REST.	I
III	Reserve line	IV	Left support line (5-8)	II
I	REST.	II	Right support line (1-4)	IV

(2) Sections will come under the command of Officers as follows:–
Left support line (guns 6-8) Lt. Fraser.
Right " " (" 1-5) Lt. Joyce.
Reserve line (" R1-R4) Lt. Peacock
Resting Section Lt. Avent.

(3) GUIDES. Section IV Guides from each Gun team to be at Coy H.Qs at 6 p.m.
Section III Guides from R1 & R2 to meet team from guns 1 & 2 at Right Batt H.Q's. Guides from R3 & R4 to meet teams from Guns 3 & 4 at Company H.Qs at 7 p.m.
Section III will move off to relieve Section II (guns 5-8) at 6 p.m. One man to hand over and one man to draw rations will be left behind with each gun position. A guide will be at Coy H.Qs to conduct No II Section to REST.

(4) No I Section will leave one man per gun team to hand over and to carry rations up.

(5) Guns, tripods, trench stores etc, will be handed over at each position. Spare parts not to be handed over. Receipts to be given. Dugouts to be left clean

(6) Lt. Avent will be responsible for relief of No 5 gun position

(7) Completion of relief to be notified to Coy H.Qs

(8) Acknowledge.

Copies 1 to 5	Section Officers
" 6	3rd Bde HQs
" 7	War Diary
" 8	File.

L.P. da Costa Lt.
3rd Machine Gun Coy.

WAR DIARY.

(WITH APPENDICES).

3rd. M. G. COMPANY.

3rd. INFANTRY BRIGADE.

1st. DIVISION.

APRIL. 1917.

WAR DIARY / INTELLIGENCE SUMMARY

Army Form C. 2118.

3rd Machine Gun Company

Vol 15

Place	Date 1917	Hour	Summary of Events and Information	Remarks and references to Appendices
CHAULNES	April 1		Working parties at Railhead for unloading supply train; Divisional Baths; and guard at local Dump. Car. Thompson - 10 officers 197 O.R. Church parade at 9.30. 2/Lieut Anderson joined Company.	Appendix I
	2		Brigade manoeuvres. Societal attacks a Battalion - and in afternoon Brigade. Boxing in evening.	
	3		Training carried on. Brigades inspected Company in the afternoon. Willatt on leave to England. Field Payne 10 /- p/man for officers & N.C.O.s. Training continued. Gym went in morning & swim to swim baths.	
	4		Training continued. No 3 section on Range. Pay parade in the afternoon.	
	5		Church parade - 9.15am. Three sections on working parties - NTR. Section on Range.	
	6			
BRIE	7		Company marched off at 8.30 am and took over Billets in TENT CAMP, BRIE. Guns mounted for Anti-aircraft work.	Appendix II
	8		Relieved B gun 92.2.d M/G coy at BRIE. Guns mounted for Anti-aircraft work. Working party on roads at BRIE.	
	9		Working party made P.E on roads on BRIE.	
	10		Working party made R.E on road at BRIE - main St Quentin road. Holes in road filled in with Trench tile dug. Much transport passing. No 2 section relieved by No 1.	
	11		On relief - scraped away mud from about 500 yds - dug new small dugouts made drains.	
	12		Work on roads continued - Bricks put down. Progress forward came to the camp	
	13		Work on road continued.	
	14		Lt Leslyngton & 20.1 m at Peronne for enquiry re ride made a road continued. Suzanne & PeRonne fumigated.	
	15		Work on road continued. Orders received from Brigade that we shall move tomorrow A N.E.R.E area.	
CURCHY	16		Company marched off to Hut Billet at CURCHY. Left camp at 12 noon. Had lunch on road. Billet for men and officers in farm huts.	
	17		Work at NESLE continued. Lt. Willatt returned from special leave.	
	18		Work at NESLE continued. Lt Willatt returned from special leave.	
	19		Company & working party from Coy at NESLE clearing away debris from ground at Railway Siding. Brigade visited Billets. Transport lines.	

Army Form C. 2118.

WAR DIARY
or
INTELLIGENCE SUMMARY.

3RD MACHINE GUN COY

(Erase heading not required.)

Instructions regarding War Diaries and Intelligence Summaries are contained in F. S. Regs., Part II. and the Staff Manual respectively. Title pages will be prepared in manuscript.

Place	Date Sep.16	Hour	Summary of Events and Information	Remarks and references to Appendices
CURCHY	20		Working parties at NESLE Railhead. Unloading up abbris, and unloading road metal from trains.	
	21		Working Party on Yesterday	
	22		Work at NESLE Railhead continued	
	23		Working parties at NESLE. Spots in the evening.	
	24		Working Party at NESLE. N.C.O's class - Infantry drill & c.	
	25		" " N°3 section training	
	26		" " " "	
	27		" " N°4 section training	
	28		" " N.C.O's class - Infantry drill & c. N°2 section training	
	29		Conference, based on MESNIL ST NICAISE during the morning. Whole parade in the evening	
	30		Training and entraining from trenches C. Tactical scheme in the afternoon. (by Major 10 officers 18 o.R. 182 other ranks) (Whitney Coy)	

W. Whitney
Lieut
For 3 M.G. Coy

Copy No. 4

SECRET.

Woolring

Operation Order No. 5.

by Lieut L.M. Da Costa

Commanding 3rd M.G. Company.

AFTER MIDNIGHT RELIEF.

No.1 Section will relieve No. 2 section on Anti-Aircraft duties on the 15th inst. at HALF HOUSE.

One guide from each team of No.2 section will be at west side of HALF HOUSE, A.26.c.6.1. at 6. 30. p.m.

2nd Lieut Gregory will take charge.

Tripods, Belt Boxes, and Trench Stores will be handed over and a receipt taken.

The Section Officer is responsible that dugouts, and emplacements are handed over in a clean condition and that Trench Standing orders are strictly carried out.

Copies.

    Section Officers 1&2

    3rd Bde H. Qrs 3

    War Diary. 4

    File 5.

28/4/1917

O.C. 3rd Machine Gun Company.

SECRET   Copy No. 7

Ref. Map. 62C and 62D.
1/20,000.

Operation Order No 3
by
Lieut L.P. Da Costa, Commdg. 3rd M.G. Coy.   Appendix I

The 3rd. Machine Gun Company will co-operate in
a Brigade Scheme on Monday, 2nd. instant.
Sections will join their Battalions, as practised
in training during the past week, with
exception of No 3 section, at Rendezvous about
M. 25.d.0.8. W. of FOUCAUCOURT at 9.50 a.m.

   No 1 section under Lt. Morgan to 1st S. Wales Borderers.
   " 2   "   "   Lt. Kypke - 1st Gloucester Rgt.
   " 4   "   "   Lt Joyce - 2nd R. Muster Fusiliers
   " 3   "   "   Lt Marks in Brigade
   Reserve at Brigade H.Q. at the disposal of
   the Brigadier.

General Idea and map is issued separately
to Section Officers.
Great care must be taken to ensure that
the ammunition supply is properly kept up
and dumps established.
Reserve ammunition will be at Brigade
H.Q. under Coy. Sergeant Major where
communication will be kept up as far as
possible.
C.O. will be at Brigade H.Q. about M.25.d.1.7.

1/4/1917.
Copies   No.
  Section Officers 1 — 4
  Bde. H. Q.   5
  File   6.
  War Diary   7

                              L.P. Da Costa Lt
                              Commdg.
                              3rd M.G. Coy.

Appendix II   War Diary

SECRET   Copy No 4

Ref. Map. AMIENS. 17. 1/100.000

Operation Order No 4
by
Lieut. L.P. Da Costa, Commdg. 3rd M.G. Coy.

- No 2 section of 3rd Machine Gun Company will relieve No 1. section of 2nd Machine Gun Company at BRIE, at 12 noon on 7/4/1917.

- Guides will be at the West side of BRIE bridge at 12 Noon.

- 2 Lt. Anderson will be in charge.

- The section will take complete kit, unexpired portion of the day's ration, and 8 boxes of ammunition per gun to gun positions. Remainder of ammunition to be left on limbers.

- Section will move off from billet at 8 a.m.

- Limbers will remain in charge of section officer until further orders are received.

6/4/1917

Copy No 1. Section Officer
     2.   2nd. M.G. Coy
     3.   3rd Bde
     4.   War Diary
     5.   File.

WAR DIARY.

(WITH APPENDICES).

3rd. M. G. COMPANY.

3rd. INFANTRY BRIGADE.

1st. DIVISION.

MAY. 1917.

Army Form C 2118.

WAR DIARY
or
INTELLIGENCE SUMMARY.

3rd M. G. Coy.

(Erase heading not required.)

Instructions regarding War Diaries and Intelligence Summaries are contained in F. S. Regs., Part II. and the Staff Manual respectively. Title pages will be prepared in manuscript.

Place	Date 1917	Hour	Summary of Events and Information	Remarks and references to Appendices
CURCHY	May 1		Training in indirect fire which carried on.	
	2		Training continued. Bay parade in the afternoon	
PÉRONNE	3		Marched via LICOURT. CIZANCOURT. ST CHRIST. ETERPIGNY to billets at PERONNE.	
	4		Morning spent in cleaning guns, spare parts, limbers &c.	
	5		Training. Inspection on Range. Other Ranks exercises in gun drill & physical training. Bathing in the afternoon.	
	6		Church Parade at 10 o'clock.	
	7		Training continued. No 2 section ambushed	
	8		Marched via BAICHET, HERBÉCOURT, ECLUSIERS. A Company Corpl. billeted in a corrrn rooms. Remainder beneath tarpaulin. C.O. attended conference at Bde HQ.	see Appendix A.
ECLUSIER	9		Training commenced. Conference at ECLUSIERS in the evening.	
	10		Training. No 3 section on Range. Capt M.G.O. visited Company.	
	11		Company on Divisional Schemes. Lecture FOUCAUCOURT and CHUIGNES	
	12		Company & Baths (indirect). C.O. and Lt.GEARY at CHUIGNES when scheme of Yesterday was demonstrated.	
			Capt. OWEN'S BULL. Cap M.G.O.'s Divisional Staff.	
			Church Parade at 10.30 a.m. with Bde. Brigadier.	
	13		C.O. on leave to UK. Training. Mt Wratten in Comp. was Polo in the afternoon. Bde XI v	
	14			
			Company. Brigade Sports at ECLUSIERS.	
	15		Training.	
	16		Training. Lt. WILLETT left Coy to command No 32 M.G. Coy. Elementals of MG fire effects. Games to 216th Coy.	
	17		Training. Conference at ECLUSIERS in Training and Divisional Sports.	
	18		Training.	
	19		Left camp at 2 pm marched via CAPPY. PROISSY. PROYART. B. LAMOTTE. Bullets dusty and very crowded. 3 men fell out on the march.	
LAMOTTE-EN-SANTERRE	20		Church Parade at 10.45 a.m. Sports in the afternoon (Brigade Transport) - Rifles reorganised - fairly good average.	
	21		Training. Rain prevented work in open. Football in evening v train final. Won C. 3. Lewis Gunners M.G.	
	22		Training. Rain stopped work in open. Brigade sports in evening.	
	23		Training - 2 section march 1st Gloucesters Regt. I match 2 not match for training in open warfare. Football, Bayoneting, Lloyd	
	24		Training. No entertainment.	

A 5834 Wt. W 4973/M687 750,000 8/16 D. D. & L. Ltd. Forms/C.2118/13

Army Form C. 2118.

WAR DIARY
or
INTELLIGENCE SUMMARY.   30 M.G.Coy.
(Erase heading not required.)

Instructions regarding War Diaries and Intelligence
Summaries are contained in F. S. Regs., Part II.
and the Staff Manual respectively. Title pages
will be prepared in manuscript.

Place	Date 1917	Hour	Summary of Events and Information	Remarks and references to Appendices
LAMOTTE	MAY 25		Brigade Field Day.	
	26		Preparation for attainment in afternoon. Entrained from CHOCQUES to LA MOTTE at 6.00 p.m.	
	27		Cleaned early & moved by A.T. road. Marched via CAESTRE and FLETRE to hutted bivouac. Ordered for leave	
P2d62 (R.34.27)	28		Cleaning equipment. Preparing motor lay.	
	29		Road march & training. On shale ground	
	30		Training. On sports in the evening. C.O. at "Tanks" demonstration near AREA 52	
	31		Road march & training	

A

12

1st Division No. G 441/

1st BRIGADE INTELLIGENCE OFFICER.
3rd BRIGADE INTELLIGENCE OFFICER.
No. 3 M.G.Company.
✳✳✳✳✳✳✳✳✳✳✳✳✳✳✳✳✳✳✳✳✳✳✳✳

Reference attached scheme.

1. Brigade and Battalion Intelligence Officers, 12 Brigade Observers, 8 Scouts and 4 Observers per Battalion, and No. 3 M.G. Company will take part in this Scheme.
    Lieut. TALBOT, 10th Gloucesters will act as Brigade Intelligence Officer, 3rd Brigade.

2. The line of the foremost Infantry of the WHITE ARMY will be shown by 5 men carrying WHITE FLAGS.
    The Line held by the Infantry of the BROWN ARMY will be shown by men carrying BLUE FLAGS.
    Strong Posts held by the Infantry of the BROWN ARMY will be shown by single RED FLAGS.

3. All personnel engaged will act in conformance with the movements of these flags. Brigade and Battalion Intelligence Officers will keep their immediate Commanders fully informed of the Progress of the Action, and of the movements of the enemy as laid down in 1st Division No. G 381 dated 3-4-17.

4. Report centres will be arranged by Brigade and Battalion Intelligence Officers to receive all messages sent back.

5. All messages and reports sent throughout the operations will be collected and forwarded to reach Divisional Headquarters by 1st D.R. 12th instant.

6. Personnel engaged in the scheme will rendezvous at 9.45 a.m. for final instructions at the following place :-

    3rd BRIGADE and No. 3 M.G.Company (WHITE ARMY) on main AMIENS - ESTREES ROAD at R.30.c. (1500 yards West of FOUCAUCOURT. Sheet 62 d.).

7. Personnel of Brigade and M.G.Coy. will bring haversack rations.

10-5-17.

Captain.
General Staff. 1st Division.

GENERAL IDEA.

A WHITE ARMY has succeeded in capturing the 1st and 2nd positions of a BROWN ARMY opposed to it on a 20 mile front, and has advanced North to the General Line of the AMIENS - ST.QUENTIN ROAD between VILLERS BRETONNEUX and BRIE by 9th May, 1917.

The BROWN ARMY 3rd position is a double line of trenches running approximately E. and W. about 600 yards N. of this line.

C - in C, WHITE ARMY has decided to attack this position on a front between WARFUSEE - VILLERS CARBONNEL both inclusive on the morning of May   at a ZERO hour to be notified later.

SPECIAL IDEA (WHITE).

From operation orders issued on the evening of May 10th the following information is received by all concerned.

1. The 3rd Brigade is attacking at 10.30 am (ZERO hour) on the 11th inst, with the 2nd Brigade on the right and a Brigade of the Guards Division on the left.

2. The 3rd Brigade is attacking with the 8/Welch on the right, and the 1/Glosters on the left, the 2/R.Munsters in support and the 1st SWB in Reserve.

3. The Right Boundary of the 3rd Brigade will be FORK ROADS M.26.a. - WOOD M.14.exclusive - COPSE in M.7.d. and 8.c. inclusive - point 75 M.2.c.
   The Left Boundary of the 3rd Brigade will be COPSE in R.30.a. - 3 MEULES R.18.a.2.8. - WOOD R.5.b. and 6.a. all exclusive.

4. The 1st and 2nd objectives of the 3rd Brigade are as shown upon the attached Map.

5. The infantry will advance to the assault at ZERO.

6. In the subsequent advance the order of the waves will be as follows :- 4, 3, 1, 2.

7. At ZERO + 1 hour the advance towards the 2nd objective will commence.

8. The 3rd and 4th waves will seize the line R.12.c.3.9. - CHUIGNES inclusive - M.8.c.2.3.
   The 1st and 2nd waves will advance through these to the 2nd objective.

9. On the capture of the 2nd objective posts with Lewis Guns will be pushed out at least 200 yards in front to cover the consolidation.

10. O.C. 3rd M.G.Company will place 4 guns at the disposal of each of the two assaulting battalions.
    These guns will be used to repel any counter-attacks which may be launched by the enemy and also to deal with any strong posts which may hold up the attack.

11. The remaining 8 guns will be employed under O.C. 3 M.G. Company to support the advance of the Infantry. Particular attention will be paid to suspected enemy strong posts at trench in R.24.c, mounds M.13.c., Copse at R.18.a and Wood M.13.b.

===================

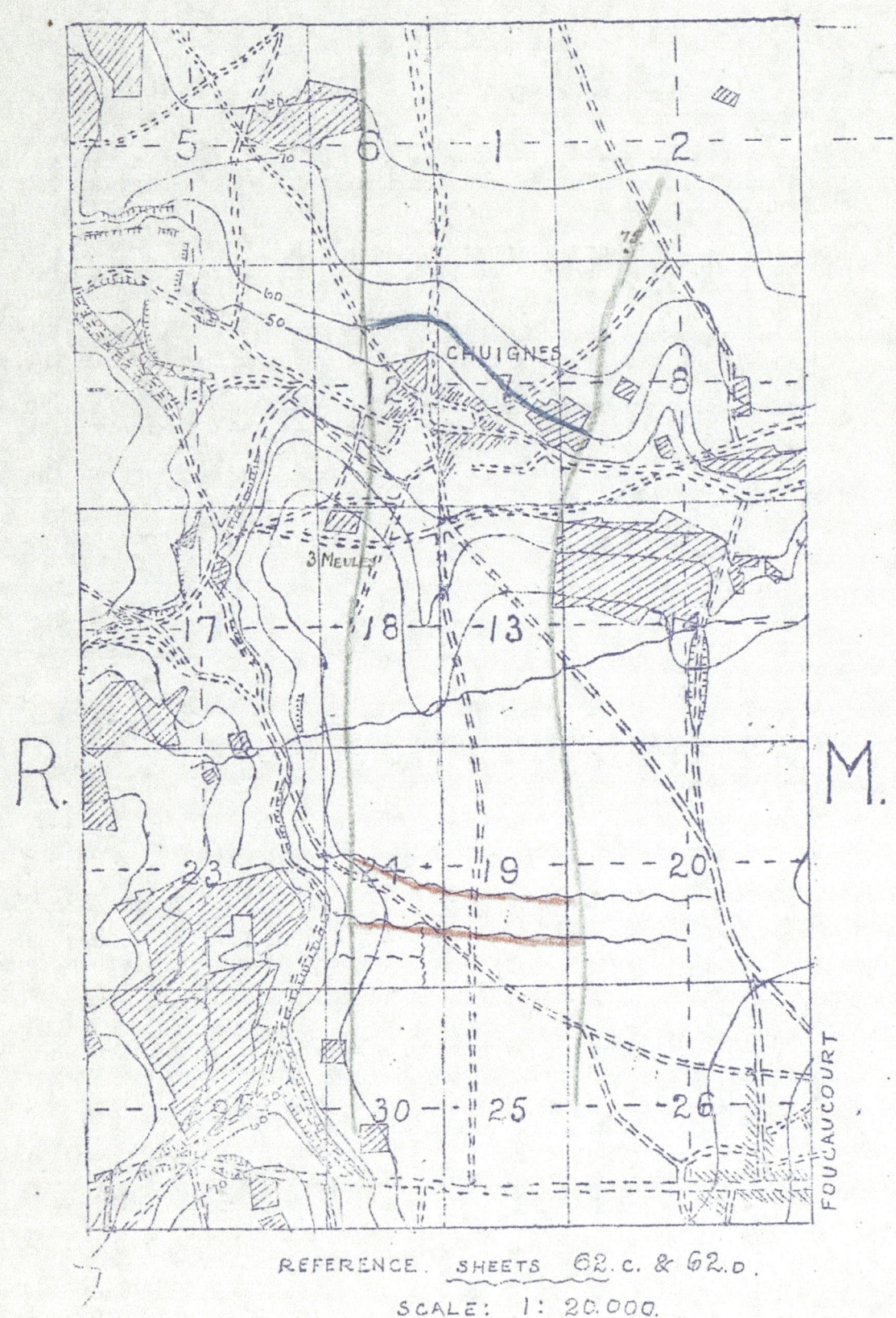

REFERENCE. SHEETS 62.C. & 62.D.
SCALE: 1:20,000.

WAR DIARY.

3rd. M. G. COMPANY.

3rd. INFANTRY BRIGADE.

1st. DIVISION.

JUNE.1917.

WAR DIARY or INTELLIGENCE SUMMARY

(Erase heading not required.)

Army Form C. 2118.

3RD MACHINE GUN COY.

Vol 77

Place	Date 1917	Hour	Summary of Events and Information	Remarks and references to Appendices
R.32 d 6.2 (Sheet 27.)	June 1.		Training of ammunition carriers. re. Pay Parade in the afternoon. Tug of War in the morning.	Coy Strength Officers 202. O.R.
	2		Route March. Captn. DA COSTA to Small Arms School as an Instructor. Baths. Sports competition.	
	3		Church Parade on Coy. Parade Ground.	
	4		Training. Ammunition Carriers. 9 Soldiers Coy-drill training.	
	5		Route March. Lt. Burney attended Lecture at Academy, Poperinghe to many officers	
	6		Training. DRO N°6 invited Coy. inspected horse lines - Contamine r. Personnel turned in afternoon.	
	7		Officers at Pin gade at 6.30 pm. Run.	
			S.O.E. Whole day off. Cars were open as B°Pldn HQ. and turned on matter interested in C-in-Cs	
			Communique: Also Special bus transport types now on 11 Mounted in silver in. Coy-turned	
			arms men was looked of when Scot had said. Baths in the afternoon. Major Z showed	
	8		or Marconi's preceded.	
	9		Training. LIEUT DAYTON and 2nd LT. BARNES and SMITH reported for duty.	
Wallon-Cappel	10		Training. Pay Parade.	
	11		Kit Inspection. Church Parade. Lieut JOYCE retimed from leave. March rear 11.45 pm	
	12		Commenced on 7.30 am. march via FLETRE, CAESTRE to WALLON - CAPPEL - Billeted in	
	13		two Farmhouses - one not too good.	
	14		Training. took field exercise for as much letter.	
	15		Training. MD.1.2 tactical exercise met Pat. Cannon. Brigadier attended Coy. HQ.	
Wormhoudt	16		Training. HD. 3rd tactical exercise met Pat Cannon. very long march. Had Coy. O. 111 officers 202. O.R.	
			Coy moved to WORMHOUDT. Arrived at 6.30 am. Billeted in Brewery. Attached to 97th Bde.	
			2 Gunners on remand.	
S. Pol. sur-Mer	17		Paraded as S.W. W. marched via BERGUES & DUNKERQUE to S. Pol. sur -MER.	
	18		C. GURNEY & Lab FRASER to KERKEPANNE by lorry. Reconnoitre new area.	
			Coy. marched the Bathed. Bathing. Reported	
	19		later. to Kerkepanne.	
Camp Kerkepanne	20		Coy. arrived at Dunkerque at 10.30. Detained at COXYDE and	
			later to CAMP KERKEPANNE. Orders received 6 was suffering from	
Camp Gadel (Coxyde plage)	21		Carts mounted at 8.30 am to camp P. GADEL. Wet Days and	
			Camp unpopulated Light needed by etc. piece and 97 ml Can - Pay parade.	

WAR DIARY or INTELLIGENCE SUMMARY

Army Form C. 2118.

320 M.G. Coy.

Place	Date 1917	Hour	Summary of Events and Information	Remarks and references to Appendices
CAMP LABEL (COXYDE BAINS)	June 22		By horse & training forward. Two cars arrived from mounted regt. Head of gun is newly typical of 2nd Bde Inder to avoid to aeroplane observation by 97th Coy. 97. Coy arranged a relieve at 9 a.m. unarmed infantry Rifle. Sand Heartening up of gun Per watchful check with Lewis cup to pieces very thinly.	
	23		Relief this a.m. at 9 a.m. from Lewis Guns Coy DE BAINS. Soldiers arrived from Regt to represent NO1.2.3 a.m. relief effected by noon. Major HANBURY joined Company and took over in Rept Sector was O.C. 2nd Bde.	
	24		C.O. went round B/motor guns with O.C. 2nd Bde. Came new orders of 2nd Bde Reps of 9 a.m.	
	25		C.O. wrote a Reppt re. cla gun w convertt and alteration to emplacement on dist/ps car to k horses & limbs.	
	26		C.O. round fresh m/c with O.C. 2nd Coy and a Sec Dunkirk. Cage to G.O. Militia Coy. Transport moved to new line of cantonment of CAMP DE BAINS. Gun of Repost into relieved by 2nd Coy.	
COXYDE BAINS	27		Company moved to HOTEL le COXY DE BAINS. Training commenced by 2 section (NO1+2) remaining 6 guns in Left wheeler.	
	28		training	
	29		training	
	30		C.O. attended conference of Coys at Bde H.Q.	

Capt Freight
11 Officers. 202. O.R.

E.R. Hunley
Major
Coy 3rd M.G. Coy.

1st Division

3rd M.G. Company

3rd Infantry Brigade

From 1st July, To 31st December 1917

WAR DIARY.

3rd. M. G. COMPANY.

3rd. INFANTRY BRIGADE.

1st. DIVISION.

JULY. 1917.

Army Form C. 2118.

WAR DIARY
or
INTELLIGENCE SUMMARY
(Erase heading not required.)

3RD. MACHINE GUN COMPANY.

Vol 18

Place	Date 1917	Hour	Summary of Events and Information	Remarks and references to Appendices
OXYPE. BAINS	July 1		Church Parade at 9.30. Brigade Race meeting on route to ST.IDESBALDE. Same were second pair - they were lighted up & lived by C.O. was also present. Madam Garnier & Monsieur Garnier (?P) Sous ct Pelish Moran to lunch now. LIEUT. MORGAN has been informed of accident. He is now in hospital with great pain.	Ary Regs 98 off
	2		Training. Capt with C.O. saw C.O. in commune regarding scheme. Bay parade arrangements made for relief by no 9 & gun teams who began on Depot Defence line.	No 11 199
	3		Ride in a.m. many errors, and pay parade at ST. IOESRALDE - Capt nr 9 & 2 Brigade were present. Irish company out trench into the sea. Relief commenced at 10 a.m.	
	4		Gun 2 in section July Class nr 3 funk hole. C.O. and 2nd in command told me observation to enemy airmen. More relieved to Brigade in its evening.	
	5		C.O. and rifle patrols saw Brigadier.	
	6		C.O. went forward brigades into brigades. Capt No.10 G-2 Captain LEYLAND (R.D.A.G.) Major Corpl n:o. Gen Both left the village in the evening.	
	7		C.O. and Lt W went. Caps take O. now C.o. at Cpt HQ.	
	8		All guns manned.	
	9		Last alarm at night.	
	10		LEFRACEC on leave. BOXYEE LAIMS shelled from early morning. At about 10 pm was received that enemy had attacked stations opposite of firm. Instructions received by O/C 3.M.G.C. to put guns into the retreat - C.O. went round hight outposts - lft Bowen & Boyes round outposts. No authorities O U N - acted noblemen - told & reserve Lt. also. All guns within - we had no casualties yesterday.	
	11		Quiet day.	
	12		Guns in action.	
	13		Lt BROMWELL reports to be evacuated to hospital for learning.	
	14			
	15		Capt in a left slipped relieved & told Cpn. No M.G.C. return names to BAYVELDE leaving camp for enemy on details as arrived. Entrained in trains for CAPE LIE.	

OXYVELOE

Army Form C. 2118.

WAR DIARY
or
INTELLIGENCE SUMMARY
(Erase heading not required.)

3RD MACHINE GUN COMPANY

Instructions regarding War Diaries and Intelligence Summaries are contained in F.S. Regs., Part II. and the Staff Manual respectively. Title Pages will be prepared in manuscript.

Place	Date 1917	Hour	Summary of Events and Information	Remarks and references to Appendices
CAPELLE	July 16		No 1 section arrived by way train from CAYEUX PLAGE. Remainder of Company entrained from EMPYRES arrived at 12 noon.	
	17		Cleaning guns. Swimming. Orders received to move tomorrow to LE CLIPON camp.	
	18		Move cancelled.	
LE CLIPON CAMP	19		Coy marched to LE CLIPON camp on the Coast. Arrived at 5.10 pm.	
	20		Physical training. Inspection.	
	21		Swimming. Physical training. Lieut BELL & Dr FRASER returned from leave.	
	22		Church Parades. Pay.	
	23		Training	
	24		Training	
	25		Heavy rain in morning. Physical training in the afternoon.	
	26		Training. Firing on beach.	
	27		Training. Film – "MOTHAGA"	
	28		"Rifesta" (name of MG Coy) commenced. (5 day.) 2/Lt HAMPTON reported for duty.	
	29		Church parades – delayed owing to rain. 15 Emigrants Row [?] received a sermon.	
	30		Coy on leave to PARIS. Pay parade.	
	31		Heavy rain delayed parades. Clean machine turned on. Training continued.	Coy Strength 11 Officers 213 OR

WAR DIARY.

3rd. M. G. COMPANY.

3rd. INFANTRY BRIGADE.

1st. DIVISION.

AUGUST. 1917.

Army Form C. 2118.

WAR DIARY
INTELLIGENCE SUMMARY
(Erase heading not required.)

3RD MACHINE GUN COY

Place	Date Aug 1917	Hour	Summary of Events and Information	Remarks and references to Appendices
LE WIPON (AFF)	1st		Received all day. To breakfast and relieved to war.	Coy Strength
	2		Heavy rain all day. C.O's conference at Bn. HQ. re closing of camp and special training demonstrated war of new Vickers' attachment for machine guns. Major SOMERVILLE, D.S.O. lectured on musketry.	A Offrs 212 OR
	3		C.O at the WAR WITH THE REDS, in the morning - returned 2nd half. Brigade/Major HANBURY turned from leave at PARIS. Officers and N.C.O. arrived - personnel carried out route march	
	4		Church parade. Coy passes. Company gas drill	
	5		Training - Training. Wall.	
	6		Training - Scheme. Wall. C.O at Conference of M.G. Officers at Divl. HQ.	
	7		Training with machine guns on (a scale). Carpenters on fire 1088. re exposion.	
	8		2/Lieutenant Joined Company.	
	9		Training - firing. Wall.	
	10		Training. Practised loading and unloading mod. pontoon on Div. HQ. by officers. Wall firing.	
	11		2 sections practiced deploying from position. By section a several levels.	
	12		Church Parade. C.O's conference at Bn HQ 12.15. Bay. 30 mar & far demonstrated as 2 p.m. Wall swimming.	
	13		Route march. Pontoon & loading.	
	14		Engaged aid parties landing and unloading by companies + staff.	
	15		Route march.	
	16		Wall training.	
	17		Wall - firing.	
	18		Route scheme - wall.	
	19		Church Parade. Swimming. Wall.	

E.C. Hawley Major
Comg. 3rd M.G. Coy.

Army Form C. 2118.

WAR DIARY
or
INTELLIGENCE SUMMARY

(Erase heading not required.) 3RD MACHINE GUN COY.

Instructions regarding War Diaries and Intelligence Summaries are contained in F.S. Regs., Part II. and the Staff Manual respectively. Title Pages will be prepared in manuscript.

Place	Date	Hour	Summary of Events and Information	Remarks and references to Appendices
LE CLIPON CAMP	Aug 21		Training	Strength 31/8/17
	22		Released in Commemoration Wall	13 Offrs
	23		Training. Sections and Battalion a Scheme Wall	222 ORs
	24		Heavy rain limited Battalion Scheme.	
			The whole "Cavenne Parade" Wall	
	25		Division inspected by General Sir H. Rawlinson.	
	26		Church Parade Day	
	27		Training. No 2 3 & 4 Section Pontoon Scheme.	
	28		Training. Wall. Very wet all morning. Ponts by R.E's attached in afternoon for machine gun instruction	
	29		Training	
	30		Training – Yes, 1 & 4 Sections attached to 1st Suffolks Bns & 2nd R Munsters Fus respectively for tactical scheme. No's 2 & 2 Sections Route March	
	31		Training firing etc. 12 30 pm 1 W.O and 10 marines arrived from marines and was attached to Company	

WAR DIARY.

3rd. M. G. COMPANY.

3rd. INFANTRY BRIGADE.

1st. DIVISION.

SEPTEMBER. 1917.

Army Form C. 2118.

WAR DIARY
or
INTELLIGENCE SUMMARY
(Erase heading not required.)

3RD MACHINE GUN COY

WD 20

Remarks and references to Appendices: Crosby Scarff? 13 C/ffm 222 OR2

Place	Date SEPT	Hour	Summary of Events and Information
LE CLIPON CAMP	1.		Training - Gun drill & Range Parties attached Various
	2.		Training -
	3.		Training - Medical parade for medical inspection. Naval men entrained on monitors at 12.30 pm and arrived party disembarked & attached to Coy.
	4.		Training. N.Z. Section attached to 1st Section for revised scheme Renwick - Porta Tienta.
	5.		Porta Tienta Scheme. Second Party of Naval men entrained at 1.30 pm. Gunnery Training - Wall. 3 munitions ended
	6.		Gunnery. Party from Monitors returned from Messines Ridge and stayed the night. 1 NCO and one Bluejacket attached the Monitors at 1.30 pm returned at 4.30 pm.
	7.		Demonstration of machine guns & Stokes Mortar to a New Party of Naval part Members, 1 officer and 10 men attached to Coy
	8.		first party detrained at 11.0 am and Second party detrained ...
	9.		Anival Parade & Pay
	10.		Brigade & Divisional ... life on fore hour. Newton Sclare. Capt. Ricard.
	11.		Training copies ... HQ re Feed Day
	12.		Field day. Dummy ... 2 hours record shooting. Army Divisional Commander present
	13.		Commencing the 10 October Captain Drennes Cashman

Army Form C. 2118.

WAR DIARY
or
INTELLIGENCE SUMMARY
3RD MACHINE GUN Coy

(Erase heading not required.)

Instructions regarding War Diaries and Intelligence Summaries are contained in F. S. Regs., Part II. and the Staff Manual respectively. Title Pages will be prepared in manuscript.

Place	Date	Hour	Summary of Events and Information	Remarks and references to Appendices
LE CLIPON	10.11.1917 15.		M.G. Training.	SS/2/S/1
	16.		Church and Bay parade. Conference on Bde HQ.	13 Off/nr
	17.		Pontoon Scheme. and M.G. training	222 OR.
	18.		Propos dates day. C.O. returned from leave. Conference Cinema tent	
	19.		M.G. Training.	
	20.		do. Walk. C.O. on may funeral train (recon trip.)	
	21.		Bde held day. Conference at 5.30 P.M.	
	22.		M.G. Sport. we were Top of Bde.	
	23.		Church parade. 2nd Bn Royal Berks.	
	24.		Baths.	
	25.		M.G. Training and Walk. Football in the evening.	
	26.		M.G. Training.	
	27.		M.G. Training	
	28.		Field. Day.	
	29.		Training. Company inspected by full fights arm	
	30.		Church parade. Pay. Lecture by Major Geml Montgomery 4th Army on French Attack.	

E. Wathery
Major

WAR DIARY.

3rd. M. G. COMPANY.

3rd. INFANTRY BRIGADE.

1st. DIVISION.

OCTOBER.1917.

Army Form C. 2118.

WAR DIARY
or
INTELLIGENCE SUMMARY

(Erase heading not required.)

3RD MACHINE GUN COMPANY

Place	Date 1917	Hour	Summary of Events and Information	Remarks and references to Appendices
LE CLIPON CAMP	Oct 1		M.G. training. Football in evening - Played 216th M.G. Coy and won.	Strength
	2		Tactical School with 2nd Royal Marine Artillery -	13 Offrs
	3		M.G. training - not firing.	223 ORs
	4		First M.G. firing (interrupted by rain)	
	5		Field day (rained)	
	6		Rained heavily - no parades possible. 2 M.G. programmes cancelled. Conference on Church parade cancelled army tactics. Lectures by programme recommendation as Ward Orderlie on operations of 2nd and 3rd St Armies & notes on Italies.	
	7		Employed.	
	8		Fine weather. M.G. training with rifle and revolver shooting.	
	9		M.G. training. Army Commander was through camp.	
	10		Physical training, camp improvement. Marshall	
	11		Firing. Lecture by Capt SMYTHE (Li'bray)	
	12		M.G. training.	
	13		Lecture by Army Commander.	
	14		Coy. Church parade - Football - Major Drawton Kenn.	
	15		M.G. training	
	16		do. Lecture by artillery officer on Fire direction.	
	17		Route March	
	18		do.	
	19		Barrage Schemes. firing. Company Concert in evening. Dummy	
ERINGHEM	20	9.15 am	Company marched from LE CLIPON Camp to ERINGHEM Rest. SPICKER GO MILLE-BRUGHA 22 JA557-19 at 3 km. Water Line	

Army Form C. 2118.

WAR DIARY
INTELLIGENCE SUMMARY

(Erase heading not required.)

3RD MACHINE GUN COMPANY

Place	Date 1916 October	Hour	Summary of Events and Information	Remarks and references to Appendices
RUBROUCK	21st		Company marched from Billets nr ERINGHEM at 8.30 am arrived Billets at RUBROUCK 11.45 am. weather fine. Route ZEGGERS-CAPPEL - ERIKELSBRUGGE camp roads.	
"	22nd		Training. Kit inspection, inspection of feet & boots. Lt Lyall then Transport officer proceeded on leave to UK.	
	23rd		Batlns - Whistles to rest for training in morning.	
	24th		Barrage Scheme (no firing). Gas helmets inspected. Respirators. Army Packed in evening ready for move.	
HOUTKERQUE	26th		Company marched from RUBROUCK at 6.15 am to HOUTKERQUE AREA. arrived Billets at E.25 C.0.9 at 12.30 pm. Route ZEGGERS CAPPEL 9 WORMHOUDT WATOU HERZEELE. Lt Gayne proceeded on leave to UK.	
	26th		Morning spent in cleaning of Billets, and overhauling guns, spare parts etc.	
	27"		Training. Instruction in Barrage work.	
	28		Church and Payroads.	
	29		Mly training. C.O's conference at Bnscn HQ.	Strength
	30		Running Competition. Inspection of Jan Black.	13 offrs
	31		C.O and Officers & N.C.Os reconnoitred the line - by motor lorry to Canal Bank - company training.	219 O.R.

E.R.Whatley Major

WAR DIARY.

(WITH APPENDIX).

3rd. M. G. COMPANY.

3rd. INFANTRY BRIGADE.

1st. DIVISION.

NOVEMBER. 1917.

WAR DIARY
or
INTELLIGENCE SUMMARY

(Erase heading not required.)

Army Form C. 2118.

3rd Machine Gun Company.

Place	Date Nov.	Hour	Summary of Events and Information	Remarks and references to Appendices
HOUTKERQUE	1.		In & Training	Strength 13 offrs 219 ORs
	2.		"	
	3.		Pay parade. Trottall new 1st m.g. Coy. C.O. went over model.	
	4.		Church parade. C.O. round the line. Lecture officers nailed model.	
	5.		Officers at model Roth.	
DAMBRE CAMP	6.		Company moved by motor bus to DAMBRE CAMP	
	7.		Lieut MARKS, BOURNER and GREGORY went up to reconnoitre positions to reconnoitre positions of two hunt situation. Lt GREGORY finished for two guns near VANITY FARM which he was to take over from Canadians that night. Lieut. MARKS and BOURNER reconnoitred barrage guns to be taken over from Canadians at night.	(Canadians (going up)
			No 2 and 3 retain and instruction of No 1 section arrived by tram at WIELTJE SIDING about 3 pm and proceeded to relieve. Two light barrage guns near YETTA HOUSES relieved at 5.45 pm. Relief of two guns a front line not completed till about 7.30 pm. C.O. with Brigade H.Q. (Cdn.) at KANSAS HOUSE. Situation quiet. Heavy shelling of battery in evening causing 1 OR wounded at dug.	2 OR Killed 1 OR DIED OF WOUND 1 OR WOUNDED 2 OR wounded.
			Sgt DEAR - wounded remained at duty.	
	8		Situation quiet. No section at VANITY FARM shelled - lost 3 killed and 2 wounded - Lieut GREGORY reported HQ in early morning and received instructions as to his advance during proposed attack next morning. The force under him to consist of 1 section, 5 extra to come up with S.W. Rabbie from IRISH FARM - under Lt LEACH; 1 section Kle Eters from Rabbie Vic John Farm area in the hand of Lt KANSAS - Lt PARKER detailed to take No 4 section in HE WRA Mchine on the left - teams 5 wounded going up.	3 OR KILLED 2 OR WOUNDED 1 OR KILLED 5 OR WOUNDED
	9		to SOURCE FARM. Lce Sgt COGLAN reliof going up	

WAR DIARY or INTELLIGENCE SUMMARY

Army Form C. 2118.

3RD MACHINE GUN COMPANY

Place	Date Nov. 1917	Hour	Summary of Events and Information	Remarks and references to Appendices
	10		As for in Company concerned, operations divided into four:-	
			1) The action of the two guns still in VANITY FARM	
			2) " " " in the Battery (NOELLA and DANGERSON - 2nd officer St MARKS and ROVER SR.)	
			3) " " " on the left under 2/Lt BARKER	
			4) " " " mobile guns on the right under GREGORY	
			1) Action of 2 guns in VANITY FARM:- Corporal COOMBES had been ordered to remain in position until officially withdrawn. At ZERO hour (6.5 a.m.) the Rm^{diers} went in and apparently reached all their objectives. At ABOUT 7 a.m. the Rm^{diers} were observed to be coming back and Corporal COOMBES ordered his men to stand to. The guns fired on Germans as they came over the ridge and this stopped their advance. They continued to fire to stop advance of the enemy until about 9 a.m. when their ammunition was exhausted. They then took up a position in shell holes prepared a delay action with their rifles - but finding themselves alone Corporal COOMBES ordered guns to be taken back & their subsector was withdrawn in good order.	
			2) Action of 6 guns in Battery:- Owing to absence of 2/Lt TAYLOR commanding the Rm^{diers} that 4 guns started to function with him - it was necessary to withdraw the guns from battery. Two were taken for N° 3 section and put under Sgt. BEAR. This battery was A battery to the left & was first sited in YETTA HOUSES B and C battery - consisting of 8 guns from N° 2 & 3/6 Companies were sited in position N° the CEMETERY - all objectives being taken reported taken - a/a consultation with the Brigade commander - the guns for no. 5 fire were laid to their SOS line at 8.40 a.m. as reported 30 to. in DOUBLE COPSE - 100 rds. minutes from A battery for 10 minutes. At 9.25 a.m. enemy were reported to be in MALLET WOOD - 13 battery were ordered to fire 50 rds. per minute for 15 minutes. At 10 a.m. A Battery was ordered to concentrate on number road W.23.b.- At 11.30 a.m. Rm^{diers} were reported to have withdrawn -	
			barrage line. 25 rds. per minute were fixed a SOS fire A & B batteries. At 1 p.m. the SOS signal went up and all 3 batteries were ordered to fire. At SOS line at 25 pr rate - which was then 25 rds. per minute - any hostile counter attack. At 1.30 p.m. all troops reported back in original line - guns adjust to line ctg Barroy line ft ZERO+3. A little later, an order to continue the line instead of firing officially. At 2.15 p.m. orders were received fire thence original barrage line.	

WAR DIARY or INTELLIGENCE SUMMARY 3RD M.G. COY

Army Form C. 2118.

Place	Date	Hour	Summary of Events and Information	Remarks and references to Appendices
	10th (cont.)		At 3.30pm the D.M.G.O. Telephoned Group Commander that he would send any filled belts that were found pending return. At 4.30pm O/C. consulted with Captain Wenlock (front commander) it was decided that owing to condition of guns and belts, it was impossible for guns & punctures probably through hit in SOS line - It was decided Lieutenants Dunne and Seagram to be dug up to be cleared rectified. Order to this effect was issued by M.S.O. at 5 p.m. Officers guns it was decided to leave 4 at the disposal of Lt.N. lines at KRONPRINZ FARM at completion of being SPANDAUed, also WORKEY were killed. Lt. BOURNE & Pte DUNNE wounded - by same shell.	Casualties 2 OR KILLED 1 Officer / wounded 1 OR
			3) Police etc. in the 2nd BARKER were ordered to proceed to pinpoint off place of R M wounded corrected with O/C. Ambulance on arrival. His orders from O/C. Company was that he was to get his guns under cover at place of assembly, not further off than them, but at a time to be selected by himself - privately between ZERO + 1 hr and ZERO + 2 hrs. And perform his own route to objection - There was - 2 gun to Pillbox at 200.40 U.S. 2 gun to VAT COTTAGES - these places were given on a guide. It was decided to proceed go up to the place of assembly later. R.M Zwarlein, which had a New ALBATROSS FARM - a shell fell among section billing & 2 gun teams - He played there till arrival of R.M. Fusiliers - He then proceeded to SOURCE FARM - A place of azimuth - into this side of PADDEREEKE - While going thenth shelly commenced - Lt R. coming got lost in the darkness when he got stuck in mud - one gun destroyed by MG fire - one submerged in a swamp - and the Third was later had fetch to PADDEREEKE. He, subsequently, decided to mount the guns just fire of SOURCE F. to Lt BARKER to report with 2 guns to O.C. Shrouded at ALBATROSS FARM (one of gun were made up of Fl which had been lost when Sgt COGLAN was hit afterwards found). At about 7 P.M. company commander rallied ALBATROSS FARM and after consultation with O.C. Gloucesters decided to send Lt BARKER with 2 guns to INCH House to hold on for a further 24 hours. Order was sent to Lt BARKER to withdraw at dusk - these orders failed to arrive. The withdrawal following morning.	
			4) Four guns under Lieut. GREGORY proceeded forward (2 came up by IRISH FARM – 2 from Battery (at ZERO (6.5am) the Sussexes section forward was SUPPORTERS to Pillbox New VALOUR FARM, renforcing W. He was	

Army Form C. 2118.

WAR DIARY
or
INTELLIGENCE SUMMARY 3rd M. G. Cy.

(Erase heading not required.)

Instructions regarding War Diaries and Intelligence Summaries are contained in F. S. Regs., Part II. and the Staff Manual respectively. Title Pages will be prepared in manuscript.

Place	Date Nov 1916	Hour	Summary of Events and Information	Remarks and references to Appendices
	10th (ctd)		advanced. Don Aston had he got to GREGORY on was gone to Lt BARKER who reported 2 guns at VIRILE FARM — 2 gun at VOID FARM. At 6.45 a Shrapnel was apparently found all spare. Lt GREGORY advised to advance. After advancing about 600 yds, on most difficult ground, Lt GREGORY sent reconnoitre VIRILE Farm and was unfortunately killed by a sniper — Sgt LEACH was billed almost immediately afterwards. No friendly troops were in sight — a long trek of many approached. An attempt was made to mount gun but, all but one, was knocked out by shell fire — they, being at this time under the knott barrage. The gun had no less than many, tracing them up. Was to was itself knocked out by a shell. Pte HUBBARD then took charge of the party, remained in shell hole to about 9 pm — he also several German with his rifle — At about 3pm, finding himself almost entirely surrounded he decided to get his gun back which he did safely — Camp took ad. wounded man with the.	
IRISH FARM.	11		Company about night here — many by train to DAMRAE CAMP on horry of 12?.	
DAM.RAE CAMP	12		Carpentered arr. 8.30 a.m. No 6 weeks care — Late in the day.	
	13		Cleaning guns of equipment.	
	14		C.O addressed Company a recent operation.	
	15		to the live 6 take up (incujunto with 216 Coy) Battery position. Physical drill, army information — including W.O. 2Lt HAMPTON handed concentration of Lewis guns to small platoon per week. transfer here Col Nero's hut.	
	16		Physical drill — leg exercises. Chery Litter, No 2 reels above 5 no 3 att. were 2D MARKS. 2Lt ANDERSON got no command of Battery. Camp skilled.	
	17		Physical drill — leg movement. Camp rolled. C.O on leave to UK. Officers in charge.	
DIRTY BUCKET CAMP	18 19		Church Parade — Lt JOYCE returned No 3 sector. — Camp shelled during night. moved to DIRTY BUCKET CAMP.	

Army Form C. 2118.

WAR DIARY
or
INTELLIGENCE SUMMARY
(Erase heading not required.)

Place	Date	Hour	Summary of Events and Information	Remarks and references to Appendices
	20th		Company on fatigue and web equipment fitted. N° 1 section to be attached to N° 1 section was at Fovant.	
	21		Route march. Inspection returned	
	22		N° 1 section returned to 3rd section was 2/5 NORTHS.	
Schools Camp	23		Company marched to Schools Camp arriving at 1.15 p.m. N° 2 sect. late in the afternoon. Co returned from leave.	
	24		Webb Packs carried	
	25		Interior arrangements.	
	26		Unit improvements — Unmarshalled Inspection of Camp.	
Putney Camp	27		Camp improvements	
	28		Contemplation commenced at 12 noon. Commenced am camp. Left about 2.30 p.m.	
	29		Camp improvements. Presented 4 medals by Lt. Colonel — Military medal to CH TOOMBS, 4qm. POTTER, 4Cpl DOWNEY, 4/05 HUSSEY. Pte GITTINGS of this Coopr — invested in 16 November.	
	30.		Camp. Shell & Musick Traning commenced. Reinforcement drafts. Cont improvement.	Strength 10 officers 238 O.R.

E Mackley Major
Cmd 3/7 Nof Regt

Armourer's shop
NILE HOUSE

A/4a 3095

Armourers shop
NILE HOUSE.

A/4a 3095

WAR DIARY.

3rd. M. G. COMPANY.

3rd. INFANTRY BRIGADE.

1st. DIVISION.

DECEMBER. 1917.

Army Form 2118.

WAR DIARY
or
INTELLIGENCE SUMMARY. No. 3 Machine Gun Coy

(Erase heading not required.)

Instructions regarding War Diaries and Intelligence Summaries are contained in F. S. Regs., Part II. and the Staff Manual respectively. Title pages will be prepared in manuscript.

Place	Date 1917	Hour	Summary of Events and Information	Remarks and references to Appendices
PUTNEY CAMP (PROVEN)	Dec 1		Camp Improvement – M.G. Training – Football – Pay Parade	Strength at 1/12/17. 10 Officers and 251 O.R.
	2		Church Parade cancelled owing to cold weather. – Football – 2/Lt Barker to R.F.C. course (anti-aircraft).	
	3		M.G. and Coy Training. – Company cross country run in afternoon – Capt Pearson reported for attachment.	
	4		Baths – Football.	
	5		Company moved to Dunkirk at B.3.a.6.3. (Sheet 28 NW) 2/Lt Barker from } to } R.F.C. anti-aircraft course. Lt Fraser, 2/Lt Hampton } for courses 2/Lt Auldon	
	6		Camp improvements. Lt Gurney transferred for M.G. Course.	
	7		Camp improvements. M.G. Training. Lt Fraser to Fraser, to England leave.	
	8		Camp improvements. M.G. Training. 2/Lt Anderson from R.F.C. Course	
	9		Camp Inspection – Pay Parade. – Capt Pearson, Lt Joyce, Parker, Hampton attended to reconnoitre new coy Bn stations failed to proceed to new M.G. Positions.	
	10		O.C. Capt Pearson, Lt Anderson & Hampton reconnoitred line – Company training.	

Army Form C. 2118.

WAR DIARY
or
INTELLIGENCE SUMMARY.

(Erase heading not required.)

Instructions regarding War Diaries and Intelligence Summaries are contained in F. S. Regs., Part II. and the Staff Manual respectively. Title pages will be prepared in manuscript.

Place	Date	Hour	Summary of Events and Information	Remarks and references to Appendices
Houthulst Forest Sector	1917 Dec 11.		Relieved no. 1. M. G. Co. in the line. Lt. Thoughton & right guns & Lt. Anderson 6 left guns. Capt. Pearson visited right guns after relief.	
	" 12.		C.O. visited right guns & Lt. Joyce left guns. Indiscriminate firing carried out by 4 guns.	
	" 13.		C.O. visited left guns at stand-to & Lt. Joyce right guns at stand-to. Capt Pearson fixed exact location of guns. 9 p.m. to midnight 4 guns fired on enemy trench.	
	" 14.		C.O. visited right guns at stand-to and Lt. Joyce left guns at stand-to. Later C.O. visited several gun emplts. the Brigadier. It was decided to change the positions of some of the guns.	
	" 15.		Capt. Pearson selected and fixed two new gun positions at Landy Mill. Late Company reliefs carried out at night. 2nd Yorkshires took over left guns and Lt. Barker took over right guns.	
	" 16.		C.O. visited Landy Mill and approved of new gun positions and selected new positions at Cairnes Farm. 4 guns fired on La Kasbah Cross Roads.	
	" 17.		Two officers from no. 2 Co. and some N.C.O.'s reconnoitred the right sector under Lt. Joyce. Two officers reconnoitred the left sector under the C.O. Fired indirect fire 4.30 to 9 p.m. on EVERIT JUNCTION.	
	" 18.		Capt. Pearson visited ISLAND and PAPEGOED FARM and Lt. Joyce visited LONELY MILL. No firing owing to patrols being out.	
	" 19.		C.O. & Lt. Anderson proceeded on leave. Heavy fire on PAPEGOED FARM guns altered. Relieved by no. 2 Company at night.	

Army Form C. 2118.

WAR DIARY
or
INTELLIGENCE SUMMARY.
(Erase heading not required.)

Instructions regarding War Diaries and Intelligence Summaries are contained in F. S. Regs., Part II. and the Staff Manual respectively. Title pages will be prepared in manuscript.

Place	Date	Hour	Summary of Events and Information	Remarks and references to Appendices
BISCHOOT Huts. E.E. 28.B.3.a.6.4.	Dec 20.		Company moved in support. Cleaning Guns & equipment & foot-washing.	Strength
EIKHOEK	21.		Moved to EIKHOEK: now in reserve.	at
CAMP.	22.		Ordinary Training and Pay Parade. Court of Inquiry into absence of 19420, O'Grady, Pte.	31/12/17. 11 officers
	23.		Church Parade and two anti-aircraft guns mounted near camp.	
	24.		M.G. Training and Steady Drill. Transport Parade for Musketry and 293	
	25.		Church Parade. Christmas Dinner at 5 p.m. Lt. Flower returned from leave.	Other ranks.
	26.		M.G. Training and Musketry for Transport.	
	27.		Ordinary Training and Lecture to N.C.Os. by Capt. Pearson M.C. Also, two working parties furnished.	
	28.		Relieved two anti-aircraft guns. Ordinary Training and Musketry for Transport.	
AS-097 20/12/17.	29.		Company moved into Support & took over billets from No.2.Coy. Lt. Graeme and 50 men carried wire to Corps Line.	
	30.		Church Parade and Pay Parade.	
	31.		Company Parade for baths and Camp Improvements.	

Offce Lt Cmdg
No 3 M.G. Coy

1st Division

War Diaries 3rd Infantry Bde.

3rd M.G.C. absorbed by 1st Bn. M.G.C.

From 1st January. To 23rd February 1918.

Army Form C. 2118.

WAR DIARY or INTELLIGENCE SUMMARY

3RD MACHINE GUN COMPANY

Place	Date JAN 1918	Hour	Summary of Events and Information	Remarks and references to Appendices
SHEET 28NW B.3.a.6.4.	1.		Ordinary Machine Gun Training and a Lecture to N.C.Os.	Company Strength 11 Officers 223 ORs 1/1/1918
	2.		Physical Training and Ordinary Machine Gun Training. One Officer and 50 O.R.'s on Fatigue.	
	3.		Training, overhauling guns, spare parts, ammunition etc from 6. Feet making in afternoon.	
	4.		Relieved No. 1 M.G. Coy in the line. Relief Complete by 8.30 am. Very clear day	
	5.		Lt Joyce visited guns at LONELY MILL & MANGLEARE at "Stand to" in the morning. Capt PEARSON M.C. visited line, and established posters of infantry posts to north of PAPEGOED.	
	6.		Capt PEARSON, M.C. visited all guns of night relief and fired new position at LONELY MILL. Lt H.S. JOYCE visited all guns of left sector. Major HAWLING returned from leave and took over command of Coy.	
	7.		C.O. visited all guns of night sector. Capt PEARSON M.C. reconnoitred ground in front of positions at PAPEGOED. Lt. H.S. JOYCE visited sector near HQ of Transport. G.O.C. visited sector.	
	8.		C.O. & Capt PEARSON M.C. laid out line for wire in front of HILL 20 & FAIDHERBE Farm X ROADS.	
	10.		Lt JOYCE visited position at Major PEARSON of "Stand to" in morning.	
	11.		C.O. and Capt PEARSON M.C. made a reconnaissance of the area in	

Army Form C. 2118.

WAR DIARY
or
INTELLIGENCE SUMMARY.
(Erase heading not required.)

3RD MACHINE GUN COMPANY

Place	Date	Hour	Summary of Events and Information	Remarks and references to Appendices
	11 (continued)		Front of our main line of resistance. Lt JOYCE visited posters at ISLANDE & CATINAT.	
	12.		C.O. & Lt JOYCE reconnoitred the area in front of right sub sect. Sector officer Lt JOYCE visited Lt. Col's in afternoon. "TEST" GAS ALARM in morning. Coy relieved by 2/5 MGC in evening. Coy relieved by B. B. & C.1. proceeded to billets to FRENCH CAMP at B. B. & C.1.	
B.3.a.6.1. S1.28.NW.	13.		Lt JOYCE proceeded on leave to PARIS. Company employed in cleaning up generally.	
S.22.a. SA.26.1/10000	14.		Company moved to billets at S. 22. a. Showed in morning.	
	15.		Company employed in cleaning limbers, guns etc. and M.G. training. Divn Band played at billets in afternoon	
	16.		Camp improvements. mn paraded leaving. Divn Cinema & entertainment in one of Company huts in afternoon.	
	17.		Wet day. Route march cancelled. Baths in afternoon.	
	18.		Route march in morning. Camp improvements. Brigadier General Bartee inspected Transport at 10 a.m. Lt MORGAN rejoined Company from Base Depôt. Lt GRATTAN reported from hospital. Lt JOYCE rejoined from PARIS	
	19.			

Army Form C. 2118.

WAR DIARY
INTELLIGENCE SUMMARY
(Erase heading not required.)

3RD MACHINE GUN Company

Place	Date Jan 1918	Hour	Summary of Events and Information	Remarks and references to Appendices
S.22.a. Sh.20 14000	20		Church parade. C.O. Lectured Company in Recreation Hut. Camp inspection by C.O.	Company Strength
	21		M.G. Training. NCO's Rep. Rendez. by Capt. Pearson M.C. Camp improvements. Orders for move to Support area received.	12 Offrs 209 O.Rs 31/1/18
B.1. d 86.90 Sh. 28 NW	22		Company paraded at 10.30 am for move to support area. Paraded strength 11 officers. Arrived at 11 am. Company billets at 12 noon in Bugard Subs.	
	23		3 working parties engaged in building shelters etc. under Brigade orders. Ls GURNEY & 243 MARKS rejoined Company from leave to UK.	
	24		Ants - aircraft fire returned by No 2 section working parties.	
CANAL BANK	25		Marked Nichts on Canal Bank. Transfer at UMBRE CAMP.	
	26		Gun cleaning. Section Officers Parade. Pay.	
	27		Working party (with S. Wales Borderers) made shelters - minimum forward areas. Church parade.	
	28		Working party. Way it Rubies - drainage. Cuttered men from 2nd Royal Munster Fusileers returned to Square by order of the Brigade.	
	29		Working party to drainage mole shelters & weapons.	
	30		Working party under 2 Brampton.	
	31		Training - firing actions on range. Cap hand monthly, medical inspection and baths.	Company Strength

V. Hankey Major
OC 3rd MG Coy

Army Form C. 2118.

WAR DIARY
INTELLIGENCE SUMMARY.
(Erase heading not required.)

3RD. MACHINE GUN COMPANY

Place	Date	Hour	Summary of Events and Information	Remarks and references to Appendices
CANAL BANK	Feb 1918		Working party (with 2nd Batt'n) [illegible] 2N TURQUIE.	Company Strength 12 offrs 209 OR 1/2/18
	1		[illegible]	
	2		[illegible]	
	3		[illegible]	
	4		[illegible] Company carried [illegible] and Rigga & Fort Heart [illegible]	
	5		Ramsey Claus has inspection by C.O. Anti-Gun appliances inspected by Brigade Gas N.C.O. [illegible] 104 Inf. C [illegible]	
	6		[illegible] 2N R.I.R. [illegible]	
	7		[illegible]	
	8		Working parties [illegible] 2.L. [illegible] on leave 6 APRIL	
	9		[illegible]	
SIEGE CAMP	10	2	[illegible] to WIEG. (Warm Huts) in SIEGE CAMP. Move completed [illegible]	
	11		[illegible]	
	12		[illegible]	

Army Form C. 2118.

WAR DIARY
or
INTELLIGENCE SUMMARY.
(Erase heading not required.)

3RD MACHINE GUN Coy.

Instructions regarding War Diaries and Intelligence Summaries are contained in F.S. Regs., Part II. and the Staff Manual respectively. Title pages will be prepared in manuscript.

Place	Date	Hour	Summary of Events and Information	Remarks and references to Appendices
SIEGE CAMP	13		Adv. guard empl. freshwater. Batt. bought. Tommy's ox - Nyasa Boy Boy captured - letters in Gen. played 2V.B. football man. 2/L HAMPTON returned from Dar es Salaam Cpl. RIDER visited Coy by day. Training.	
	14		Training. Colonel RIDER instructed Coy in Column work.	
	15		Training. Coy. route marched 7. (inoculated nos 2 in West (?))	
	16		Kit camp inspect. Church Parade. Football match. Cpl. R.T.A. Coy. bn. war.	
	17		Training. Letter to Sergeant - Journey from or turns over - 3 man started on towards HQ.	
	18		Coy. parade WB. Parade 1 sergeant inspection in camp.	
	19		Training. To Camp & system b. coys. defend by Games. Interactive football.	
	20		Training - Training up for the main Bayonet - handle machine gun. rope. En. war huts. appendix 2/L 2/L Col. tackle + Aux. GARRISON attention approx. - Cpl. PERRSON on leave.	
	21		Brown out trooper at Par 8 point = weeks on SIEGE JUNCTION - BRIELEN-BRIEUX RAILWAY conf. camp (US Lx16 (?). Con unprepared to the marine hit	
COMIL CHALK	22		To 6th bigger habitat rec. cleared cleaves. Officers appointed. HANBURY learned sergeant to do . Buried out Bag on first command. Concerned (no bn to tea) Left no Right action of Depare pary - Petro officer & quite inspect Saw Canton rump of ground direction of East to Para. Howry times to nl to true meter before - bag. to Lo sumter - Vt Regal. to T.P. My son Percent. - Human from pr. cashew on Ration mirth were Cr. BARKER - Army - a officer (6.45 carrying for RE). 2/L HARRIS fo Bn. the fr. Ox. (name) Entrances from the of N. the Center - 2/L.	
	23			
	24		SNEAPHGE to attack - loaded - Gun Captn Coy fee water hand away. Passenger of Commander to represent to potable - be it looks hand away. Care 2/L for of casual foot & ? Commanded	

Army Form C. 2118.

WAR DIARY
or
INTELLIGENCE SUMMARY.

(Erase heading not required.)

3RD MACHINE GUN Coy.

Place	Date	Hour	Summary of Events and Information	Remarks and references to Appendices
CANAL BANK.	24 /4/17		Company on ordinary duties when new Brigadier General BODEN — Divisional Supplied system of guns. New outs — arranged right (adopted from german night) Chamanned to G.O.	Afternoon to new outs —
	25		Training in Rushing parties. 40 n.c. every parties for one Commanded Canal Bank. Conference on Curricula with G.S.O.1 and D.M.G.O.	Rainy day —
	26		Training on Battery tactics. 40 men Canal Bank & European troops. Orders received to money of SLAB POST by 6 P.M. Orders for SLAB post cancelled. Met the Brigade major. Lt GRATTAN returned from leave.	Lt GRATTAN
	27		Gave Lewis gun practice — hr Channing at 12.30 on a.c. mm of Batter. R. Joyce from leave	
	28		Training — Lewis Drill. Gun drill. Classes from Units. Equipment as before in view to Usual Scheme organising R.S.M. as usual	Company Strength.

Your obedt servt
Maj. 3rd MG Coy.

www.ingramcontent.com/pod-product-compliance
Lightning Source LLC
Chambersburg PA
CBHW081423300426
44108CB00016BA/2289